METAMORPHOSES REIMAGINED

Metamorphoses Reimagined

Michael Marder

With art by Damien MacDonald

Columbia University Press
New York

Columbia University Press
Publishers Since 1893
New York   Chichester, West Sussex

Copyright © 2025 Columbia University Press
All rights reserved

Library of Congress Cataloging-in-Publication Data
Names: Marder, Michael, 1980– author.
Title: Metamorphoses reimagined / Michael Marder.
Description: New York : Columbia University Press, 2025.
Identifiers: LCCN 2024061223 (print) | LCCN 2024061224 (ebook) | ISBN 9780231212540 (hardback) | ISBN 9780231212557 (trade paperback) | ISBN 9780231559447 (ebook)
Subjects: LCSH: Ovid, 43 B.C.–17 A.D. or 18 A.D. Metamorphoses. | LCGFT: Literary criticism.
Classification: LCC PA6519.M9 M355 2025 (print) | LCC PA6519.M9 (ebook) | DDC 873/.01—dc23/eng/20250209

All drawings by Damien MacDonald.

Play/pause symbol on pages 240 and 241 created by Travis Avery
(Wikimedia Commons, CC BY 3.0).

Cover design: Milenda Nan Ok Lee
Cover art: André Derain, *The Dance*, 1906. Public Domain. photosublime / Alamy Stock Photo

GPSR Authorized Representative: Easy Access System Europe,
Mustamäe tee 50, 10621 Tallinn, Estonia, gpsr.requests@easproject.com

For Anaïs—

the memory of past metamorphoses

and the anticipation of those to come

CONTENTS

PREFACE XV

Prelude: Chaos (Liber I, 1–30) 1

The First Metamorphosis, or Man Is a Wolf to God
(Liber I, 210–240) 3

Stone(s) Age (Liber I, 380–415) 6

Daphne's Fugues (Liber I, 452–567) 8

Io: The Nonmetamorphosis (Liber I, 568–688) 16

Syrinx: Becoming-in-Place, Becoming-Plant (Liber I, 698–712) 18

The Sisters of Phaethon: The Vegetal Shape of Grief
(Liber II, 330–365) 20

... and the Animal Shape of Grief:
The Swan Song of Cycnus (Liber II, 366–380) 23

Callisto: The Most Beautiful She-Bear (Liber II, 401–530) 25

Crow Trouble (Liber II, 531–632) 27

Another Sort of Metamorphosis: Asclepius and Ocyrhoe
(Liber II, 633–675) 30

CONTENTS

Battus: Becoming-Stone (Liber II, 676–707)   32

Metamorphosing Into a Statue: Aglauros (Liber II, 708–832)   34

When a God Steals Himself: Europa's Bull (Liber II, 833–875)   36

Interdeath, Interbirth: Cadmus and the Sowing of
Serpent Teeth (Liber III, 1–137)   38

Actaeon: The Revenge of the Hunted (Liber III, 138–252)   40

Fiery Manifestations: Semele (Liber III, 253–315)   43

Trans-Tiresias (Liber III, 316–338)   46

Disembodying Metamorphoses: Echo and Narcissus
(Liber III, 339–510)   48

Frenzied Becomings I: Dolphins and Other Marine
Motifs Borrowed from Lydian Sailors (Liber III, 572–700)   52

Frenzied Becomings II: Pentheus, or the Voice of Reason as a
Wild Boar (Liber III, 511–733)   54

Human Blood/Plant Sap: On Pyramus and Thisbe
(Liber IV, 55–166)   57

Mars and Venus: Exposure (Liber IV, 167–189)   60

Shrub Diaries: Leucothoe (Liber IV, 190–273)   62

Two Becoming One: Salmacis and Hermaphroditus, with Some Formulas
and Formulations (Liber IV, 274–388)   65

Twilight (Liber IV, 389–415)   68

Metamorphosing Minds: The Madness of Athamas and Ino
(Liber IV, 416–562)   70

For "What Remains of Me": Cadmus's Wife and Becoming-Snake
(Liber IV, 563–603)   73

To Become a Mountain: Atlas (Liber IV, 604–663)   75

Andromeda and Perseus: Becoming Free
(Liber IV, 664–739)   77

CONTENTS

From Living to Dead Corals, from Woods to Wood
(Liber IV, 740–764)   81

Pulped Nonfiction (Liber V, 1–156)   83

Perseus, Again: Heart of Stone (Liber V, 157–250)   85

Becoming Liquid: A Riddle (Liber V, 255–267)   87

Pyreneus: Excerpts from a Self-Help Book (Liber V, 268–293)   89

9/IX: The Daughters of Euippe (Liber V, 294–319)   91

An Island Meditation (Liber V, 320–361)   93

Tearful Metamorphoses: Cyane (Liber V, 410–437, 462–470)   97

Seasonal Existence: Proserpina's Questions
(Liber V, 385–409, 564–571)   99

Arethusa: Becoming the Other (Liber V, 572–641)   101

For Arachne: A Few Threads to Follow (Liber VI, 1–145)   104

Niobe: Becoming Scarce (Liber VI, 146–312)   107

Becoming Abundant: Lycian Peasants
(Liber VI, 313–381)   110

Skinned: Marsyas's Grammar Lesson (Liber VI, 382–400)   113

Becoming Whole: Pelops (Liber VI, 401–411)   115

Tereus & Co.: A Whirlwind of Metamorphoses—Fire,
Snakes, Autophagy, Birds (Liber VI, 412–674)   117

Changing Strategies, Metamorphosing Moods:
A Nearly Tautogrammic Reflection (Liber VI, 675–721)   124

Proverbial Wisdom: Medea (Liber VII, 1–158)   126

The Art of Becoming Immortal (Liber VII, 159–293)   128

The Art of Becoming Mortal (Liber VII, 294–349)   131

Up and Down: Air and Earth—A Meditation
(Liber VII, 350–403)   133

CONTENTS

The Capture of Cerberus (Liber VII, 404–452) 135

Getting Infected: Pandemic Diaries (Liber VII, 453–613) 140

Cross-Species Immigrants: An Interrogation Transcript (Liber VII, 614–660) 144

Becoming Unfaithful: Cephalus and Procris (Liber VII, 661–865) 148

Dreams from My Owner: A Memoir (Liber VIII, 1–151) 152

Ariadne Variations (Liber VIII, 152–182) 155

How to Soar Above the Labyrinth of Your Mind: Icarus's Wings (Liber VIII, 183–235) 157

To Perdix, the Inventor (Liber VIII, 236–259) 159

Diana's Boar: A Phytological Ritual for the Animals That We Are (Liber VIII, 260–450) 162

Meleager: Becoming Ashes (Liber VIII, 451–545) 165

Island Afterlife: Perimele (Liber VIII, 546–610) 167

Tree Hospitality: An Exegesis (Liber VIII, 611–724) 170

Sometimes: Proteus, the Daughter of Erysichthon, and Erysichthon (Liber VIII, 730–874) 173

Phallic Metamorphoses (Liber IX, 1–97) 178

Flooding: Reflections from the Event (Liber IX, 98–133) 180

Clothes-Skin, Skin-Clothes: Hercules (Liber IX, 134–272) 182

Becoming Atmospheric: Lichas (Liber IX, 211–229) 185

Notes on Position: Alcmene (Liber IX, 273–323) 187

Dryope: Becoming a Cut (Plant) (Liber IX, 324–393) 190

Becoming Young (Again), Growing Older: Iolaus and the Sons of Callirrhoe (Liber IX, 394–438) 194

Byblis: The Externalization of Desire (Liber IX, 439–665) 197

CONTENTS

The Trans/Formations of Iphis (Liber IX, 666–797)   202

Don't Look Back: Orpheus and Eurydice (Liber X, 1–85)   205

Coming, Becoming—A Cypress Tree (Liber X, 86–142)   208

Of Plants and Planets, of Stars and Seeds: Ganymede and Hyacinthus (Liber X, 143–219)   210

Sin and Crime: Venus and Cerastae (Liber X, 220–242)   212

Pygmalion, the Morning After (Liber X, 243–297)   215

Myrrha: The Thrashing About of "Nature" (Liber X, 298–502)   217

Running: Atalanta and Hippomenes (Liber X, 503–707)   220

Adonis, Adonai, Anemone Coronaria (Liber X, 708–739)   223

Orpheus and His Critics (Liber XI, 1–84)   225

The Midas Touch: Script for a Commercial (Liber XI, 85–193)   228

Building-with, Building-against: How Troy Fell Before the Fall of Troy (Liber XI, 194–220)   230

The Tenacity of Substance: Peleus and Thetis (Liber XI, 221–265)   233

A Cycle of Violence: Daedalion (Liber XI, 266–345)   235

Becoming a Fossil: The Wolf of Nereid (Liber XI, 346–409)   237

Being No More: Alcyone and Ceyx (Liber XI, 410–748)   240

The Infuriating Destiny of Becoming an Immortal Animal (Liber XI, 410–748)   243

A Happy End: Iphigenia (Liber XII, 1–39)   245

"Dwelling," Online (Liber XII, 40–63)   247

On Deicide: Cycnus and Achilles (Liber XII, 64–145)   249

Tra-ta-ta: Trauma, Transition—Caenis/Caeneus and Neptune (Liber XII, 146–209)   251

Lapiths and Centaurs: Weaponization and Disfiguration (Liber XII, 210–535)   253

CONTENTS

Periclymenus: A Parody of a Parody, or in the Footsteps of
Proteus and Thetis (Liber XII, 536–579)   256

The Death of Achilles in Fragments (Liber XII, 580–630)   258

Weapon-Oriented Ontology (WOO): The Arms of Achilles
(Liber XIII, 1–398)   260

Hecuba's Lament: The Howl of the Place (Liber XIII, 399–575)   264

Becoming-Many: Memnon (Liber XIII, 576–622)   266

The Daughters of Anius: A Blessing (Liber XIII, 623–647)   270

The Daughters of Orion: A Blood Offering for the Wounded Earth
(Liber XIII, 648–699)   272

Polyphemus and Galatea: Land and Sea (Liber XIII, 700–897)   274

Phytomorphosis: Glaucus (Liber XIII, 898–969; Liber XIV, 1–79)   277

The Sibyl's Monologue (Liber XIV, 80–153)   280

Becoming-Foreign-to-Yourself: Achaemenides
(Liber XIV, 154–222)   282

Aeolus: The Ruler of the Winds (Liber XIV, 223–319)   284

Picus, or the Keyboard Pecker (Liber XIV, 320–434)   286

Acmon Turning Into a Bird: A Joke (Liber XIV, 435–511)   288

An Apulian Shepherd: Bitter Words, Bitter Fruits
(Liber XIV, 512–565)   290

Re: A Funereal Hymn for Aeneas (Liber XIV, 566–608)   292

Vertumnus, Vertimus: The Turn of Becoming
(Liber XIV, 609–697)   293

Marble Thoughts: Anaxarete (Liber XIV, 698–764)   296

The Apotheosis of Romulus: Blood for Celestial Peace
(Liber XIV, 765–851)   298

Homeland Insecurity: Myscelus (Liber XV, 1–59)   301

A Vegan Feast of Words: Pythagoras (Liber XV, 60–390)   303

CONTENTS

The Phoenix Memo (Liber XV, 391–478)   308

Running Out of Words: A Wounded Body Politic—Hippolytus (Liber XV, 391–546)   309

Being Double: Cipus (Liber XV, 547–621)   312

Orbi et Urbi: To the World and to the City—The Approximations of Power (Liber XV, 622–744)   315

The Indigestibility of Fate (Liber XV, 745–870)   319

The Work Undone: Ovid (Liber XV, 871–879)   321

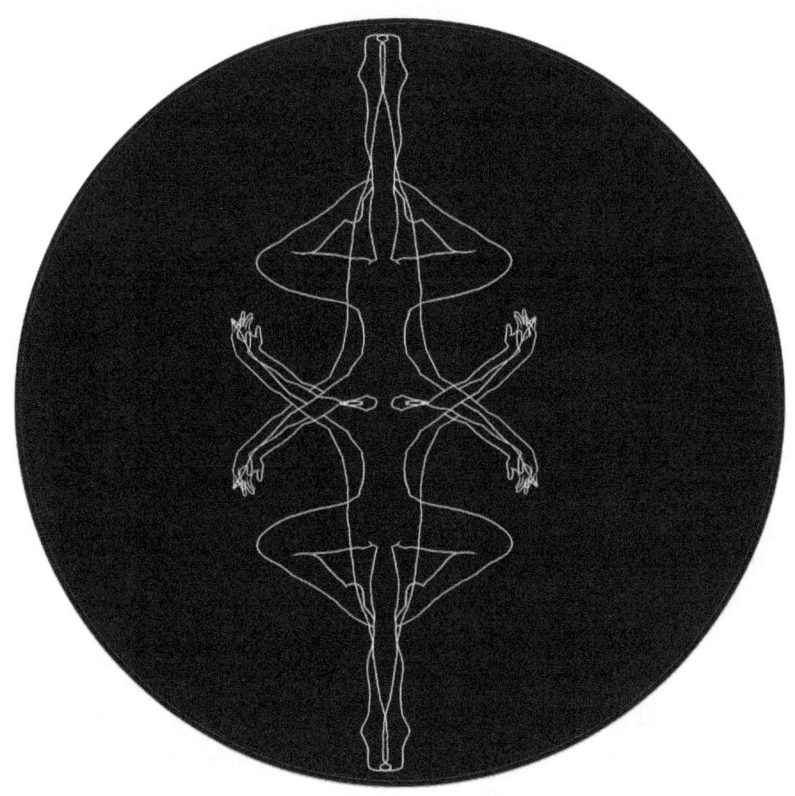

PREFACE

Written just over two thousand years ago, Ovid's *Metamorphoses* is one of the key works of Western culture. It is also a work that challenges some of the fundamental assumptions of the culture it belongs to, namely that the human is the pinnacle of creation, that the world is organized in a hierarchical and immutable whole, that change and becoming are the secondary and epiphenomenal events in the vast panorama of existence, and that the realms of nature and culture are set apart from each other. At the dawn of Christianity, which also questions rigid distinctions between the human and the divine, Ovid portrays reality consisting of perpetual transformations: of humans into stones, plants, and animals; of the gods and stones into humans; of animals into stars or constellations... Often metamorphoses are partial or lead to mismatches between the bodies and the minds of the metamorphosed entities, when, say, a human mind persists in a vegetal body, or the mind of a beast takes hold of human corporeity, which is not such a far-fetched possibility. These and related features of *Metamorphoses* make the text strikingly relevant and contemporary in the twenty-first century in light of the intellectual currents associated with posthumanism that try to recover many facets of existence already present in Ovid's masterpiece. Unless it is "our" twenty-first century that is strikingly relevant to *Metamorphoses* . . .

This is a "remake" of the fifteen books comprising Ovid's original text in multiple genres, ranging from letters and essays to poetic passages and dramatic dialogues, from diary entries and confessions to prayers and the newsreel, from meditations and loose fragments to pieces of exegesis and lamentations. (Let it be noted already that what I have just called the "original text" is far from original, seeing that the Roman author reelaborates, embellishes, or altogether modifies already existing myths deeply rooted in pre-Roman traditions. In this sense my gesture is faithful to Ovid, despite its occasional unfaithfulness to the letter of his text.) Some of the materials gathered here envision "the morning after" the transformations, picking the narrative thread where Ovid leaves off. What does Lycaon do after he becomes a wolf? How can Echo and Narcissus be reunited? What is the fate of Arachne after she has been transformed into a spider? Others re-create the mythic events depicted by Ovid in an alternative manner: in first-person confessions, such as those of Ino and Athamas, or in daily diary entries, like the ones of Leucothoe. Others still offer unconventional interpretations of parts of Ovid's poem, for instance, the idea of cross-species interbirth and interdeath in the myth of Cadmus sowing serpent teeth or the inversion of the relations of subservience and domination in the story of Europa's theft by Zeus/Jove.

Through diverse genres with which I experiment, I cultivate the metamorphoses of language itself. Indeed, the very choice of genre is in each instance closely attuned to a particular metamorphosis it is called upon to convey, and often genres are mixed in hybrid assemblages, say, of poetry and philosophical prose, of scholarly analyses and dramatic dialogues, or of inventory lists and literary fragments. Oftentimes it is impossible to explain and justify this choice at a rational level: the materials, the matters themselves, dictate it. As for language's metamorphoses, one of their aspects has to do with translation—not only the English translation of Ovid's Latin, but also with Ovid's own implicit and explicit translation of Greek mythologies into a Roman worldview. Careful attention to the original text is made possible by the bilingual edition of *Metamorphoses*, which is available as volumes 42 and 43 of Loeb Classical Library and which has provided me with an indispensable resource in writing this book. Here the meanings of names are crucial, seeing that by turning into other-than-human beings, humans live up to their proper names: Daphne, who becomes a laurel tree, is already named "laurel"; Arachne, who morphs into a spider, is named "spider"; and so forth.

The metamorphosis of language I have in mind is not limited to the rather technical elements of translation. The question that silently resonates throughout this text is: How to make, or to let, metamorphoses (and *Metamorphoses*) metamorphose? Resorting to multiple styles, sometimes bending English grammar and punctuation, or recording the sounds and the near silences that the metamorphosing creatures emit or that they sink into, I strive not only to reflect metamorphoses in my writing but also to encourage writing itself to metamorphose so as to accommodate these transformations better, more fittingly and vividly. Depending on the metamorphosis at stake, language dries up in ultrashort sentences, abutting the inorganic. It flows like water without final periods when touched by the fluidity of identity (of sexual identity, for instance, as in the case of Tiresias). Or, again, it branches out in various directions in the course of becoming-plant.

Across Arcadian hills and Boeotian palaces, between Phoenicia and Thebes, transposed from Greek and Roman antiquities to today, you are in for an exhalating ride. The goal of these exercises is not to bring Ovid closer to us but to bring us closer to him—in fact, so close that in our contemporary events and phenomena we would discern the folds and ramifications of an ancient text, the text of transformations, of metamorphoses interwoven as threads in the fabric of life and death, of lives and deaths. Grief and bellicosity, fear and compassion, greed and love, jealousy and devotion, among many other emotions and psychic states, will complement the physical landscapes, where the adventures of metamorphosis will transpire. Throughout, the figure of the human, the human as a figure of life, will be a transit point between our immemorial organic and even inorganic past and the other-than-human future, which, at many turns, may circle back to that past. Could this be the only sense of the human worth keeping today? Could it be a moment of liberation, which metamorphoses seek and wordlessly announce?

METAMORPHOSES REIMAGINED

PRELUDE: CHAOS
(Liber I, 1–30)

Chaos. A primordial heap made up of "the warring seeds of ill-matched elements," *discordia semina rerum*. An impossible vision: difficult to sustain, to frame, to lend a shape to. Matter and form, form and content, are not yet combined in it. This lack defines it. But a vision it is. An optics of the origin—the lens, though which the myth of origins (hence, the myth of myth) is viewed.

Chaos. A dim glimmer of the immemorial past. An obscure premonition of the future. An abyss of the present. Un-conscious.

Is the past of chaos immemorial? Or does it occupy (better: does it pre-occupy) the entire sphere of memory, seeing that a chaotic heap reappears between kaleidoscopically changing forms in every process of becoming, in each event of metamorphosis, of the alteration and alternation of existences? Is metamorphosis a reminder of the immemorial, a memento of absolute amnesia, a memory of what cannot be remembered, of what is dis-membered, discombobulated, disjointed yet piled together, of a time (if a time it was) when "no form of things remained the same," *nulli sua forma manebat*?

PRELUDE: CHAOS

A time of otherness, as well as of indistinction, of mélange, of the mishmash of elements . . .

> Chaos. Where? When? Do these questions make sense, still or already? Before the beginning, in the middle, at and after the end. For everything ends (without ending) in chaos, too: a gigantic heap at the end of times. A dump, which tolerates neither metamorphosis nor metabolism, neither alteration nor alternation, beyond the distinction between the same and the other.

THE FIRST METAMORPHOSIS, OR MAN IS A WOLF TO GOD

(Liber I, 210–240)

The first metamorphosis is never first. It will have been preceded. By chaos, above (or below) all. (See the reflection above.) There is, however, the first metamorphosis in the order of the text: the transformation of a god (Jove/Jupiter/Zeus: Are these transformations of a divine proper name that stands for the common name of god—*deus*, *dios*, *dieu*—in translation from Greek into Latin and on into Romance languages further signs of metamorphosis?) into a human being. A god who incarnates as a human so as to witness the inequities and the sheer depravity of humankind. Sounds familiar? Divine metamorphosis, the metamorphosis of something or someone already in a state of perfection and therefore not supposed to suffer any changes, is the first link in the winding chain of transfigurations—of humans into trees, spiders, wolves, stones . . .

In effect, the inaugural metamorphosis is double: its duality troubles its claim to being first. When Jove turns into a human, Lycaon, the king of Arcadia, becomes a wolf. Lycaon, the forefather of all werewolves. Violating the sacred laws of hospitality, killing and cannibalizing hostages whom he was supposed to receive as his guests at home and whom he instead incorporates receiving them in his flesh, as his flesh, ready to shed blood to find out the truth beyond the shadow of a doubt, *nec erit dubitabile verum*, Lycaon acts as a wolf before he morphs into one. What are the telltale signs of his transformation? Garments turning into shaggy gray hair? Arms now shaped like legs? No, his animal features retain the traces of prior forms, *vestigia formae*. The main difference is the loud howl that resounds instead of speech.

The nocturnal silence of Arcadia. Covered with frost in the deep of winter, Arcadian villages feel lifeless, their stillness reflected in myriads of tiny crystals sparkling on rooftops and mountain slopes under faint moonlight. Nothing breaks this silence save for his howling, aggressive yet desperate. He is a frantic, distressed werewolf. It was words that he wanted to utter, not howls. Mad words, murderous words, swearwords, but words nonetheless. How can he pursue indubitable truth now that he is unable speak? Were all those murders in vain? Were the tests to which he submitted his divine guest for naught? To be sure, he will keep doing the same: terrorizing poor helpless sheep, tearing their bodies to pieces, getting inebriated at the sight, smell, and taste of blood. He will continue to do what he has been doing in his human incarnation. Just not in the name of truth. Or, maybe, in the name of *another truth*—that of a hungry stomach, of sharp fangs and claws, of metabolic hospitality.

A howl pierces the dead of night to announce an impeding orgy of death. Long, fearful, and fear-inducing. Then another one. And yet another. He is surprised with what he hears, with the sounds he cannot stop emitting, as though experimenting with his vocal cords in the hopes of sounding otherwise, of sounding human. Was howling a brief interlude between one word and another, between words and silence, between one silence and another? Will speech roll off his tongue ever again? He has expected to hear himself speak; instead he hears himself howl. Is the ear that hears his own howls the same ear that used to hear the utterances of his mouth?

5
THE FIRST METAMORPHOSIS, OR MAN IS A WOLF TO GOD

For a moment, both exceedingly brief and endless, there are neither claws nor paws, neither thick gray fur nor gleaming eyes. There is only a tiny space, a resonance chamber between his foam-covered lips and pointy ears. He had been a wolf all along. He shape-shifted into a wolf. But he did not become who he was until he heard himself howl, time after time. Each howl announces him to himself, precisely as who he is, even as it announces him to the world, to the hushed villages, fields, and mountains.

———

Homo homini lupus, "man is a wolf to man," a Latin proverb says (and Thomas Hobbes confirms). *Homo homini deus*, "man is a god to man," Ludwig Feuerbach retorts, mockingly. How about *homo dei lupus*, "man is a wolf to god?" The signature is Ovid's.

STONE(S) AGE
(Liber I, 380-415)

Since Babylonian, Egyptian, and Greek antiquity, global destruction by fire or water instilled fear and trembling in people's minds and hearts. But dread in the face of planetary devastation was mixed with the hope of revival, the rebirth of life from the ashes or from high waves. What are the shapes of postapocalyptic renaissance? What does it look and feel like? How is becoming jump-started on the abyssal verge of nothing?

Between art and nature, between technique and growth, between Deucalion and Pyrrha—the son of Prometheus and the daughter of Epimetheus—stones come to life so as to restore humankind through –jection: ejection from the earth, projection into the air. Unlike other creatures, they (we) are saved not by evolution but by revolution. Flung up, rocks are detached from their native element, the earth, the body of the great mother: *magna parens terra*. Rejected. Thrown, they move *contra natura*, against nature *in* nature. Art is this very movement, and it needs nature to move within. Always against-within. The descendants of Prometheus and Epimetheus must join forces to make it happen.

Stones fly, then. A moment later they land, no longer the same as they were when they were hurled upward. Between their takeoff and landing, time itself is fast-forwarded. The inorganic becomes organic. Softening: crumbling into fine mineral dust that will nourish plant life. Softening: displaying a different shape, less rigid, fleshlike. Softening: giving in to relentless erosion, to the insistence of the waves, to the friction of air, to the promise of elemental and biological relations. Only greatly accelerated.

Stones are not without life, not without moisture, the humid portion (*pars umida*) of their being, the lichens and moss that cover them. The fleshiness of rocks. And life is not without its stony support, not without an inorganic, mineral substratum, concentrated in the bones and the skeletal structure of the planet crawling with life. With time, bones turn into stones. It is not that big of a stretch to imagine how stones turn into bones, of the earth and of those she births.

... Rumbling. The sounds of coming unglued from the body of the earth. Later, swishing by in the air. Later still, they speak in men's and women's voices, depending on whether it is a man's or a woman's hand that hurled them. The initial vociferations are plosive, pulmonic consonants blocking the vocal tract. They are airless, suffocated, voiced like a stone dropping: *tttt, kkkk, ddddd, bbbbbbb, pppppp*: *tttttookkk, dddddroppppedddd*. Mineral words, ancestral speech...

But speech also softens. Like stones.

... Soft consonants pronounced by stone-people: *ssssss, ffffffff, sss-soffffft*. These are the souvenirs of their travels through the air, swishing by. Vocal souvenirs. The softening of minerals, the softening of speech... Which is not to deny the hardness of our race—*genus durum sumus*, "we are tough people." The stone age that follows on the heels of gold, silver, and the other metal ones.

Speech softens to the point of singing.

... *Ooooooo, aaaaa, uuuuuu*. A song: stones taking to the air, returning to the atmosphere. As people. In the rounding of the mouth, of the lips, the cycle of renaissance is complete.

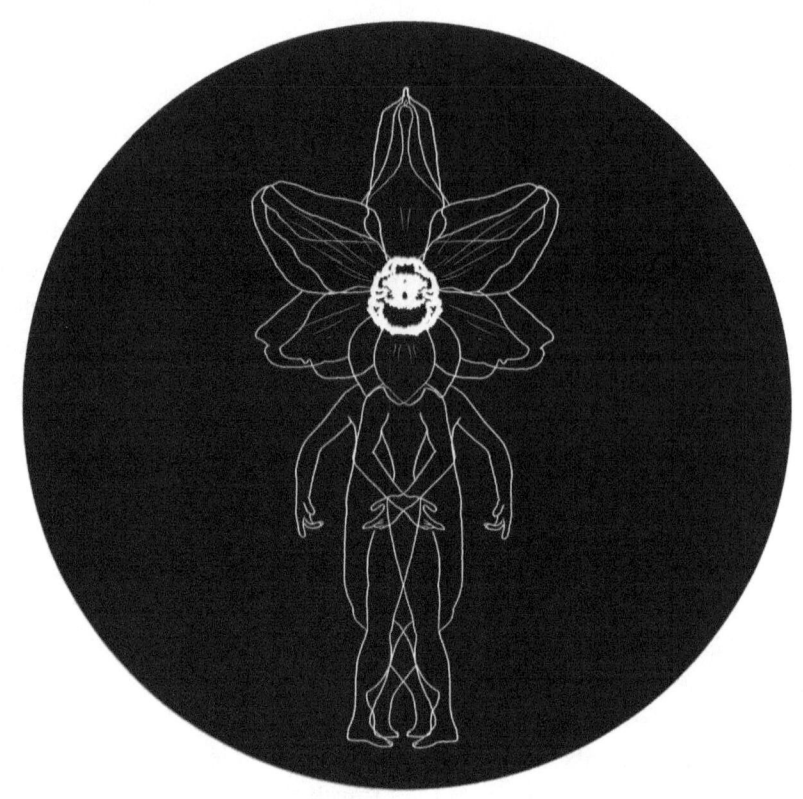

DAPHNE'S FUGUES

(Liber I, 452-567)

Fleeing from him, she flees from herself, from her divine or semidivine nymph self, clothed in a human form. Because he, the god of order who is chasing after her, claims the right to determine that which must be her form, imposed upon her as a structured and stiff identity. She transfigures herself (and her self, but let's not hurry to come up with diagnoses, such as "dissociative fugue"). She escapes from and toward her destiny. And toward her name: finally, she may live up to it. Δάφνη, Daphne, Laurel, Bay Tree. There are myriads of transformations between and among these apparent semantic equivalents, testifying to how translation is inevitably, invariably metamorphosis. Hers is an almost archetypal case of metamorphosis. She is desperate; she finds herself in an intolerable situation, where the only glimmer of hope is, precisely, to lose herself (and her self), to become other, but also to live up to herself—for instance, to her name, which already is and says a great deal—otherwise. Almost archetypal, but not quite. Something gets jammed in the machine of metamorphosis, the machine that *is* metamorphosis, which functions smoothly even as it inconspicuously undermines its own operations. By the jamming of the machine, I do not mean *the logic of metamorphoses* (Ovid's and of a more general variety) where change itself does not change, where the form of change remains constant across all changes of form, and where, further, continuity prevails over rupture, that is to say, where something unchangeable persists beneath, above, or behind every mutation and behind mutability itself. Were only these issues prominent in the story of Daphne, it would have been really archetypal. There is another element, though, within the twists and turns of the narratives in which she figures, from Phylarchus and Parthenius of Nicaea through Pausanias to Nonnus of Panopolis and Ovid, that adds weight to the meta-unchangeability of metamorphoses. This element is a fixation on eternity.

In the thickets of Ovid's text, eternity (better: the desire for eternity) is a constant before and after Daphne's metamorphosis. The young nymph wants to be a virgin forever, as she asks her father to let her "enjoy virginity" (*virginitate frui*) in a manner similar to the goddess Diana (*Met.* 1.486), or Artemis, Daphne's patroness, according to Phylarchus. She gives voice to the desire to be eternally pure, unstained, untouched. Absolved and absolute. In its turn, the laurel, into which she metamorphoses, lends a body to her desire: evergreen, bay leaves are the symbols of eternity, oblivious to seasonal rhythms and cosmic cycles. Hence, Apollo: "as my youthful head is never shorn, so, also, shalt thou ever bear thy leaves" (*utque meum intonsis caput est iuvenale capillis, tu quoque perpetuos semper gere frondis honores*) (*Met.* 1.563–564). Later on, Saint Hildegard of Bingen will associate the evergreen branch with another eternal virgin, Mary, "the greenest branch," *viridissima virga* (*Symph.* 19.1), on which redemption will blossom in the vegetal form of her son. In her undying purity, *she*—Daphne, Mary . . .—will crown the heads of gods and heroes or carry the radiant savior-flower. She will be substantive, she will be substance itself, in spite of or thanks to, her metamorphoses. Above or below, she will persist, glorifying and supportive. Forever the same.

Sharing stability in their ideally static and unchanging nature, virginity and undying evergreen life are the materializations of the idea of eternity, the metaphysical idea par excellence. They know no passage of time. And yet, eternity materialized is a stumbling block on the path of becoming; it is indigestible, indecomposable, nonbiodegradable. Like plastic that, despite its apparent plasticity and pliability, breaks into ever smaller bits of debris. Daphne is willing to exchange her body for another corporeity: to preserve, on the one hand, her life in its eternally virginal state and, on the other, virginity as the animus of her life. "Destroy the beauty that has injured me," she appeals to her progenitor, "or change the body that destroys my life" (*qua nimium placui, mutando perde figuram*) (*Met.* 1.547). Her appeal needs to be heard in all its gravity: Daphne prays for her countenance, her fatally beautiful figure, to be disfigured or reconfigured in order to maintain the life that this figure and its appeal devastate, that they overlay, suppress, and suffocate. Metamorphosis is a tool, an instrument of salvation, a piece of salvific technology, a soteriological machine permitting the kernel that truly matters—namely, everlasting, evergreen, virginal life—to stay unscathed at the price of the dispensable shell.

...and so, you begin your endless apprenticeship in vegetating. Ever a beginner, a novice, ever. Forever and ever. A bay tree, not at all kept at bay. Vigor and paralysis, vitality and torpor, metamorphosis and eternity. You feel both, you *are* both at once. There is no more absconding in space, your toes rooting in the earth, anchoring you, cutting short your fugacious journey upon the terrestrial surface. But you are escaping more effectively than ever before, in time, through time, as vegetal time, albeit impervious to the alternations and alterations of the seasons. You follow different rhythms—particularly, distinct breathing rhythms—that augur the previously unexperienced cadences of existence. Slower, yet more elusive. You are learning the art of the fugue, a contrapuntal composition of your life: torpor and vitality, paralysis and vigor. Fleeing from yourself, or yourself fleeing? I bet that yours is a fugue *from* the human and *of* the human, from and of the one who has no objectively determinate sense. Silently, wordlessly, with nothing other than the rustling of your leaves (green glory, a culinary delight...) you are teaching us the meaning of being-human: yourself only in a perpetual flight from yourself.

Daphne's genealogy is shrouded in mystery. Parthenius relates that her father is Amyclas, the mythic king of Sparta (*Erot.* 15.1). Pausanias thinks that she hails from Arcadia, the daughter of the river god Ladon and the earth goddess Gē (*Paus.* 8.20.1). According to Diodorus, she is the daughter of Tiresias, the soothsayer from Thebes (*Bibl. Hist.* 4.66.5). Herself an oracle and a poet, she was the true author of Homer's verses: "it was from her poetry, they say, that the poet Homer took many verses which he appropriated as his own and with them adorned his own" (*Bibl. Hist.* 4.66.6). Ovid names the river god Peneus as her father and locates her in Thessaly (*Met.* 1.425), a hypothesis previously proposed by Hyginus (*Fab.* 208).

Equally mysterious is Daphne's vow of virginity and her relation to Apollo. Pausanius states that she "avoided all the male sex" (*Paus.* 8.20.2), which is why she and other maidens killed Leucippus ("White Horse"), who, having fallen in love with Daphne, pretended to be a woman (merely donning women's clothes, no metamorphosis there!) with the view to befriending and gaining her confidence. Jealous of Leucippus, Apollo was responsible for the exposure of his lie, which coincided with the exposure of his sex (*Paus.* 8.20.4). Diodorus is convinced that Daphne was a prisoner of war, handed over to Apollo as a present (*Bibl. Hist.* 4.66.1). Ovid suggests that Apollo started pursuing Daphne after his heart was pierced by the golden arrow of love, while hers received the leaden arrow of indifference (*Met.* 1.470–471).

Her provenance is a tangle of appellations and places. It is a dump, dominated by the name of the father or of the fathers, who are impotent to establish and to guarantee the daughter's definitive origin. Could it be that what Daphne attempts to escape is the dump, a haphazard accumulation of toxic materials and ideas, of indifferent nondifferentiation, of patriarchal signifiers and metaphysical notions, of things that elude decay and decomposition? From within and from without, the dump weighs her down; it is piled over and amassed inside, suffocating her. To be able to breathe again, she resorts to vegetal respiration, reigniting obstructed metamorphoses and metabolisms.

A bastard daughter, Daphne is without a *whence*, just as, on the run, she is bereft of a *whither*. Between points of departure and destinations unknown: X–Y. Before metamorphosing, she dwells in this in-between, in the gap of metamorphosis that, deviating from the genealogical tree, draws a tree of its own and that lets her become and keep on becoming a tree. Mimesis is the talent of the human animal—say, of Leucippus, who (the animal that he is) only imitates a woman out of his passionate attraction to Daphne. Metamorphosis is the gift of the human plant, or of human-plant, the hyphen condensing in itself the vagaries of becoming. Mimetically, you look like someone else; with metamorphosis, you *are* that someone else. And it is so much easier to become the other if you are other to yourself, your origin unfixed...

Two problems crop up at this point.

1. Doesn't the difference between metamorphosis and mimesis repeat and encompass the metaphysical difference between essence and appearances, with the fresh proviso that essence is subject to change? Doesn't the purported difference between the plant and the animal produce the same effect? From a vegetal perspective, mimesis and metamorphosis are one and the same: essence resides on the surface of changing appearances that, the opposite of superfluous, are of the essence.
2. The ease of metamorphosis is explicable, at the subterranean level of its very roots, with reference to the violence, the violent silencing, overwriting, inscription and erasure (erasure in inscription and inscription in erasure) of lives. Daphne is already other to herself because of what has been taken away from and piled onto her, from the multiplications of patronyms to the unacknowledged appropriation of her verses by Homer, from the narration of her life and vegetal afterlife by the male authors of Antiquity to her insertion into a story that she has little to do with—the trick Eros plays on Apollo, or the war in which she is taken prisoner and handed as a gift over to the god.

Coupled with her desire for eternity, the refuge Daphne seeks in vegetal becoming, if not in the vegetality of becoming, is of a piece with that from which she is fleeing. Both her metamorphosis and her violent overwriting are facilitated by the absence of a rigid identity, which is not to be confused with the absence of firm principles, those last bastions of metaphysics. Causes, effects, and countereffects are scrambled, their relation left indeterminate. In a dump and in metamorphosis.

The bark enveloping your trunk. Is it a shield? The outward exhibition of your indifference? A prosthesis lending you strength and physical support?

Your unfading leaf. Is it really your hair, vegetalized and eternalized, supporting and thwarting planetary metabolisms?

DAPHNE'S FUGUES

The roots that grow from your toes. Are they prosthetic? A replacement for the umbilical cord, now connecting you to mother earth? An anchor for your unending flight? Cords that electrify your efforts of fleeing otherwise?

The branches that your arms have become. Are they evading embraces? Or are they capable of embracing all that is: the air and the sky, the rain and sunlight, the birds and the insects they host? Embracing before being embraced?

To you, I can only direct questions without expecting anything resembling an answer. Only in this way, by means of questions shorn of answers, a question incessantly transformed into other questions, can I hope to live up to metamorphosis, to live up to the lives caught up in a whirlpool of what is still called, by force of habit and rather absentmindedly, metamorphosis.

If Ovid is to be believed, Daphne has been penetrated by an arrow, which Venus's son had sent (*Met.* 1.463), the arrow that, contrary to Eros's usual pranks, had awakened indifference in her. Has she been traumatized by this initial penetration carrying the interdiction of approximation, of proximity, of touch? Is vegetating Daphne's response to that trauma, her idiosyncratic mode of dealing with it, working through it? And yet, Apollo keeps touching her, already in her incarnation as a tree, "feeling the trepidations of her breast under the newly formed bark" (*sentit adhuc trepidare novo sub cortice pectus*) (*Met.* 1.553). He "gives kisses to the wood; yet the wood also shirks from his kisses" (*oscula dat ligno: refugit tamen oscula lignum*) (*Met.* 1.555).

Being a tree, Daphne is exposed and protected from touch, paradoxically more exposed and more protected, more vulnerable and more unreachable, than before. Terrified and on the run, she has, according to Nonnus's account, sought refuge in her mother, the earth, "yawning," "gaping wide open" to receive Daphne back in her bosom: "γαῖα χανοῦσα" (*Nonn. D.* 33.214). Her roots are then hidden from sight and from touch, while her trunk, branches, and leaves are laid bare to the eye and the hand, for a caress as much as for the strike of an axe, for kisses as well as for "delimbing," the removal of branches that will be made into wreaths. As a strategy of concealment, it is dubious, to say the least.

To appreciate Daphne's move, to valorize her vegetal gesture, it is necessary to start thinking vegetally. She did not burrow into the earth like a worm or a mole, for example; she rooted there. Rooted in her mother. This return to the maternal—or, in part, *into* the maternal—is already a vegetal choice, rebelling against everything that sets her loose from that source, against everything that cuts the tie of the umbilical cord or the ligature of the root. In Ovid's narrative, it is to her father, the river god Peneus, that Daphne appeals for help (*Met.* 1.545–546), and, with her prayer heeded, her metamorphosis commences. Whether it is to her mother or to her father that the hounded nymph cries out, her appeal is a breaking point in the narrative. After this dramatic moment, she ceases fleeing like a chased animal; rather, she flees *into* animality or vegetality (the difference between the two is insubstantial here), rejoining a chain of metamorphoses where any given living figuration is provisional. Taking refuge in the elements, be it the earth yawning open under her feet or flowing water, she welcomes vegetality at the core of her being before actually becoming a plant. Fleeing into the open.

What kind of earth receives and excretes you? How does your evergreen glory express the eternity of uranium, microplastics, to say nothing of the abundant lithium you are exposed to? Which smog-filled skies do your branches embrace? Do your roots imbibe wastewater, industrial discharge and agricultural runoff and sewage effluent? What befalls you then? Other metamorphoses, largely undetectable, lurking behind the euphemisms *plasticity* and *adaptability*?

The fifteenth book of Parthenius's *Sufferings in Love* begins with the chapter titled Περὶ Δάφνης. "On Daphne," but also "Around Daphne." "On Laurel," or "Around Laurel." Encircling her with words, narrative structures, poems, myths. Moving about, dancing around her, apparently immobilized as a tree, in a tree, is what the authors, classical and contemporary, have done. Circling around or above her, vulture-like, without end, retracing the perimeter of what is supposed to be properly hers, and chasing her down. As if they have really caught up with her. Apollo himself has passed the baton to them—and to us, who continue this hermeneutical pursuit in full conviction that we have nailed her down, cornered and exposed her, who has opted for vegetal exposure.

Consider the closing lines in Ovid's poetic account. After Apollo has described the glorious role laurel will play in Roman ceremonies, "unto him the laurel bent her newly fashioned boughs in a nod, as if shaking her head, the crown" (*factis modo laurea ramis adnuit, utque caput visa est agitasse cacumen*) (*Met.* 1.565–566). Daphne is said to nod in the affirmative (*adnuit*), to agree with the god, to underwrite his words that overwrite her wordless expressions. Yet, she also shakes (*agitasse*) her crown violently, saying *no*. This is more than troubled, instantly disavowed, or misinterpreted consent—a dump of significations. Having metamorphosed into a tree, Daphne has no head; likened to hair, bay leaves grow on the branches her arms have become. Laurel's head is a crude hermeneutical error, a projection of something onto nothing. Which is not to assert, by any stretch of the imagination, that the laurel neither thinks nor feels. In fact, she thinks-feels with incomparable acuteness and sensitivity outside the spherical enclosure of the head (*caput*). For their part, Apollo, alongside the authors and the commentators writing about—on—Daphne, rejoice in their impression of having cornered her, dancing around her apparently submissive head, which is nothing at all.

Indirectly, *via negativa*, the end of Ovid's narration gives us indications for what a new beginning might look like. Every successful interpretation of Daphne, every earnest attempt to write her life or her lives, will be marked by what from the teleological perspective of accomplishment is a sheer failure. From every such attempt, writers and commentators will resurface empty-handed, confirming that Daphne has fled again, reaffirming her flight. Well, not exactly empty-handed, but saddled with growing, ramifying, decaying, regerminating, metamorphosing questions, tending toward her, wherever she might be, rather than snaking around her, where she is not. In the midst of these questions, it would be unforgivable to skip over the question of metamorphosis: the heritage of metaphysics (of *meta-* as such) it transmits and, in the course of transmitting, interferes with; the histories of violence it stems from and reacts to, bolstering and undermining them; the dump it both attracts and repels. Contrapuntal subjects, mutually opposed yet intertwined themes, as in any fugue. If Daphne's is an almost archetypal case of metamorphosis, then the question of metamorphosis will be folded into all the others that are destined toward her. That is, toward the one who, or that which, remains in the wake of her flight.

IO: THE NONMETAMORPHOSIS
(Liber I, 568-688)

Dearest Io,

I salute you. I admire your courage, worlds apart from the stupid ideal of heroism. You've suffered through a becoming that is no becoming, a metamorphosis that is a non-metamorphosis. How many have buckled under the weight of similar circumstances?

Ever since Jove cast his eye over you, he thought that you were *iuvenca*—a young woman, a girl, as well as a young cow, a heifer. That is what you were to him; that is what you were destined to become.

Your father, the river Iachus, wept over you because he let go of you. (No mention of your mother.) You were lost to your father and to yourself, though not to Jove who kept you as his *iuvenca* in human and in bovine forms. He kept you throughout, despite having to pass you on to someone else.

Even when the god called you a maiden, *virgo*, he envisioned no one but *iuvenca*. His jealous wife confirmed this vision of you. It was after Juno suspected Jove of infidelity that he transformed you into a heifer.

A white heifer. Your newly acquired color meant to dissimulate his own dirty thoughts under a veil of innocence. It was also meant to appease Juno, who wanted to receive you as a gift. And, of course, to make you highly visible, noticeable from afar, easily guarded by Argus with his hundred eyes.

Seen by others, you were invisible to yourself. You had no experience of your new body: trying to stretch your arms in supplicating prayer, you displayed your hoofs; trying to speak, you mooed. When you caught sight of yourself as reflected in your father, the stream, whose hand you licked and tried to kiss, you were terrified; when you heard your bovine voice, mooing, you shuddered in fear. Were you unfamiliar with your nature as a young woman, as that other *iuvenca*, desired by gods and men? And with yourself freed from the status of an object of another's desire?

I salute you! I admire you, dearest Io! Not least because, when speech ceased, when your tongue failed you, you discovered writing. Literally. You substituted speech with letters, *littera pro verbis*. What a change! What an exchange! You traced letters in the dust with your hoof. You wrote your story for others to read. And for yourself to grasp, in the first instance. You wrote yourself: the writer and the written, all in one. You committed yourself (your story, your life or your lives) to signs you left in the dust without the assistance of a hand, quill or ink, paper or parchment, stone or stylus. Hold on! Maybe you did so with the help of stones ground to fine powder, softened. They have swished by on these pages already. These details are secondary; what matters is that you wrote. You did not merely become a cow, a girl, a heifer, *iuvenca*; you became writing itself. And that is already not nothing.

Vegetally yours,
Oi

SYRINX: BECOMING-IN-PLACE, BECOMING-PLANT

(Liber I, 698–712)

Syrinx's path ended in a marsh. The end of one road was the beginning of another: after extensive travels—an intensive journey. "Water was the impediment in her course" and a prompt to travel inwards. Her feet found firm support no more. She got bogged down in moist soil. Water and earth: elemental indecision, blurred boundaries. A part of her was now below-ground. The place's texture and the composition of the soil dictated the kind of metamorphosis she would undergo: she would become a plant, in touch with the sky and the soil and the worlds in-between.

In a marsh, Syrinx morphed into marsh reeds. One among many, many, many. *Where* she was determined *who* or *what* she would metamorphose into. This is vegetal becoming at its purest, or at its muddiest, since a plant always becomes in a place, with and as that very place.

As a reed, Syrinx brought together the soil and water; she turned an obstacle to her progress into the communion of elements. And let's not forget air. Pan's sighing over the reeds, which his hand grasped instead of Syrinx, "stirred soft air," so that the plants "gave forth a low and complaining sound." Self-centered, he thought she was talking to him, but it was elemental conversations she was conducting, allowing air, water, earth, and fire to speak through her.

Acting upon his presumption, Pan completed her metamorphosis, crafting a musical instrument out of her. A pipe. A natural metamorphosis gave way to a technical invention. His fingers sliding along the extension of her plant body; his lips hugging each of her openings . . . Henceforth, it was his breath, the air he exhaled, that she had to welcome, to accommodate in her hollows, to receive and to conduct. Whenever he played with her. Whenever he played *her*.

But the memory of the place
where she became marsh reeds—
the memory of the place that became her—
lingered on.
As did the memory of the elemental communion,
which she made possible and which made her—
Syrinx-the-reed-pipe—possible.

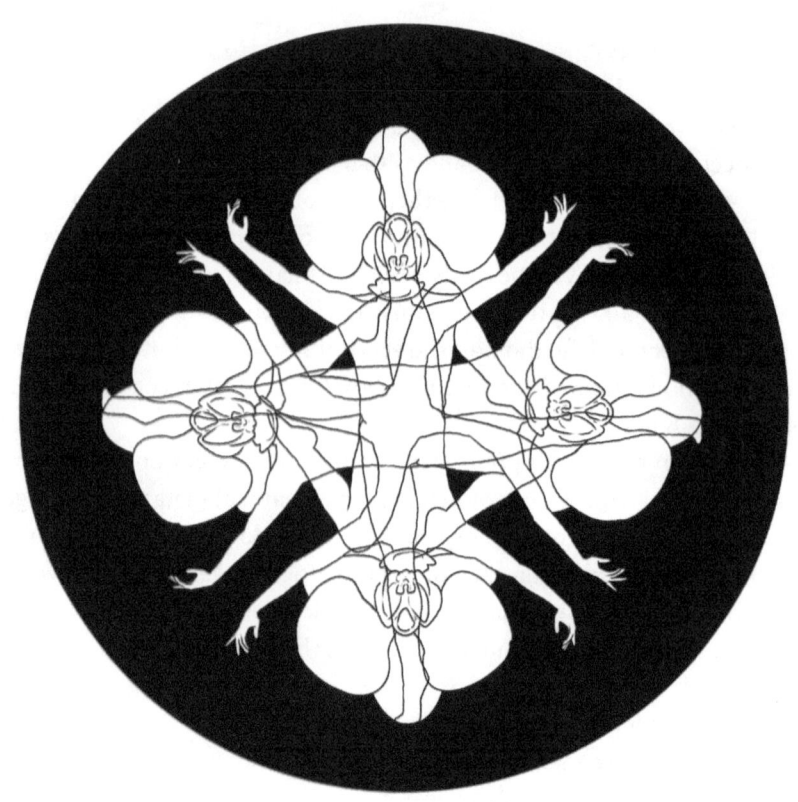

THE SISTERS OF PHAETHON: THE VEGETAL SHAPE OF GRIEF

(Liber II, 330–365)

Eager to outshine his father, the sun, an amateur charioteer incinerated everything: the earth, rivers and seas, the sky. Fiery destruction, all over again. All (is) over. The elements do not change into one another; they are consumed by the flames, metabolized by fire. Their very differences are burnt up, covered over with the indifferent gray of ash.

> Chaos returns. "If the sea perish and the land and the realms of the sky, then we are hurled back to primeval chaos, *in chaos antiquum confundimur.*" Says the earth. The death-bearing fire of devastation no longer regenerates life but dumps the earth into the sky and the sky into the earth. It confounds, disorients, suffocates.

THE SISTERS OF PHAETHON

Phaethon's father Helios (or Phoebus) mourns his son, as does Phaethon's mother Clymene, an Oceanid nymph, and her daughters, the Heliades. How to mourn a child who, scorching the world, is himself scorched to death? How to keep mourning a child, who, playing with fire, was barely distinguishable from our contemporary humanity?

Phoebus hides his face: mourning as withdrawal from others and retreat into oneself, as a nonappearance of the one who makes everything and everyone appear.

Clymene weeps on her son's tomb, shedding tears on his name and fondling it against her breast: mourning as the replacement of the lost object with the name, which is a symbolic surrogate, healing even in the depths of grief and despair.

The Heliades seem to do what their mother does, but an inexplicable thing happens in the course of their "useless tribute to the dead." Theirs is a mourning that transfigures, that, instead of inspiring either the mourners' retreat into themselves or the outpouring of grief tied to an engraved name, causes them to become wholly other. The feet of one grow cold at her brother's grave; the second is held fast by "sudden roots;" the hair of the third turns into foliage; the others discover long branches in place of their arms: mourning as metamorphosis.

The sisters' grief takes the shape of a plant. It suffocates and paralyzes them, makes them cold and slow, almost deadening them. They are stuck in their sorrow, fixated on it. The work of mourning—unworkable. Yet, they also grow in the place of the dead. Rooted there, they feed on decaying flesh, the flesh of their brother but also of their memories, of affects, of psychic life, of their prior human form. Their mournful growth speaks to the nonfinality of death, to the revival of scorched earth and of the scorched scorcher himself, if in another shape.

Plant memory is etched into annual growth rings, not into letters on a marble monument that are bathed in the mother's tears. The bark, *cortex*, that covers the sisters' bodies spares no more than their lips, the lips that keep whispering and that receive the mother's mournful kisses. Human speech in a plant body. Verbal consciousness in wooden forms. Later, much later, the vision that the Heliades unveiled will be Dante's nightmare, sounded by "these loud, unhappy voices" of sinners turned into bushes in *Inferno*. From their broken twigs, "words and blood," *parole e sangue*, gush forth together (*Inf.* XIII, 25–45), alluding to one of the medieval signs of the approaching Apocalypse. Blood also drips from beneath the Heliades' bark after their mother tries to "tear it off from their bodies, breaking off slender twigs with her hands." Her already infinite grief amplified, she refuses to accept the death of her son *and* the apparent loss of her daughters. She tears them to pieces in an attempt to save them, to save their past selves, to save herself, to save an illusion of permanence.

Nostrum laceratur in arbore corpus: "it is our body you are lacerating in the tree," they retort. Bark is not a lifeless cover, hiding the sentient flesh of old; it is who we are. Our body . . . in the tree. Our body, the tree: singular and plural. These are the last words the lips whisper before they, too, are covered by bark. They stop speaking. And they continue to speak, through their mournful vegetal shapes, through flowing plant tears that, hardening into amber, line the bottom of nearby streams and rivers. The Heliades are now pines, pining over, commemorating and resurrecting their brother, whom they recall more vividly than a monumental slab of marble bearing his name. They let the dead live otherwise by feeding on decaying organic matter, lending it the forms of a tree, which *is* the charred corpse's afterlife. Vegetal grief is, by the same token, revival, resurrection in the flesh, in vegetal flesh, congruent with grief and with the flowing, then hardened, amber tears it leaves behind.

... AND THE ANIMAL SHAPE OF GRIEF: THE SWAN SONG OF CYCNUS

(Liber II, 366–380)

Are you grieving so intensely that you become an animal? Screeching in pain, baying in agony. Distraught. Out of your mind. Which is to say: out of your body.

Your voice is the first to go. Your human voice. By going, it comes: with an inhuman pitch and animal intensity. Losing your voice, you gain it, your grief gains on you and takes the place of your voice, your calmly articulated words and phrases. *Nooooooooo . . . N-n-n-n- ooooooowwooooo . . . ooooowwwwwoooo . . .* Your voice becomes "thin and shrill," gradually dissolving, dissipating. And you are dissipating in and with it. Getting thinned out into something else, passing through the sieve of grief, through nonbeing. Into another form of being?

Let's see (or listen). You are thinned out but are not altogether disappearing. On the contrary, thanks to your suffering, your presence grows starker than ever. Your presence to others, if not to yourself.

Next your hair is hidden by plumage, your neck stretches out, membranes appear between your reddened fingers, you grow wings on your sides. Each one of your feathers is a shield and a wound. The wings of your mourning do not carry you aloft. You have little trust in the skies of Jove, where the one whose death you are bemoaning was killed. Your animal grief reconfigures the world of the elements: you are at home closer to water, abhorring fire, cautious about the upper strata of air.

It is your mourning for your lover, Phaethon, that molds you into a swan. Makes you ever more beautiful, gracious, even in the midst of sadness and pain, of solitude and irrecoverable loss. The song sung in your shrill voice declares the other's death and the approach of your own, the other's death as your own. You have died to yourself as a human being, to be reborn as a bird. In mourning the other, your lost lover, you are mourning yourself—your past human self, which was, perhaps, a mistake, a persistent misrecognition, an error of judgment you had gotten accustomed to. Not anymore.

CALLISTO:
THE MOST BEAUTIFUL SHE-BEAR
(Liber II, 401–530)

—Who are you? What has become of you?

—Agrrr, agrrrr, grrrr

—Is that you, Callisto, *kallistē*, "the most beautiful one?" Oh, Jove, you whose rape of Callisto robbed her of her human countenance, and you, Diana, who, enraged, sealed her fate—restore her voice at once! Let the she-bear, the splendid, shining *Ursa*, speak!

—Grrreetings. Woe to me; I'd rather roar at my fate.

—Aren't you Diana's shadow, her alter-ego? Didn't the Greeks celebrate and worship her (that is, you) as *Artemis Kallistē*, the most beautiful Artemis?

—I am her; she is me. I've punished myself for the crime perpetrated against me. And, it pains me to say this, it was my husband, Jove, who

raped me in the guise of . . . me, myself, "having put on the image and the dress of Diana."
—Horror! You were raped, as though by yourself, and then castigated yourself for the act!
—I was afraid of myself. I am still afraid. Every time I glance at the surface of the pond, I see the face of the rapist staring back at me. What used to be my own face. Disfigured. Reconfigured. "How hard it is not to betray a guilty consciousness in the face!"
—A crime? Guilty consciousness?
—The insignia of Jove's wantonness left on my body, in my body, as my body. A son, Arcas, a flesh-and-blood trace of that night, after which I am not *virgo* anymore. The night, after which every day that passed brought me close to being a she-bear, *ursa*.
—What did you do then? What have you done?! Did the chisel of your trauma sculpt an animal out of you?
—An animal, sure. And a star. Several stars: a whole constellation of them. Just when Arcas, who grew up a hunter, was about to kill his she-bear mother, knowing not who I was, the hand of a god saved us both, "setting us up in the heavens and making us neighboring stars."
—You were less than human *and* more than human. Simultaneously. More or less.
—Yes and yes.

Shortly thereafter, silence descended. A vibrant silence, bathed in shimmering light.

One star speaks to another, one constellation communicates to another, through the light it reflects across space-time. The light that arrives and is received, twinkling, after a long delay. And an overwhelming darkness all around.

An infinitely repeated "Yes and yes," even if there is no one there to respond to anymore.

CROW TROUBLE

(Liber II, 531–632)

Augury is ornithomancy, the art of detecting omens in the behavior of birds. These signs are indirect: they have to do with the patterns of the birds' movement in the air, with how feathered bodies inhabit space, hovering in it, and telling observers about the time to come. When these signs are too obvious, spoken, foretold in a loud voice, birds get into trouble. Voice cannot replace the body's position when it comes to speaking of the future, if not to the future. "A talking raven, though white before, had been suddenly changed to black." Why? "His tongue was his undoing," *lingua fuit damno*.

Another talking bird, a crow, does not desist, cawing in our ears and echoing in our heads: "Scorn not the forewarnings of my tongues." There is more than one tongue, then. Glossolalia. Even when it is a bird who is speaking in tongues. She cannot stop talking and urges all to listen, while knowing full well that this crass augury, this too literal a foretelling of the future, is dangerous. Speaking on, she bids birds not to speak, lest they get in harm's way. "My punishment ought to be a warning to all birds not to invite trouble by talking too much." For instance: of the impending apocalypse, nuclear doom, land submerged by the ocean and unbearable climates.

The cause of the bird's undoing is speech. The reason for which a princess, Coronis, the daughter of King Coroneus, is transformed into a crow is her beauty, barely distinguishable from her form. Abrupt metamorphoses are cataclysmic events meted out as punishments, while also quietly operating the machinery of salvation, saving those who go through them from a sure death. Intimating that death is nothing but ongoing metamorphosis. While they combine seemingly disparate forms of life, metamorphoses separate speech from appearances, *logos* from *phenomena*, that are then often mismatched, producing, say, human speech in a bird's body. More than that, appearances and speech are pinpointed as the sources of damnation, the causes of one's undoing: the brilliant, glowing, beautiful forms of Coronis; the crow's elaborate speech that changed the color of her feathers. Phenomeno-logy in ruins . . .

As a crow, Coronis is able to avoid the unwanted advances of Poseidon. The milieu, the entire environment, works with her in seamless synergy. The hot and soft sand of the beach doesn't retard her steps. High above, the air receives her into its embrace. Her flight turns into a flight; fleeing, she flies away.

The raven will have none of this. "On your head, I pray, be the evil that warning portends; I scorn the idle presage." Idle presage: articulated in words. The art of ornithomancy is another thing entirely. Read the motile configurations of feathered bodies in the air, not letters typed or sounds mouthed.

Birds act. Besides foretelling the future, they bring it about. The raven, who cursed Coronis—warning about warnings, both denying and acknowledging their power, disavowing warnings and redirecting them elsewhere—informs Phoebus, Coronis's lover, of her infidelity. Far from "an idle presage," the report is effective: gripped by jealousy, the god kills Coronis, who dies together with her unborn child. "Two now die in one": *duo nunc moriemur in una*. Except that the child does not die. (Is—despite all appearances to the contrary, despite the coinage of the verb *intermorior*, to interdie—death *never* sharable, or is it not shared just in this peculiar instance?) Saved from the funeral pyre and raised by the Centaur, a "foster child of heavenly stock," he will be, in another sort of metamorphosis, Coronis's afterlife, the continuation of an existence that has come to an end.

ANOTHER SORT OF METAMORPHOSIS: ASCLEPIUS AND OCYRHOE

(Liber II, 633-675)

Another sort of metamorphosis awaited Coronis, who gave birth in death to a child destined to be *salutifer orbi*, "a health-bringer to the whole world." Resurrected and keeping vestiges of his mother, Asclepius will go on to become a resurrector, a healer, the god of medicine, to whom "mortals owe the life of their bodies." Another sort of metamorphosis is a metamorphosis undergone in the other, as the other: that of the mother in and as her son. So goes the prophesy of Ocyrhoe, the Centaur's daughter, who, moved by "prophetic madness," carries on speaking, conveying in speech the fate of the foster child and her own father. Another sort of metamorphosis is held in store for the Centaur, she suggests, the metamorphosis of an immortal god into a mortal being—and back: "So, from a god shalt thou become but a lifeless corpse; but from this corpse shalt though again become a god and twice renew thy fates." A metamorphosis that, at the time when these words were written, will have been already Christian. Another sort of metamorphosis is, thus, in itself multiple, referring, more exactly, to other *sorts*: of one mortal into another mortal; of a mortal into an immortal being; and of an immortal into a mortal. Brushing our first impressions aside, mortality is a gift for an immortal being who faces eternal agony and "longs for a power to die," *posse mori cupies*. The power to give up all power, all potency, potentiality and actual existence. Another sort of metamorphosis still is what lies ahead of Ocyrhoe. For divulging the secrets of the future, she is transformed into a horse. As a daughter of the Centaur—half-human, half-horse—she

ANOTHER SORT OF METAMORPHOSIS

feels kinship with the mare she is morphing into ("a kindred shape") but bemoans the final determination of her own existence, the denial of her intermediate state or status: "But why completely? Surely, my father is half-human." Or, at least, this is what Ovid surmises from Ocyrhoe's *confusaque verba*, her "confused words," at the outer edge of human speech.

—Human half completely father my but why is, surely?

In a split of a second, there are neither words nor animal sounds, "but vociferations as of one trying to imitate a horse."

—*Neigh, neigh; eee-go-go; hee-hee; nee nee; ih-hi-i-i; ihaha; pffffrrrr*

BATTUS: BECOMING-STONE
(Liber II, 676–707)

Battus, Battus,
what have you done?
you, the touchstone of treachery and greed!
asked, for a handsome reward, to cover up divine theft,
you broke your word in expectation of a greater prize yet.

Battus, Battus,
your very name was a promise and a limitation: tongue-tied.
you were anything but.
"That stone will tell of your thefts sooner than I,"
Lapis iste prius tua furta loquetur.
your silence was short-lived, and for the worst of reasons.

Battus, Battus,
what has been done to you?
A BROKEN WORD HAS MADE YOU INTO AN INTACT STONE.
Since a stone was supposed to speak first,
and the one who betrayed the thief was you,
you were already a stone, as soon as you opened your mouth.

Battus, Battus,
what kind of a stone have you turned into?

BATTUS: BECOMING-STONE

"Into a hard rock, to this day called a touchstone,"
In durum silicem, qui nunc quoque dicitur index.
You are the index—of lies and truth, of promises broken and kept,
often despite ourselves.

Battus, Battus,
you are the touchstone, testing ground, a gauge, bearing the traces
of metals with their alloys, words, qualities, statements,
etched onto your rocky body in a flash and in a clash,
with degrees of resistance and surrender
determining your worth,
as a clue to the worth of that which hits you.

METAMORPHOSING INTO A STATUE: AGLAUROS

(Liber II, 708-832)

Mercury has a penchant for turning people into slabs of stone. Which is rather odd for a god who is as light as the air, on which he glides. Responsible for the metamorphosis of Battus into a hard rock, the god goes on to turn Aglauros into a dark statue.

Corpses may actually be fossilized and petrified after thousands of years; the magic of metamorphoses speeds this process up, condensing *longue durée* into an instant. But a statue? Whose chisel creates it? Although the materials are the same, Battus is not Aglauros. Nature (*natura/phusis*) on the one hand, to one side of the abyss; technique (*artificium/technē*) on the other. And yet the two hands belong to the same uncanny being. It is life itself that chisels the statue named Aglauros, and it is as a technical means for evaluating gold alloys that the touchstone, into which Battus is transformed, serves.

Consumed by envy, Aglauros blocks the threshold of her sister's room to prevent Mercury from entering. "I shall never stir from here till I have foiled your purpose," says Aglauros to the god. Rather than symbolic, her statement turns out to be literal. (Hyperliterality is the shibboleth of myths and mysticisms.) Mercury grants Aglauros's desire—she will stay put forever—which is also the cruelest of punishments. As a popular saying goes, "Be careful what you wish for, you may just get it."

Unlike a rock, a statue is an expression of a body in space, assuming a position, a pose. Aglauros's pose is one of defiance and of a blockage, a one-woman blockade—though, in the end, it is her own life that is blocked, transformed into a granite block. Her psychic fixation on the purported happiness of her sister results in her being physically fixed, unable to *move her limbs* as a somatic manifestation of her inability to *move on*. Absolute inhibition. An expression of a body in space bears in equal measure on life and death. Or, with regard to Aglauros, on life-death, still before her becoming-statue: her "secret misery," her "useless suffering," *inritata dolore*.

The sequence of her metamorphosis is very precise. Initially, her bent limbs grow "motionless with dull heaviness"; her "knees stiffen"; a chill is felt in her extremities, even as her flesh is rendered pale and bloodless; finally, "the deadly cold of winter" spreads through the rest of her body, reaching her breast and choking off speech and breath. Heaviness, stiffness at the joints, cold extremities and pallidness, respiratory failure and cardiac arrest: death and dying merge in a single vision of demise, marked by the cessation of vital functions and rigor mortis setting in. But the corpse Aglauros has become is not allowed to decompose. Hers is eternal rigor mortis. Un-passing, impassable, impossible. Like her mental fixation and its corresponding inhibition.

WHEN A GOD STEALS HIMSELF: EUROPA'S BULL

(Liber II, 833-875)

Europa, the Sidonese princess, was seduced, raped, and whittled away by Zeus (or Jove) who appeared before her in the guise of a bull. Or so the story goes. What hides underneath its veneer? What follows is a reflection on the other side of mythic mirror.

Driven by love (*amor*), rather than desire (*cupiditas*), Jove metamorphoses into an animal. Love animalizes a god. He keeps his power—a bull, who displays and plays with his muscles in front of Europa. In all his bovine splendor, though, he is nothing more than a creature, having given up divine majesty for the sake of love, with which such grandeur is incompatible. Jove's creaturely power is divine powerlessness; he must stop being all-powerful, enervating and debilitating himself to descend to the level of his beloved, if not below her. Physically beneath, his back serving as her seat, as the supporting plane for her buttocks and thighs. And metaphysically, too.

To steal Europa, then, Jove steals himself from himself, enfeebling his own divine image with an animal incarnation. Rapt, enraptured. As a bull, he mixes with the rest of the herd, joining his voice to the mooing of cattle. What does a god think in the shape of a bull? What does he feel? Which bovine thoughts and emotions visit him? He must keep his love alive, for otherwise there is no sense in his metamorphosis. All the same, he is drawn to the grass of the pastures, to the flowers Europa hands over to him as much as to the hand holding them: "Presently she drew near and held out flowers to his snow-white lips. The disguised lover rejoiced and, as a foretaste of future joy, kissed her hands." This foretaste mixes with the taste of flowers and fresh grass; the bull's body and voice mix with the rest of the herd. Before she is lost to her family, he is—to himself.

Europa grabs the bull by the horns, adorning them (again!) with flowers arranged in entwined garlands. And she sits atop his back. When they cross the sea, each of her hands will grasp these parts of the bull. For stability and support, no doubt. Claiming them as her possessions, perhaps.

He is tame and apparently harmless. It's a part of his plan: not to scare her off, not to spook her with his might, which cannot dwell excessively close to love, we are told. Is it possible that his tameness, "his brow and eyes [that] would inspire no fear," were more than aspects of his cunning, or, if they were just that, then they betrayed a cunning that had outsmarted itself? Could Jove-the-bull be tame because he is debilitated, because he has debilitated himself, in the name of his love and on the hither side of pretense?

Stolen by Jove, Europa is free. Released from her family ties and from her native land (indeed, from all land), she towers over the god who has humbled himself for her sake. It is in this vein that we should read the last, apparently purely poetic and superfluous line of Ovid's narrative. *Tremulae sinuantur flamine vestes*, "Her fluttering garments stream behind her in the wind."

> A line that is, itself, free from the preceding text
> and from the empty space extending after it.

Fluttering in the wind, her garments are a sign of freedom, of elemental liberation set against marine horizons, of the waves and the salt-suffused air, where, far from all past certainties, she can embark on a journey unto herself.

INTERDEATH, INTERBIRTH: CADMUS AND THE SOWING OF SERPENT TEETH
(Liber III, 1–137)

Bidden by the father to find his sister, Europa,
Cadmus had no choice but to go into exile.
And a "happy exile," *exilio felix* (what an oxymoron!), he would be
outside his native Phoenicia and outside every order of being.
A founder of Thebes, he had a hand in the joint death—
the interdeath—of an oak tree and a threatening serpent,
"the neck and tree pierced together,"
by his spear.
In the same manner, the phoenix bird,
linked to Cadmus's beloved Phoenicia,
"receives his name from a palm tree,
dies together with it [*intermori*],
and is reborn of itself" (Pliny, *Historia naturalis* XIII, ix, 42).
An interdeath gave way to an interbirth:
like plant seeds, the serpent's teeth, sown in plowed earth,
yielded a crop of men,
in a mix of vegetal germination, animal matter, and telluric parturition.
Then, interbirth flipped back into interdeath,
faithful to the mortal seeds
that had given rise to a warrior breed:
each newly germinated human killed the other

in civil strife that spared but five Sparti (the sown ones).
Mutual wounds are the shared birth pangs
of a city born of death,
distributed among the body of the earth, plants, animals, and human shapes.
A common destiny is palpable
in intermortality that,
phoenix-like,
triggers Phoenicia's revival in Boeotian Thebes.

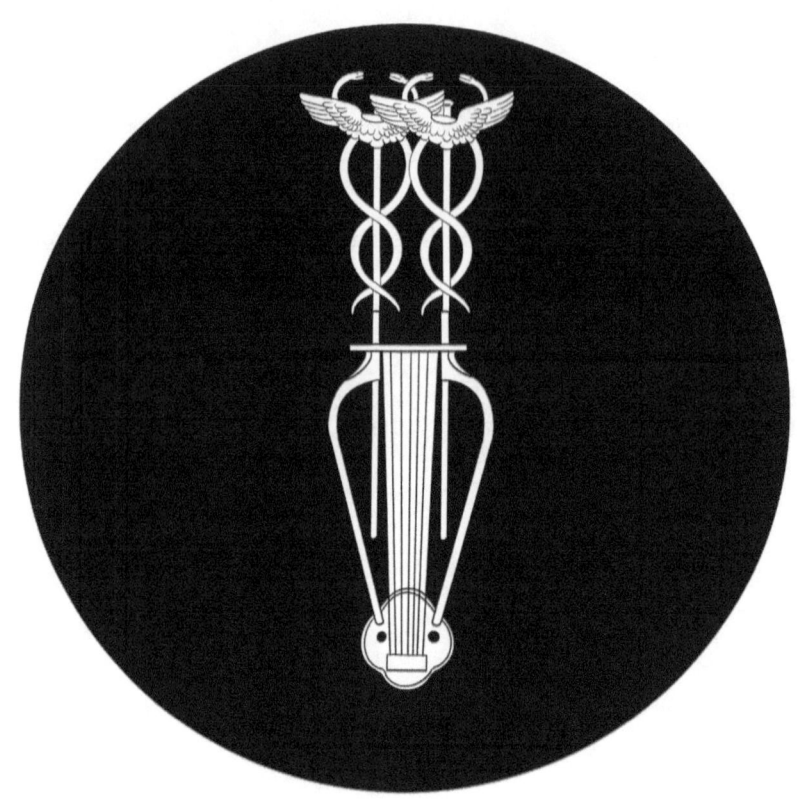

ACTAEON:
THE REVENGE OF THE HUNTED
(Liber III, 138–252)

March 1, 2022

At the moment, when I am addressing you, Actaeon, it is already too late. You have been eaten alive by your own faithful dogs, who did not recognize you in the deer you had become. Your eyes do not see a thing; I doubt that they have *ever* seen anything save for your prey. For, it is equally late for the countless victims of your hunts, the "many slaughtered beasts," with whose blood the woods of Boeotia were stained.

A poet tries hard to absolve you, to blame bad fortune, a mere mischance. There is poetic, divine justice, in what has befallen you.

ACTAEON: THE REVENGE OF THE HUNTED

Copious animal blood soaking those hills was avenged, when your own was spilled after you assumed the shape of a hounded stag. When all's said and done, maybe it was not actually too late ...

I am composing this missive to you, who will never read it, during Carnival, the time of inversions and duly authorized perversions. Metamorphosis is an ongoing Carnival of sorts. Here, instead of art's imitation of nature, it is nature that "by her own cunning imitates art," *simulaverat artem ingenio natura suo*. Here, the downtrodden rise up and former masters become servants. The hunters are hunted down; prey triumphs. All this transpires in your body, *as your very body*.

You did not deserve one thing, though. You kept your faculties, your human faculties, I mean: "Only his mind remains unchanged" in the body of a stag. There is a dash of pretense, make-believe, a carnival in such a nasty mismatch of a body and mind visited upon you by a vengeful goddess. But such pretense is tragic; it goes right to the core of tragedy. I am sorry that you had to live through it just before dying as a beast of prey torn apart by the very hounds who have served you so faithfully.

Your terrifying fate was not yours alone. Well before your time, Gilgamesh narrates Ishtar's violent treatment of her shepherd lover, whom she turns into a wolf, hunted down and killed by other shepherds and their dogs. So, too, Aqht, whose name still rings in yours, was devoured by eagles at the behest of the goddess Anath, who wanted to obtain his hunting bow. And how many lovers of Ishtar and Anath, how many Aqhts and Actaeons, have there been afterward? How many will there still be? I begin to think it is for their sake, for the benefit of future Actaeons, that I am writing this letter, which you will never read.

What you wanted to say—but couldn't—corresponded to the ratiocinations of your pristine human mind: "I am Actaeon! Recognize your master!" Your hounds could not smell your *ego sum*; instead, they got the whiff of your scared deer flesh. Your mind said—without saying—unrelinquished mastery, but your body said—wordlessly, too—submission, as you sank down on your "knees in suppliant attitude, just like one in prayer." You were torn, more so than your flesh was by the dog's teeth, between these incompatible silent statements, between the *I am* and the *you are*. You were.

It's getting late here, time to finish my letter to you, to the *you* divided between yourself and the other you have become, between the hunter and the hunted. The Carnival is over, its flashy paraphernalia scattered around, littering the ground. Next comes Lent with its mortification of the flesh. What is the Lent of the Carnival that is metamorphosis? Metaphysical stability? Mastery? The dominance of *ego sum*? Your becoming the hounds and the deer, biting into your own flesh with a thousand death-bearing muzzles, in an effort (exerted in vain) to forestall becoming?

Unsigned

FIERY MANIFESTATIONS: SEMELE
(Liber III, 253–315)

However brilliant, the manifestations of a god before mortals are necessarily attenuated. Divine glory is diminished, so as to permit the infinite to come into contact, to be in touch (even of the erotic variety), with the finite. In a sense, to address itself to the finite, to relate to it, the infinite *becomes* finite. It is then that the infinite respects humanly appreciable appearances that, unfolding within fragile limits, seem solid and secure.

The illusion of security instills in Semele—another one of Europa's sisters, to whom Jove is also attracted—her "trust in beauty," *fiducia formae*, which Juno will strive to undermine. The Latin association of beauty with form implies that the ugly is formless or amorphous and, more significantly for us, that a beautiful appearance must be appropriate to the forms apprehended by the one, to whom they appear. What is divinely beautiful will not be so according to the parameters of human perception, dumbfound by the power of such manifestations, which will be received, at best, as sublime. What is felinely beautiful will similarly defy the boundaries of humanly appreciable forms.

Manipulating Semele's trust in beauty, Juno reveals the relativity of each form of perception and each perception of form (proper to a god, a human being, an animal, a plant...), not to mention the unavoidable transformations that prepare the terrain for strange encounters. At the level of manifestation itself, transformations or metamorphoses involve, in addition to the mutations of forms that destroy any residual trust in beauty, adjustments of that which makes appearances as such possible, notably fire with its two principal "powers" of light and heat. Too bright and too hot for mortals to behold and to handle, divine fire—especially that of Jove, the god of the sky, thunder, and lightning—must be dimmed down. A god is doomed to appear in the human sphere in what, from the standpoint of divinity itself, is twilight.

Jove's true form, the beauty all his own, is terrible and intolerable for Semele, or for any other mortal, for that matter. That is why, as Juno feigns that she is but an old woman, she convinces Semele to ask Jove to disclose his most glorious appearance to her. The goddess regulates appearances and their various valves with unmatched craftiness: muted and soft here, unbearably stark there. It is Juno who prods Semele to beseech Jove to show himself "in such guise as Saturnia beholds you when you seek her arms in love." In short, to be a divine exhibitionist.

Lest we forget, the appearances or the apparitions of a god pertain not only to sight but also to touch—hence, Jesus's *Noli mi tangere!* "Touch me not!" addressed to Mary Magdalen upon his resurrection. They emit not only light but also heat, affecting not just the eye, but the entire body. "Beholding" divinity is *eo ipso* being struck by it, blinded and burnt. So Semele's "mortal body did not bear the onrush of heavenly power, and by a conjugal gift she was consumed" (*donisque iugalibus arsit*). "By a conjugal gift," *donisque iugalibus*, may mean:

a. the poisonous gift Jove's wife Juno gave to his lover, Semele;
b. the full measure of passion, lit between Jove and Semele;
c. unrestrained divine self-giving to the senses;
d. the marriage of life and death, in which the former is handed over to the latter.

Fire rages in each of these gifts or variations on the gift: the fire of jealousy and of desire, of appearances and life, of the funeral pyre and a god's glory. Uncontrollable fires, immoderate, excessive.

If, furthermore, Semele is a figure of the earth in Thracian language (a figure preserved in the name of the Baltic earth deity Žemelė or in the Slavic word for the earth, *zemlja*), then we are back at square one: the devastation of the terrestrial sphere by a heavenly blaze. Once more chaos returns (it has never left). Nor does the seed (*seme*, *semja*) fall far behind: the seed is of the earth. But it is saved, as Semele's unborn child (Bacchus) is cut out of her dead body and sewn into the thigh of Jove, where he will complete the period of gestation. Saved and hidden away, moved from one concealment into another, extracted from the lethal excess of fiery manifestations, finding refuge in another earth, or in another instantiation of the earth, and hence of itself.

TRANS-TIRESIAS

(Liber III, 316–338)

...in Thebes, there lived Tiresias, a prophetic figure, in whom the transformations that transcribe *metamorphosis* into Latin lay bare the transsexual, rather than transspecies, nature of change: when he "outraged two huge snakes mating in the green forest, from man (o miracle!) he was changed into a woman, and in that form spent seven years," and this experience meant that Tiresias "knew both sides of love," which gave them access to the Absolute (generally absent from human lives, partial and fragmented as they are) that accounted for their exceptional wisdom, envied by the gods themselves, who, like Jove and Juno, consulted with them on sundry matters in dispute, and that was undisturbed by the physical blindness, which an angry goddess visited upon Tiresias but which afforded them a panoramic vision of being, suppleness, and flexibility (for instance, the flexibility of shifting back to another sex after striking the serpents with the staff) rivaling the plasticity of plants—especially vegetal sexuality with its sudden reversals of the flowers' sex, hermaphroditism (be it serial or simultaneous), and other physiologically induced alterations in reproductive morphology—the panoramic vision of being that, not limited either to the present or to the past, included the revealed knowledge of the future (*scire futura*) on the assumption that this future was growing continuously, without the slightest interruption, from the same root as the other modalities of time, namely from the Absolute extratemporal source of time, to which Tiresias was constantly connected, nourished by it in their transsexual bodies and souls, thanks to the gods, the animals, and the unmentioned plants, steering them to another fate than the one that would have been theirs were they to have been a mere man born in Thebes . . .

DISEMBODYING METAMORPHOSES: ECHO AND NARCISSUS

(Liber III, 339-510)

—evanescence—naissance—scene—sense—nse—se

Evanescence—painful and gradual. Painfully gradual. And graceful, nonetheless?

You are fully conscious of your disappearance. Your body is ebbing away (liquescing: this is the domain of river nymphs and gods, after all), syllable by syllable, sound after sound. Yet, something sticks around. A voice without either lips or a mouth, without a tongue, a throat, vocal cords, or lungs. A reflection without anyone or anything reflected. Unless the one reflected is a fragile flower.

DISEMBODYING METAMORPHOSES

Surviving your own evanescence, you realize: rather than death, this is a way of transitioning out of your body. Not into another body. Not into the body of the other. But out of the flesh that will remain irreplaceable, non- or un-substitutable in its metamorphoses.

You will be leaving traces of your irreplaceability, even and especially by way of replacing others, supplanting or supplementing others, replicating their words. Their last words, mainly. Echoing them.

NARCISSUS: Is anyone here? *Ecquis adest?*
ECHO: Here! *Adest!*
N: Come! *Veni!*
E: Come! *Veni!*
N: Here let us meet! *Huc coeamus!*
E: Let us meet! *Coeamus!*
N: Embrace me not! May I die before I give you power over me! *Manus conplexibus aufer! Ante emoriar, quam sit tibi copia nostri!*
E: I give you power over me! *Sit tibi copia nostri!*

There is total accord here—in these invocations of the *here*, where Echo and Narcissus are and are not together—and, at the same time, utter discord. An immediate coincidence of accord and discord makes communication impossible. (If anything, communication is a *mediated* coincidence of these polar opposites.) A failed dialogue comprises two monologues that give off the appearance of responding to one another: the monologue of the self, enamored of itself alone, and the monologue of the other, reiterating the words of the other, in whom one is hopelessly lost. Let us now rewind these intersecting monologues, of the self and of the other.

N: Why would I want any power at all over you? I do not need you.
E: Need you!
N: This meeting was a mistake.
E: A mistake...
N: I am glad you also think so. I should not have come here.
E: Come here!
N: Here? Right here (and over there, as well), I find no one to talk to.
E: No one to talk to.

DISEMBODYING METAMORPHOSES: ECHO AND NARCISSUS

When the all-knowing Tiresias was asked whether Narcissus would live to a ripe old age, he responded cryptically: "If he never knows himself," *si se non noverit*. Loving, valuing, and listening only to himself, did Narcissus get to know himself? Arguably he did not, because self-knowledge, rare as it is, arrives at our doorsteps from the others, whether they are friends or foes, and from ourselves as other to ourselves. Glancing with unrequited attraction at his own reflection in a pond—"He looks in speechless wonder at himself"—he does not know that he is espying himself. Objectively, he has met himself; subjectively, he parted ways with himself. Tiresias is wrong: only if he knew himself, would Narcissus have reached a ripe old age.

—What an absurdity! Who can echo a flower, the flower that has grown instead of his body?
—Echo herself grows silent around Narcissus after his supplanting with a plant. More precisely: she echoes his silence. Shhhh . . . Just listen.
—But a flower? Can you think of anyone less narcissistic? Can you imagine anyone more open to the outside world? What a discrepancy!
—A flower contemplates the world in speechless wonder, relating to its floral self as to the other and to the other as to itself. Draw your conclusions, will you?

Narcissus yearns to melt into an image so as to be with the image he is in love with. He also wishes for the beloved image to be substantial, tangible. So much so that he deems "to be a body that which is but a shadow." He strives to lose his body and to clothe with corporeity what is but a shadow. Another missed encounter . . .

N: Alas! *Eheu!*
E: Alas! *Eheu!*
N: Farewell. *Vale.*
E: Farewell. *Vale.*
E (ASIDE): If only I could declare what I think, I would have told you that our *farewell* is a *hello*, a face-to-face, an ear-to-ear, or a face-to-ear of a

pure reflection and a just as pure reverberation. Shedding the bodies that separated us like a snake sheds its skin or a tree its leaves in the fall, we get together with each other and (why not?) with ourselves. Remember what you said from the depths of your despair, dear Narcissus: "Oh, that we might be parted from our own bodies!" *O utinam a nostro secedere corpore possem!* A secession from my body: this is what I had been dreaming of in my most sincere desire to be with you, to be yours. This is what I've achieved and now I await you, ready to receive you with open arms. All right, I do not have arms, but I am eager to receive you with my very openness, the openness that I am, the openness I have become.

To reunite Echo and Narcissus, conjure up a synesthetic experience without experience, a reflected reverberation and a reverberating reflection. A voice without voice going hand in absent hand with an eye without eye. A togetherness without togetherness.

FRENZIED BECOMINGS I: DOLPHINS AND OTHER MARINE MOTIFS BORROWED FROM LYDIAN SAILORS

(Liber III, 572-700)

Bacchus, domine nostrum, our unruly lord,
grant us ceaseless flows of wine: La Rioja, Château Margaux,
and every other variety;
let our minds be enveloped and uplifted by your spirits,
magically transforming our bodies into swine, parrots, dogs, gods,
so that those of us who are still sober would wonder about the rest:

FRENZIED BECOMINGS I

"into what strange creature are you turning?"
in quae miracula verteris?

Oh, god of libation and carefree delight,
make us move like water in water, or at least like dolphins,
frolicking in clear waves,
"leaping about on every side" of the boat of this world we refused to
    steer
in the right direction.
speak "words of cheer" to us,
causing us to "emerge from the water,
only to submerge ourselves in its depths again,"
emerguntque iterum redeuntque sub aequora rursus.

Nostrum domine, Bacchus, take away our hands that
insatiably seize chunks of the real as land, houses,
and every other form of property;
"shrink them in size to things that one can no longer call hands"—
to fins that balance and propel us toward the endless ocean's ends,
where water is only water, ungraspable,
"drawn in and blown out of our broad nostrils,"
acceptum patulis mare naribus efflant.

Oh, twice-born son of the one who seduced Semele,
allow our limbless bodies to dance on the waves of sense and
    nonsense,
"sending up showers of spray" over the abysses of meaning
that receive us.
in our wild inebriation, give us signs of matter's spirit and spirit's
    matter,
of the infinite in the finite, of laughter howling in the face of death,
of "what divinity is in that mortal body,"
quod numen in isto corpore sit.

FRENZIED BECOMINGS II: PENTHEUS, OR THE VOICE OF REASON AS A WILD BOAR

(Liber III, 511–733)

His was the voice of sober reason, vehemently opposed to the new cult of Bacchus and deeply skeptical of Tiresias's prophetic capacities. Pentheus, the king of Thebes and Cadmus's grandson, complains about the bacchanalias he witnesses: "What madness has dulled your reason, you sons of serpent's teeth, you seed of Mars?" The warmongering madness of Mars, producing ready-made soldiers out of the teeth of the serpent, apparently does not count as such, according to Pentheus's logic. For him, the apogee of craziness is ecstatic dancing to the sounds of "clashing cymbals" and the "pipe of crooked horn."

> ... this gang of drug addicts and neo-Nazis.
> —V. PUTIN, FEBRUARY 25, 2022

The barely concealed frenzy of reason itself is its excess: P speaks too much, he cannot stop talking, compulsively and largely to himself, not knowing what it is that he is saying. Maybe because he is so scared of losing it, of letting go of reason, which made him and his warrior compatriots insensitive to the terrors and trumpets of war, *non bellicus ensis, non tuba terruerit*.

> ... whoever might be tempted to meddle in the ongoing events, whoever tries to stand in our way or create threats for our country ...

should know that our response will be immediate and lead you to consequences you have never encountered in your history.
—V. PUTIN, FEBRUARY 24, 2022

The so-called voice of reason is committed to nothing but war: commemorating past hostilities, devising military plans in the present, and outlining future threats.

- Past: "for you it was once seemly to bear arms ... not garlands," *quos arma tenere ... non fronde decebat*
- Present: "but now our Thebes falls before an untried boy," *at nunc a puero Thebae capientur inermi*
- Future: "if it be the fate of Thebes not to endure for long, I would the enginery of war and heroes might batter down her walls," *utinam tormenta virique moenia diruerent.*

- Future: *après moi le déluge* ("after me, the flood"—Louis XIV: the sun that is the Sun King having set, who will be there to dry all that excess moisture?)
- Present: we are under attack
- Past: heroic fight, the principle of noncontradiction, friends vs. enemies, *not* vegetal mélange and symbiosis

And for our country, this is ultimately a matter of life and death, a matter of our historical future as a people. And this is not an exaggeration—it is true.
—V. PUTIN, FEBRUARY 24, 2022

P heads into enemy territory, getting closer to everything he so abhors and despises. The sounds of bacchanalia are loud, nearly deafening. He is enraged, resistant to rapture, "spying with profane eyes upon the sacred rites." Yet something is going on with him, in him. Has he metamorphosed? Changed, if not in his own profane eyes than in those of others? He is taken for a wild boar by the very woman who gave him birth. Could a mother, however ecstatic, have misrecognized her son? Does his unyielding reason prevent his self-recognition in the animal other? Is it the frenzy of this very reason that assumes the shape of a wild boar?

> Modern Ukraine was entirely created by Russia or, to be more precise, by Bolshevik, Communist Russia. This process started practically right after the 1917 revolution, and Lenin and his associates did it in a way that was extremely harsh on Russia—by separating, severing what is historically Russian land. Nobody asked the millions of people living there what they thought.... You want decommunization? Very well, this suits us just fine. But why stop halfway? We are ready to show what real decommunization would mean for Ukraine.
> —V. PUTIN, FEBRUARY 23, 2022

What comes next is gruesome—disturbingly so. Pentheus, the wild boar, is torn to pieces, "limb to limb." While his body is dismembered, his mind is torn between the man he thought he was and the animal he has become: *membra viri*, says Ovid, not *membra apri*. It is by avowing the absolute unity and truth of reason, of an identity, of history, of an interpretation that one succumbs to merciless fragmentation. The dismemberment of the one (of the One) bent on dismembering the entire world.

HUMAN BLOOD/PLANT SAP: ON PYRAMUS AND THISBE

(Liber IV, 55-166)

Color is the most superficial thing of all. It is what, right off the bat, strikes the eye. It hands the object over to vision and hides what is underneath.

The subtle metamorphosis in the tale of star-crossed lovers, Pyramus and Thisbe, centers on color. At the end, "the fruit of mulberry tree, which once were white" turn "dark from the bloody stain." A trace of tragedy, this change of color is a turnabout that, while taking place on the surface, evinces an alteration at the level of essence.

Everything in the story of Pyramus and Thisbe, who never consummate their love, moves through cracks, holes, openings, and wounds.

HUMAN BLOOD/PLANT SAP: ON PYRAMUS AND THISBE

1. Living in adjacent houses, they communicate through a chink in the wall between them. Through it, words and whispers and breath are exchanged, turning the inorganic division into a living membrane—a surface that is, precisely, breathable and permeable.
2. The lovers agree to elope from their houses, to go out into the open, and to meet next to a tall mulberry tree "hanging full of snow-white berries" by "a cool spring." Another opening—the spring—is there where water is gushing out of the earth, the union of the terrestrial and aquatic elements foreshadowing the comingling of the lovers' bodies.
3. When, judging by a bloodied piece of clothes he finds on the ground, Pyramus thinks that Thisbe was killed by a lion, he kills himself by drawing a sword into his side in the shadow of the tree, crying out to the mulberry: "Drink my blood too!" The wound, from which blood spurts like a fountain, is a third gap that will, in death, reunite the lovers.

The mingling of blood on the blade of the same sword, with which Pyramus and Thisbe put an end to their lives, contrasts with the mixing of blood in the tree, which is *creative*, above all, of a new color. When Thisbe spills her own blood on the same spot, she begs the tree to "keep the marks of our death." As it is with Phaethon's sisters, the tree is a living monument, "the memorial of our twinned murder," *gemini monimenta cruoris*. In the mulberry tree, *as* this tree, Pyramus and Thisbe are with one another after their individual deaths. Here surfaces are not just perforated; liquids, including blood, are osmotically imbibed in the contact of membranes with widening and narrowing pores, not walls.

Chromatic metamorphosis affects vegetal surface and depth alike. Pyramus's blood stains mulberries, even as it is also soaked up by tree roots.

Berries: surface, appearances.
Roots: depth, essence.

Yet the two indicate one and the same change, translating deep essence into appearances and the apparently superficial appearances into essence.

Human and vegetal hues and colors are reshuffled, changing places. The berries that are initially white darken to red or purple (ripening?), while, upon discovering Thisbe's damaged shawl, Pyramus grows "deadly pale." He becomes as white as mulberries were; they become as red as his blood. An uncanny cross-species, cross-kingdoms metabolism underlies chromatic metamorphosis, including, crucially, the metabolism of essences and appearances, both human and vegetal.

MARS AND VENUS: EXPOSURE

(Liber IV, 167–189)

Everything lies exposed in sunlight. Everything and everyone. Hung out to dry. In the light and the heat of the sun.

The sun brings to visibility and sees the world. He (if it is a he) is the first one to see everyone and everything, *videt hic deus (Solis) omnia primus*. Including the extramarital affair of Venus and Mars. A scorching gaze. A gaze silently saying both *yes* and *no* to the vision of others.

A web of light. Catching every single body, it exposes its catch without delay. For everyone and everything to see. No matter how much this sight hurts your eyes. No matter how much it hurts your soul.

MARS AND VENUS: EXPOSURE

Exposure is indiscriminate, sweeping, relentless. Plant or animal, stone or human, a god or an insect: all are subject to it. The goddess of love and the god of war are, too. Exposed in their naked embrace.

More ancient than the power of exposure is only the force of germination in the obscurity of the chthonic realm. This power causes you to be naked, even when you are dressed. To say nothing of when you are undressed.

Exposure espied by others provokes a sense of shame. Would you be ashamed under the gaze of the sun? Before a plant? Or, as a philosopher has inquired, when a cat looks at you?

The jealous husband of Venus, Vulcan duplicates the web of light with a fine copper net, "thinner than a spiderweb," in which the lovers—Venus and Mars—are entangled in their love nest. Caught twice: in threads of light and of copper. Exposed twice, as well: before the sun and before the other gods, whom Vulcan invited into their chamber. Two exposures in one, in diurnal luminosity and before the judgment of others. Two exposures, phenomenological and moral.

Where is metamorphosis in exposure? In the light—of the sun and of judgment—you appear as what you are. You are available. The goddess of love and the god of war became what they were in their mutual embrace and in their exposure as the love of war and the war of love. Shamefully so, *turpiter.*

Everything appears in the light. And disappears in it

SHRUB DIARIES: LEUCOTHOE
(Liber IV, 190–273)

DAY 1

This day is like any other in my life, and yet it is different. I am having trouble pinning down what has changed. It bothers me. A nagging feeling, very annoying. Maybe because what has changed is not a thing. It's as if there has been a shift in the atmosphere, in the very light.

DAY 2

I feel that I am being followed. Again, not by anyone in particular, but by a sunray. I am in the spotlight without wanting to be. The moment I step out, the spotlight recalibrates, putting me in its crosshairs. I am tired of playing hide-and-seek with it. I should definitely get some sleep, some rest from this incessant light. It prevents me from sleeping, though. When I close my eyes, when I put an eye cover on, it's still too bright, I still feel the spotlight I am in. All I want is darkness. Should I hide in the basement?

DAY 3

My mother came to talk to me tonight. She seemed to be the same and different, like the atmosphere, like the light. After a while, "she kissed me as a mother would have kissed her dear daughter." My mother kissed me on the forehead, as she does every night. But her lips were so hot! I was concerned she had fever. And as soon as her lips touched my skin, I felt this incredible scorching heat spreading inside me. It moved down from my head to the neck, over my breasts and further down, down, down . . . I got scared. Averted my eyes and bid my mother goodnight in a hurry. Now I am confused.

DAY 4

I am writing this entry on what has turned out to be the worst day of my life. The veil (of light) has been lifted, and I peered at what was behind it in horror. My mother was not my mother. The creature I took to be my mother was "the eye of the world," *mundi oculus*. Everything became clear, hideously clear. She was him; he assumed her form. He: the sun, the one eye scanning the sky. That was the reason behind the trailing spotlight, the blistering heat of the kiss . . . My fear grew so deep in me, was so overwhelming, that I "became my fear." And he, who just a moment ago pretended to be my mother, became himself, in all his splendor. He became himself *before* me and *in* me, in and before my fear, which is now my whole body, my entire self. After that, impenetrable darkness enveloped me. I am crying and writing myself to sleep.

DAY 5

Rereading what I jotted down in my diary yesterday, I cannot believe I went through something like this. My memory is now a black hole, or an insufferably bright spot. I am incapable of facing it: if I do, it will destroy me. And to add insult to injury, my sister Clytie is jealous. Of what? Of whom? She is burning with the love of him who revealed himself to me yesterday and with hatred toward me. This is more than I can handle. I don't want to die: I wish I were never born.

DAY 6

Clytie has informed our father of everything. It's so silent in the house now—the calm before the storm that is coming.

DAY 7

Darkness. Soil everywhere: below and above, to the left and to the right. Outside and inside of me. I am cold. What does it mean? That I am freezing. Or that if someone were to touch my lifeless corpse, it would feel cold to the touch. But there is no more I to be freezing and there is no one to touch me, except the earth. Why am I here? Why "am" "I" still here???

DAY 8

Why am I here? My father. He got mad at me. Buried me "deep in the earth, and heaped on the spot a heavy mound of sand." Buried me alive, when I was still I. When I was still me. Who am I now? What am I? An "it?"

DAY 9

There is nothing else to confide to this diary, which no one can keep in any case and no one would read. The same cold, silent oblivion. Wait a moment. Faint warmth. Could it be him? Him? The sun? Trying "by his warm rays to recall those death-cold limbs to the warmth of life?" Even in death he is not letting me be. Or rather not be. I can do nothing but melt all the faster under the influence of his heat. Melting into the earth, melting, melting, melting. Becoming her.

DAY?

Faint sounds. Muffled. The soil buzzing, moving gradually, displaced in chunks. Are those worms, white grubs, sowbugs working through the soil? Or parts of me? Am I sending roots down into the earth? And what is that inching up? Or who is that? Above, sand has replaced the soil, a heavy mound that was piled over my dead body. Light filters through its grains. Light and more audible sounds, uttered in *his* voice: *tanges tamen aethera*, "you'll also touch air." I am touching it—touching them—both air and light. With all my branches and leaves. Just as I am touching the humid earth with the tips of my roots. The rest is not up to "me" to report. "Then did a shrub of frankincense, with deep-driven roots, rise slowly through the soil and its top cleaved the mound."

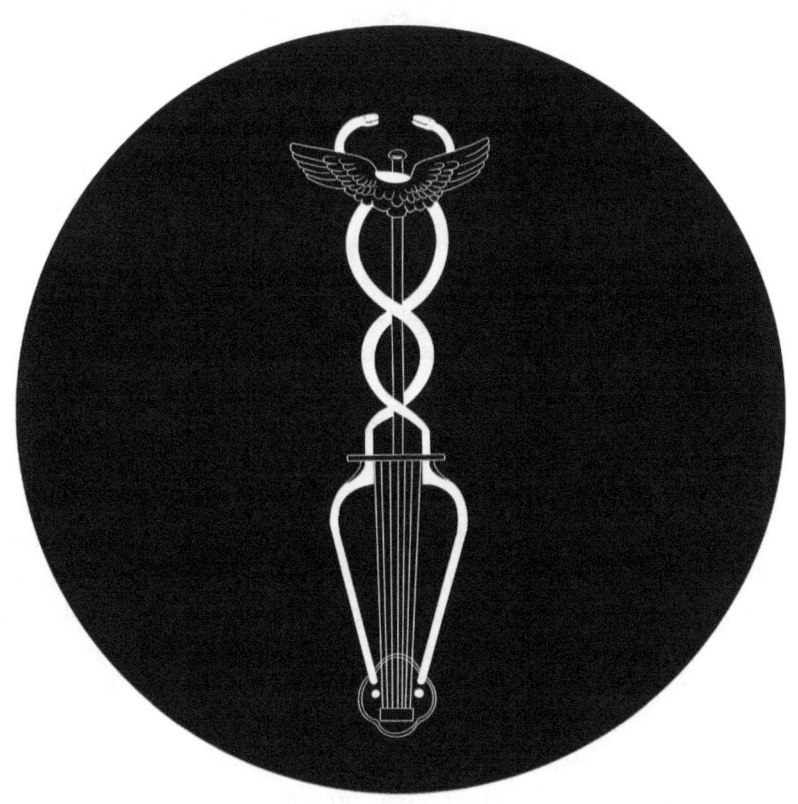

TWO BECOMING ONE: SALMACIS AND HERMAPHRODITUS, WITH SOME FORMULAS AND FORMULATIONS

(Liber IV, 274-388)

The story sounds straightforward enough: Salmacis and Hermaphroditus, a woman and a man, fuse into a single being. Two become one;

$1+1=\mathbf{1}; 2 \to 1; S \cup H$

In contrast to the myths of hermaphroditic human origins, such as those narrated in Plato's *Symposium* or in the Hebrew Bible, hermaphroditism is not the dawn of humanity, but an outcome—the outcome of a misunderstanding. After her advances are rejected by Hermaphroditus, Salmacis acts out of despair, embracing the object of her affection while he is bathing naked in a clear pond. As she wraps her limbs around him, she prays to the gods never to be parted from him ever again, a prayer that is heeded *literally*: "their two bodies, joined together as they were, were merged into one."

But the story is more complicated than it seems.

First, because of divine misunderstanding. Salmacis's passionate request is granted her in such a way that she grows unhappier still. The gods take her at her word and fulfill her wish exactly as stated. Is this a nasty joke they play on her? Are the gods really unable to distinguish between the literal and the symbolic senses of nonseparation? Or do they, like Mercury in response to Aglauros, want to make an ironic point, to teach Salmacis a lesson about the nightmarish shape of dreams realized and vows kept? About the nature of linguistic expressions, of words strung into grammatically correct sentences, that are incorrigibly ambiguous, irreducible to simple (or not so simple) formulas?

Second, because of the semantic mix-up between the senses of being together and being one. Togetherness is proximity that maintains the distance between two and, therefore, keeps their relation alive [$1+1=2$]. Oneness also involves two, albeit not in relation to each other, let alone each to her- or himself:

$$\mathbf{1} = 1+1$$

Beyond her one-sided, unrequited love, Salmacis finds a two-sided being, two-in-one, "with one face and one form for both."

Third, because each one is already, in itself, more than one [$1>1; 1\neq1$]. Before the mishap at the pond, Hermaphroditus bears a blend of his father's and mother's names (Hermes + Aphrodite; $H \cup A$). This blend is reflected also, in part, in his body: "in his fair face mother and father could be clearly seen." So, in each one of the two, there are already two, and in each of those, there are two more, and so forth [$1 \to 2\ldots$]. One is an infinite set [$1=\{(1+1), (1+1), (1+1), \ldots\}$].

Both Salmacis and Hermaphroditus (though, strictly speaking, there are no "both" anymore) are devastated after their fusion. They embody the unity of sexes, the Absolute actualized, which renders a relation impossible. Being or becoming the Absolute leads to profound disappointment, worse yet than the dissatisfaction one feels when the Absolute is unattainable. In the total unity of their new state, prior partial unities appear as merged halves: half-man, half-woman:

$$(1 = 1+1) \rightarrow (1 = \tfrac{1}{2} + \tfrac{1}{2})$$

"Whoever comes into this pool as man, may he go forth half-man [*semi-vir*]." The two who, or that, become one turn into halves of that one. Objectively and subjectively so. The Absolute is more elusive than ever before.

TWILIGHT
(Liber IV, 389–415)

A day dies, steadily metamorphosing into night. Every day does. "The day has ended, and the time has come when you could not say 'it was dark or light'; it was the borderland of night, yet with a gleam of day." As the sharp outlines of things fade away, the turns of celestial fire (Heraclitan *puros tropai*) come to visibility.

Itself the metamorphosis of day-night, twilight is the time of metamorphoses, even when they seem to happen in broad daylight. As they unfold, you cannot say, "it is a human or a tree," "it is a human or a rock," and so forth. But if metamorphoses are always under way, then all shapes are dubious, inhabiting in perpetual twilight the borderlands of being.

Alcithoe and her sisters, the Minyades, metamorphose at dusk. They have been spinning texts and weaving textiles all day long. Doing the work of high culture in defiance of Dionysian rites. Cultural artifacts, however, revert back to the nature they have been extracted from, traversing the unstable boundaries between plants, animals, and humans. ". . . and past all belief, their weft turned green, the hanging cloth changing into vines of ivy." Nature, which had metamorphosed into culture, has metamorphosed back (and forth) into vegetal nature.

TWILIGHT

Whether we want it or not, the work unworks itself. The weaving unweaves itself all by itself into vines; the weavers are rid of their human countenance. The unspooling of culture is the rewiring (or the rewilding) of nature. After textile filaments, it is the sisters' turn to change into someone else. They are called *vespertiliones*, evening creatures flitting about in the twilight, who owe their name to the evening, *vespere*. Bats. The sisters metamorphose into twilight-dwellers, partaking of that which is the ambience of every metamorphosis. Though now they are winged mammals, they eschew the outdoors: "houses, not forests, are their favorite haunts." They still obey the law of the household in the twilight zone between economy and ecology.

METAMORPHOSING MINDS: THE MADNESS OF ATHAMAS AND INO

(Liber IV, 416–562)

I. INO

OK, I confess: confessing is hard. You peel yourself raw, reveal your juicy flesh for others to see and to taste. After a few licks, you let them bite into you the same way you bite into yourself, sinking the teeth down, all the way down to the kernel. To the center of who or what you are. Assuming that there is something there. Anything. It is the hardest thing of all: to do your soul striptease, to remove the outer layers, for nothing, for the nothing that your innermost being is.

METAMORPHOSING MINDS

Do you know what it feels like to be bitten by a poisonous snake that leaves your flesh alone and aims right at your mind? "No wounds their bodies suffer; it is their minds that feel the deadly stroke." Your suffering is mental at any rate, whether your body is hurting or your mind. It helps, though to localize your pain, to say, 'It's my stomach; it's my neck . . .' and to focus on curing the ailing organ. I had no such luxury. They say it was a Fury, sent by Juno, who drove me mad. No, it was Athamas. His own madness made me insane. As though by contagion. He thought I was a lioness, pursued me as he would a beast of prey. When he caught up with me, he snatched our son from my hands, my little Learchus, *parvum Learchum*, and "whirling him round and round through the air like a sling, madly dashed the baby's head against a rough stone."

Would you not go crazy at this sight? You could say I lost my mind. At least my human mind I lost, that's for sure. I started running, with the body of my other son in my arms, to try and get away from myself, from my memory, from what I had just witnessed. But there was no "myself" left after what Athamas did to me, after what he did to Learchus. I howled in agony.

This world was no longer for me. I was no longer for this world. Inside, I was as dead as my son, never mind the frenzy of running. My body was moving as though by inertia, by itself, without the least interference, mine or anyone else's. And it was carrying me and my surviving child, Melicertes, to a watery abyss.

They say "madness made me strong." No, it was sanity that made me weak, unable to defend my son and myself from Athamas's vain wrath. I got rid of the shape of mind that had held me back, the mind that was all too human, all too understanding, prone to justifying and forgiving, submissive. Next I had to shed the body that went along with that mind, the body that wanted physical certainty, firm ground beneath its feet, the body constricted by gravity and weight.

So I took a leap from the tallest cliff into the raging sea. And together with Melicertes, I became divine. Somewhat like Empedocles, who jumped into the active crater of Mount Etna, to attain godlike existence. Water here; fire there. But the outcome is the same: the elements "take away . . . that which is mortal," *abstulit . . . quod mortale fuit*, and preserve a metamorphosed mind. Because minds have shapes. And mine got changed forever. Into nothing? The Nothing? Is this what has been speaking to you through "my" confession?

II. ATHAMAS

I don't know what's gotten into me. It felt like an alien power. I became possessed. Thought that I was in the wilderness, in the woods, and that Ino, Learchus and Melicertes were a lioness and her two cubs. In a royal palace, of all places! I was the king of Boeotia. Had unlimited power, obeying no one and fearing nothing. And here I was, possessed by I-know-not-what. Could it be this unlimited power that made me insane? But then it was not alien; it was in me, slowly germinating, blossoming with its poisonous flowers, and finally yielding its horrible fruit, which took the fruit of my loins away. My mind had been metamorphosing for a long time without me noticing it, inebriated as I was with my absolute power. No, it was not an alien force that took control of me; it was I, myself, who took full control of others—and lost it entirely.

What am I still doing here? She killed herself and Melicertes after I killed Learchus, sparing myself. Or did I? Did I not kill myself the moment I crushed my son's skull on that slab of marble? I saw a beast in my wife and sons, because my own "sovereign" mind had become beastly: I saw myself in them. I badly wanted to do away with myself, which is why I murdered my own child, whom I took for a lion cub. Since then I have been roaming the earth as a lion or a wolf would. Still in my human body but with the mind of the wild animal I had become. More precisely, of a wild animal *as it is construed by people*. That is why I am still thinking, speaking, and writing in human terms, using letters and words, ideas and concepts. No lion would purposefully kill his child. Only a human beast would.

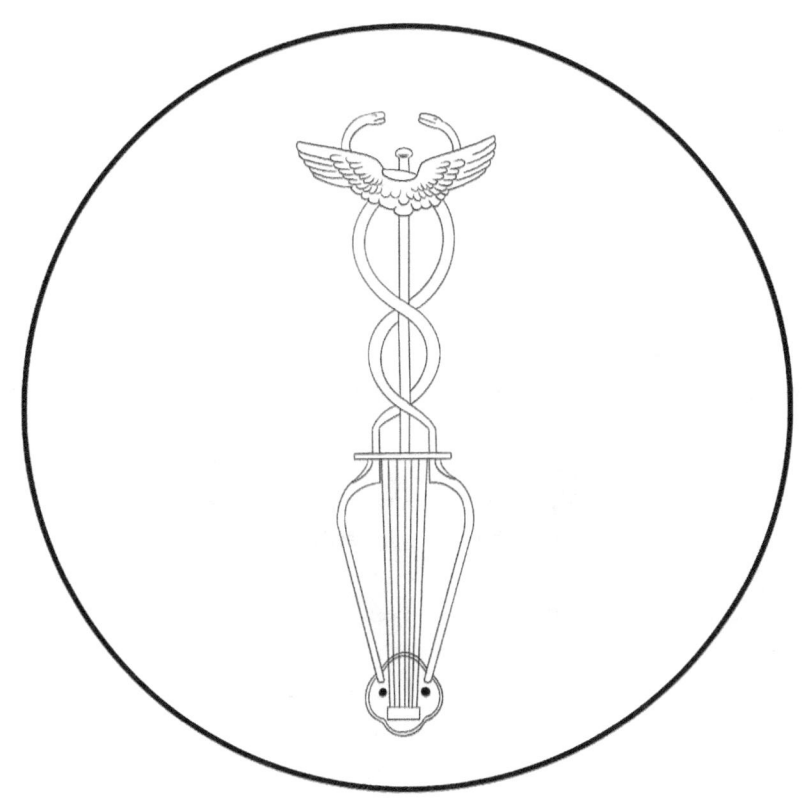

FOR "WHAT REMAINS OF ME": CADMUS'S WIFE AND BECOMING-SNAKE

(Liber IV, 563–603)

—What would our dialogue have been like if we could still speak in words, instead of hisses, dear wife?

—I don't know, Cadmus... I mean, now I don't know what knowing is, or maybe I never knew. We can try to imagine a conversation of ours, if imagination still has any sense. Although... this word, "imagination," has remained with me; it *has remained me*. Along with many other words attached to it. They just stretched out into a lllllloooooonnnnnggggg and winding line, after the fashion of our bodies. Snake bodies, snake words, loaded with the memory of being human. That's why we don't hurt humans, "remembering what we once were."

—Look! Listen! We are doing just that now: imagining our dialogue. Engaging in it. Addressing each other by imagining it together. God knows through whom, but we are doing it. Maybe that's what a dialogue is: a tongue split into two, one tongue forked, *lingua in partes fissa duas*? No, better than that, a dialogue is the two of us, our slick selves entwined around each other. One must become a snake to realize this. Otherwise, one stands no chance.

—Ever since you started turning into a snake, we both became obsessed with this worry—with what remains of you, what remains of me, what remains of us. Sssssssur-vival. We are still obsessed. With each human part of you, of me, of us lost, you wanted to freeze the frame, to stop the moment, to survey and to savor the losses and (no, not the gains!) the unchanged. The unchanged, for the time being, in the midst of a hurricane of changes. Calm and stable, like the eye of a storm.

—Yes, I remember. More than anything, I remember how I wanted to keep what was left of the human me through you: through your touch. That was the ultimate confirmation. I asked you: *me tangere*, "touch me," touch my still human face and hand, the countenance and the organ of action that make us human.

—Now there is no hand to touch. No hand to touch with. And no face. But we are in touch, you and I, absolutely in touch, like never before. Stretched out, intertwined; intertwined, stretched out. Body and mind, mind and body. Yours and mine, ours.

—So what remains? Does it matter?

—What remains is what will be. What will be, what will become of us. Of survival.

—How do you know?

—I've told you already: I do not know what knowing is. Socrates was the wisest of humans because he knew that he knew nothing. We, posthumans, might not be the wisest of anything, but we are honest enough to admit that we don't even know what knowing is.

TO BECOME A MOUNTAIN: ATLAS
(Liber IV, 604-663)

Mighty Atlas! This letter flies to your heights from your own domain, the edge of the earth (*ultima tellus*) and the seemingly endless sea (*pontus*) beyond it. Or as another poet said, from where "the land ends and begins the sea." The Atlantic realm, *regnis Atlantis*, the sea of Atlas. I am where you are, at the elemental threshold, on the verge, which, if you examine it closely, is actually fractal verges between the earth and the sky and a vast body of water and the solar blaze above it. "Thinking like a mountain" in your case is spanning the elemental fourfold: lifting the earth up to support with your head heavens and its stars; bathing your stony bones in the waves; receiving the energy of the sun to help grow your vegetal cover, the woods into which your hair and beard metamorphosed. You make the world livable by making room for existence, by spacing it, by making sure that the sky does not collapse onto the earth and that vegetation thrives on your slopes. But at what price? In your human, or quasi-human, form you denied hospitality to Perseus to then become a mountainous ecosystem, imposing yet welcoming all into your midst. Aren't we doing the same to the whole planet—expelling life from it? Then, again like you, we massify ourselves, amass the nondecomposable products of our industries, and turn ourselves into the earth, into its crust, from which we draw the name for the current geological era. The Anthropocene. The Atlasocene? The Anthropatlasocene? But, unlike you, we are not redeeming our initial hostility to life with a new hospitality: the earth that we decompose, or fail to decompose, into is sterile, toxic even.

At best we aspire toward "sustainability," the sort of hubris that dares imagine humanity holding up, sustaining the intricate web of ecosystems the way you hold the starry sky with your head. And what a head it is in our case! One filled with algorithms, calculations of costs and benefits, geoengineering designs, interplanetary species and machine-brain interfaces. This head cut off from the rest of the body, like the head of the Medusa you've glimpsed, tells us: "Mine the mountain, but not too much. Or mine it elsewhere, on asteroids or on other planets." A *caput* that is breeding ideas such as these is caput, no doubt about it... And it endeavors to reshape what it sees around after its own image. Chopping things up, mutilating them. How could it ever compare with your magnificent peak? Everything is topsy-turvy here: the head is where the feet should be. Who sustains whom? Is it you, the mountain and the woods that grow on your slopes and the sea beneath it and the airy expanses above, or is it a fraction of a fraction of a weird species, *Homo sapiens*, without a clue of what wisdom (*sapientia*) is, clueless either about itself or about the rest of the lifeworld? I do not want to burden you with more than what you already have to bear, Atlas. That said, may I send together with this letter to you a small request, a minor wish, really? If humanity still stands a chance to learn or relearn thinking, could it be not as haughty as a mountain, but as unassuming, low-lying, and horizontal as moss?

>With the embrace of the unembraceable
>from a humble inhabitant of your realm

ANDROMEDA AND PERSEUS: BECOMING FREE

(Liber IV, 664-739)

Chained to a cliff: the primal scene of unfreedom. It has been unfairly and subtly gendered in the mythological imaginary. Painful loss of liberty has been primarily associated with Prometheus (note how this loss resonates in the excess of a passive voice saturating these very lines), who had been punished by the gods for his theft of fire by being chained to a rock, the eagle feeding daily on his liver. But what about Andromeda? The daughter of an Ethiopian king, Cepheus, she is "bound by the arms to a sharp cliff," *ad duras relegatam bracchia*, awaiting her sacrifice to a sea monster. That is where Perseus sights her, as he flies over the African coast. Only if her parents offer her to Poseidon's dreadful representative will they spare the lives of their subjects.

The first of my many blessings is the fact that I was born in this great nation, a little over 50 years ago, in September of 1970. Congress had enacted two Civil Rights Acts in the decade before, and like so many who had experienced lawful racial segregation firsthand, my parents, Johnny and Ellery Brown, left their hometown of Miami, Florida, and moved to Washington, D.C., to experience new freedom. When I was born here in Washington, my parents were public school teachers, and to express both pride in their

heritage and hope for the future, they gave me an African name: "Ketanji Onyika," which they were told means "lovely one."
—TEXT OF THE OPENING REMARKS BY JUDGE KETANJI BROWN JACKSON, NOMINEE TO THE SUPREME COURT, ON THE FIRST DAY OF HER CONFIRMATION HEARINGS BEFORE THE SENATE JUDICIARY COMMITTEE, MARCH 21, 2022

Perseus fights the sea monster to liberate Andromeda. Today's Andromedas can fight for themselves. But the monster is far from gone; he is multiheaded and multisuited, clad in high-quality business attire and well versed in the language of civil servants. He cannot be defeated in one fell swoop—this much Perseus has demonstrated to us. So what's the strategy?

STEP 1. SMOKE AND MIRRORS AND SHADOWS

Perseus flies high above the seas. "When the monster saw the hero's shadow [*umbra*] on the surface of the sea, he savagely attacked the shadow." Perseus then "attacks the roaring monster from above, and in his right shoulder buries his sword."

> For four years, Democrats systemically voted against many well-credentialed nominees that were diverse professionally, geographically, religiously and ethnically. Was it racist or anti-woman for them to do so? I don't believe it was. Democrats did it because the nominees didn't agree with living constitutionalism. Just as Republicans have opposed nominees based on their judicial philosophy.
> —SENATOR CHUCK GRASSLEY OF IOWA, SENATE JUDICIARY COMMITTEE HEARING, MARCH 21, 2022

> Over the course of my almost decade on the bench, I have developed a methodology that I use to ensure that I am ruling impartially and adhering to the limits on my judicial authority.
> —JUDGE KETANJI BROWN JACKSON, "ANSWERS FOR THE RECORD," SENATE JUDICIARY COMMITTEE HEARING, MARCH 21, 2022

> If he came and said, I'm going to put the best jurist on the court, and he looked at a number of people and he ended up nominating a Black

woman, he could credibly say, OK, I'm nominating the person who's most qualified. He's not even pretending to say that. He's saying, if you're a white guy, tough luck.
—SENATOR TED CRUZ, "KETANJI BROWN JACKSON IS POISED TO MAKE HISTORY," NPR TRANSCRIPT, MARCH 22, 2022

When they go low, we go high.
—MICHELLE OBAMA, 2016 DEMOCRATIC NATIONAL CONVENTION

STEP 2. NIMBLY ELUDING THE BLOWS AND FINDING VULNERABLE SPOTS

Smarting under the deep wound [*vulnere . . . gravi modo*], the creature now reared himself high in air, now plunged beneath the waves . . . Perseus eludes [*effugit*] the greedy fangs by help of his swift wings, and where the vulnerable points lie open to attack, he smites with his hooked sword.

Three hundred and thirty pages of this. Three hundred and thirty pages of nimble elusion and seeking vulnerable spots!

127. Should federal courts invoke Younger abstention in cases with two private plaintiffs? RESPONSE: Please see my response to Question 126. . . .

163. Should rights be viewed through a broad level of generality or a narrow level of generality? RESPONSE: I cannot answer an abstract question because Article III requires that judges consider only questions of law that are presented in the context of particular cases and controversies.
—SENATOR CHUCK GRASSLEY OF IOWA, "QUESTIONS FOR THE RECORD," AND JUDGE KETANI BROWN JACKSON, "ANSWERS FOR THE RECORD," SENATE JUDICIARY COMMITTEE HEARING, MARCH 21, 2022

STEP 3. THE FINAL TRIPLE PUNCH

"Meanwhile Perseus's wings are growing heavy, soaked with spray." Resting on a rock, half-hidden by the waves, he holds on with his left hand while "thrice and again he plunges his sword into the vitals of the monster." At this the shores and the high seats of the gods re-echo with wild shouts of applause (*litora cum plausu clamor superasque deorum inplevere domos*).

In a new Marquette Law School Poll national survey, 66% of adults say that, if [they were] senators, they would support the nomination of Ketanji Brown Jackson to the Supreme Court, while 34% would oppose her nomination.
—*MARQUETTE UNIVERSITY LAW SCHOOL POLL RELEASE*, MARCH 30, 2022

Just three Republican senators—Susan Collins of Maine, Lisa Murkowski of Alaska and Mitt Romney of Utah—crossed the aisle to support Jackson.
—SARAH BINDER, "AMERICANS SUPPORTED JACKSON. WHY DIDN'T MORE REPUBLICAN SENATORS?" *THE WASHINGTON POST*, APRIL 8, 2022

Whoa! It's about time!
—PRESIDENT BIDEN, SOUTH LAWN OF THE WHITE HOUSE, APRIL 8, 2022

FROM LIVING TO DEAD CORALS, FROM WOODS TO WOOD

(Liber IV, 740-764)

Suppleness, pliability, plasticity:
These are some of the qualities of the living.
Warm moisture suffusing the body, or
Its aquatic milieu.
Fresh twigs and brilliant green leaves are soaked
With water and solar fire,
Their "living core," *viva medulla*,
Celebrating the marriage of the elements.
Until . . .
Until the moment they become the objects
Of the Gorgon's petrifying gaze.

FROM LIVING TO DEAD CORALS, FROM WOODS TO WOOD

When Medusa's severed head rests on leaves and twigs,
They acquire "a strange stiffness,"
The stiffness of death, returning to inorganic existence.
The elements are divorced from one another:
Moisture is gone, vegetal body dried up, hardened, *indurvit*.
The woods become wood, lumber, timber.
The corals are bleached and equally stiff:
"A pliant twig beneath the sea
Is turned to stone above."
Corals are corralled in the warming seas,
Arrested in their exposure to air and sewers.
Who is Medusa? Or what? Who converts every *who* into a *what*?
Is her gaze not ours,
Surveying land and sea, forests and meadows,
With the same rigidifying indifference
Or possessive desire?
Even with the head severed, with "the human" demoted or deposed,
    declawed or deconstructed,
Even after the capital punishment of the Anthropocene,
The rests of its ugly techno-body smeared over the surface of the
    earth,
The gaze does not lose its deadening power.
No sooner it espies someone in its field of vision
Than those who are espied perish.
When they are chopped to pieces, when their throats are slit,
When they are depleted or deoxygenated, burned up or deep frozen—
They die a second death.
Was it worth caring for the Gorgon's severed head,
For the command-and-control center of the world machine,
Lest it "be bruised on the hard sand,"
At the expense of the living?

PULPED NONFICTION

(Liber V, 1–156)

Scene 22, B, Take 4

Blood is everywhere. Spilled, splattered, gushing, "spouting forth," "sprinkling a well-spread table," drenching a whole house. Is this a scene from *Kill Bill 1*? From *Inglorious Basterds*? *Once Upon a Time in Hollywood*? Another Tarantino movie? Or could it be Ovid, describing Perseus slaughtering demigods and heroes at a feast?

As he aims his bow at Perseus, Athis is counterattacked: "Perseus snatched up a brand which lay smoldering on the altar and smote the youth, crushing his face to splintered bones." "Amphimedon, eager to join in the fray, slipped and fell in the blood, with which all the floor was wet." Idas is struck by the spear of Phineus, and "as he was just about to hurl back the javelin which he had drawn out of his own body, he fell failing, his limbs all drained of blood." Another participant of the banquet has his hand pierced by the spear "and pinned to the wood. There fastened, Abas thrust him through the side; nor did he fall, but, dying, hung down from the post, to which his hand was nailed."

This is not run-of-the-mill gore. It is pulp fiction (or *Pulp Fiction*). Excruciatingly detailed depictions of extreme violence spectacularize death, reveling in it. Such violence is not a means for attaining this or that end; it is, literally, a bloodletting. In the melee of death, where it is impossible to distinguish friend from foe, there is only one message, one conclusion, still available for understanding: You are alive in this very instant, and you may be dead the next. Isn't a transition from life to death a metamorphosis of sorts? A butterfly breaking out of its cocoon—the cocoon torn, disfigured, defaced, beaten to a pulp, bled...

Perseus's fight is pure Tarantino, or proto-Tarantino; Tarantino is pure Ovid, or crypto-Ovid. One epoch is transmuted into another retrospectively, retroactively, *and* prospectively, proactively.

It is tempting to conclude that in Ovid's Tarantino moments, the reader (who, in her mind's eye, sees the scenes staged with a variety of props and special effects, the camera panning, zooming in and out of bloodied bodies and body parts, to the soundtrack of shrieks and gasps mixed with Ennio Morricone's musical score) is desensitized to senseless violence. But desensitization is not quite the right term. The too-much of bloody gore leads the reader or the viewer to take ironic distance toward the spectacle. A tragedy bleeds into and blends with its opposite. *Incipit* tragicomedy!

Cut!

PERSEUS, AGAIN: HEART OF STONE
(Liber V, 157-250)

You. Yes, you, Perseus. You are not shy when it comes to turning people into stone, using your trophy, Medusa's severed head, as the weapon of choice. Her gaze is not hers, but yours. It has always been all about *you*.

Although you ask friends to avert their eyes, you do not differentiate among those who are to be targeted: knowing neither barriers nor particulars, your (her) gaze is toxic or radioactive. They are all no more than homogeneous throngs to you, "opposing crowds," a mobile multitudinous mass, on which you exercise your own fascist brand of crowd control.

They are those you fought in Ethiopia: Indian, Libyan, Syrian, Mendesian (Egyptian), some Thracian, and Ethiopian youths, nobles, and demigods. Who are they to you—you, a Greek hero, the legendary founder of the Perseid dynasty that ruled Mycenae in northeastern Peloponnese?

You beheaded Medusa because you were scared of *her* power, of femininity. Fearful that she might castrate you, deflating your phallic delusion of grandeur, you enacted your castration anxiety on her by the act of decapitation. To quell the dread that you felt before the African and Arab "crowds," you immobilized their best and brightest, transferring your own petrification onto them.

How did you face them? You stood with your "back against a great stone column, protected in the rear." *Ad magnae saxa columnae tutaque terga gerens.* (What did you think they would do to your rear? Would it be so much worse that having the supposedly protective substitute that is the "great stone column"—of your "reason," your law and order—up there? Throw yet another anxiety into the mix!) And you showed her cut head to them, turning them into marble statues. A stone pillar behind you; stones ahead. And in the middle? In or at the core? Stone, a heart of stone. Numb, benumbed. Too afraid and too proud to be flexible, to bend, to incline, to feel anything, to expand *and* to contract (the heart beating), to breathe.

Your stony heart did not take pity on Phineus, who begged you to spare his life—Phineus, who "repented," who not only let himself feel fear but also come close to and touch the bodies of others, *proxima tangit corpora*, which you had turned into marble. And to punish Phineus further, you put his fear, his emotion, "the very tears upon his cheeks" on permanent display in the statue he became, eternally exposed. Now, everything you despise and excoriate in yourself is projected onto and immortalized in him.

But you—you!—harshly punish yourself by cutting yourself off from the feminine and the non-European, from living-breathing bodies and affects, from inclinations and approximations. Without them you are nothing. Yes, nothing. You spread around nothing but nothing. When the world, meaning, and sense, history and science, politics and religion, are "all about you," they are all about nothing. The impeccable nihilism of self-aggrandizement.

BECOMING LIQUID: A RIDDLE

(Liber V, 255-267)

Here is a riddle. Which animal gives birth to a water source? A jellyfish washed up on the seashore? (We are still floating around corals and medusa or medusae, at least in our imagination.)

None other than Athena solves the riddle: "The fame of a new spring has reached my ears, which broke out under the hard hoof of the winged horse of Medusa." The Muses, Mnemosyne's daughters, confirm the rumor: "The tale is true, and Pegasus did indeed produce our spring" (*est Pegasus huius origo fontis*). Water gathers in the trace of an animal, the cavity left by Pegasus's hoof on the body of the earth. The spring is a meeting place of the elements: of water and the earth, of the air (on which the winged horse glides) and the fiery force of his limbs. It is Pegasus's legacy, the liquid memory of animal body.

BECOMING LIQUID: A RIDDLE

At first glance, glacial lakes do not seem to have much in common with the new spring, which Athena graced with her presence. But aren't they also cavities in the body of the earth filled with water, the cavities that monumentalize the cooling and the warming of the organism that is the planet? Winged, amphibious—global warming is racing through the atmosphere and the oceans and the earth, leaving liquid (and not so liquid) traces everywhere.

At a closer glance, our Pegasus turns out to be petroleum, crude oil pumped from the entrails of the earth. Granted: oil is nothing like pure water. It is nevertheless the liquid trace of untold numbers of animals and plants who lived millions of years ago and whose remains have in the meantime liquefied. "The tale is true," though other goddesses and gods visit these springs or wells. And other hoofs break the ground, from which these wells or springs gush forth, the heavy techno-hoofs used for drilling and fracking.

The two glances merge in stereoscopic, panoramic vision. The vistas are truly frightening: liquid rests of living beings are incinerated, filling the air, the oceans, and the earth with the rests of these rests, their residue in the form of CO_2 or synthetic plastics, the byproducts of crude oil. The elements do not meet; on the contrary, they fall apart. Glaciers melt and disappear, irreversibly so, in the trail of this conflagration. The planetary-scale organism is feverish, responding with still more heat to the inflammation provoked by our extractive and destructive desire for energy.

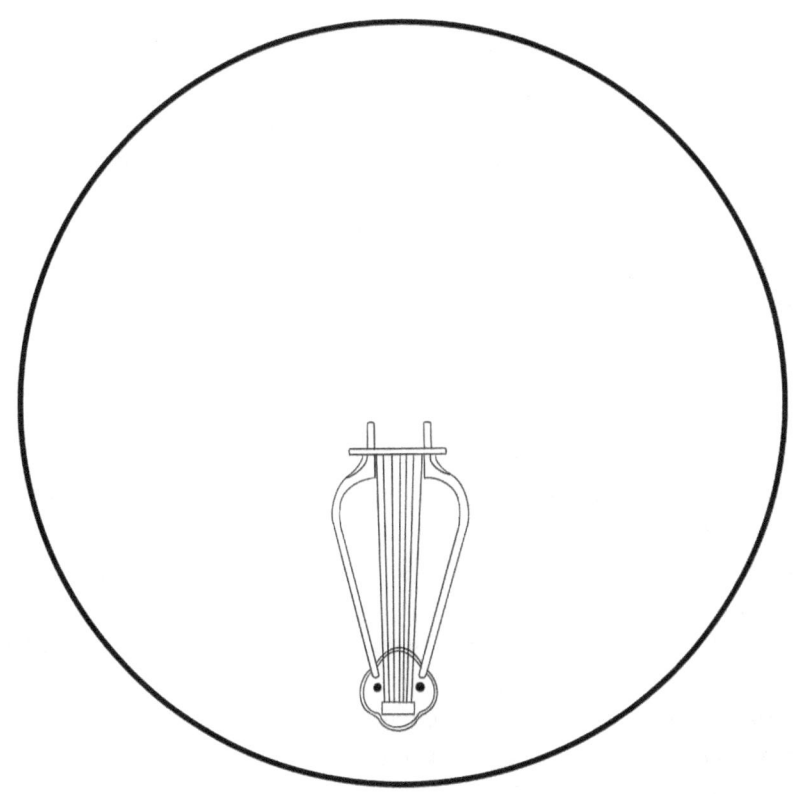

PYRENEUS:
EXCERPTS FROM A SELF-HELP BOOK
(Liber V, 268-293)

Everyone is an artist, including you. Don't be surprised; you just haven't realized your potential yet, your creative genius waiting to see the light of day and to flower. You don't even suspect that it's there. For a modest fee, I will instruct you in the arts of identifying as an artist and monetizing your newly discovered talents.

To begin with, get in touch with your inner self. Honor your inner animal, wild and untamable. You are the lord of your domain, a "ferocious king" of your castle. Survey your land, every corner of your inner world. Take the time to acknowledge that this, too, is *you*. Your personality is as deep as the highest peaks of the Pyrenees.

Now that you have inspected and claimed your domain, invite the Muses into your home. Offer them shelter and the safety of your roof in these times of inclement global weather. Repeat this mantra (no matter if you don't understand a word of it): *nec dubitate, precor, tecto grave sidus et imbrem vitare meo.* Let the mantra resonate in your head, taking *its* place under your roof.

Exercise your artistic expression. Daily, without any barriers, filters, or self-criticism. Write, draw, dance, sing, sculpt anything that comes to mind, anything you see or feel. One by one the Muses will fly into your world, inhabiting it. Inhabiting you. Host them. Lead them into every room, every chamber of your inner dwelling. Ask them to be at home there. Enjoy their company. Naturally, your enjoyment of the Muses will yield works of art.

Know that the Muses are capricious guests. At the first available opportunity, they will try to get away from the castle of your existence. To unlock your creative potential, lock the Muses up. Shut your doors closed. Hold onto to them; don't let them flee.

Still, "donning their wings," they may fly away. If they do, chase them. Repeat a new mantra, "What way you take, the same I will take also." *Qua via est vobis, erit et mihi eadem.* Take a plunge on your creative side. Though you may lose it altogether, your art will be superb.

9/IX: THE DAUGHTERS OF EUIPPE
(Liber V, 294-319)

Turned upside down, 9 is less than itself: 6. Losing the unit it commences with, IX is more than itself: X.

Philosophers have placed numbers on a par with the eternal ideas. But numbers have shapes; their shapes are their bodies; and, like all other bodies, they grow (tails or limbs), contract, mutate. Spatial orientation matters. Is a number facing left or right? Is it standing on its head (0: is all head, 5, 6, 8) or on a birdlike leg (1, 4, 7, 9)?

Assuming a precise spatial position is even more important for Roman numerals: XI and IX are different numbers, though the symbolic components of their bodies are the same.

Do numbers *have* bodies? Or *are* they their bodies? Nine will respond.

9/IX: Once upon a time, there were nine sisters. Nine births their mother Euippe had given for them to exist in the world. Actually, I do not care nine of what we are talking about: apples or oranges or humans or rocks or lizards. They were nine, and so I accompanied them everywhere, this sisterly throng, this *turba sororum*, in the same manner as I accompany nine of anything. Or of anyone. They were proud of being so many, "swelling with the pride of numbers," *intumuit numero*. Swelling with the pride of *me*. The sisters identified with me—they were nine, which is already quite a flock, and the rest paled in significance. They did not realize that, through me (through the unique combination of my loyalty and indifference) they could turn into nine of something else. I can add also this: they knew that I clung to another group, the muses. When the daughters of Euippe challenged those other nine sisters to a singing contest, they relied, at least in part, on me. "... and our numbers are the same." They wanted to be like the muses, better than the muses. I will not tell you how the contest went; just the outcome. Do you hear those birds, those magpies "nine in number, lamenting their fate" (*numeroque novem sua fata querentes*)? It is them. I, the number nine, am their form and transformation, their body and s... whole. And not only theirs. But what of *my* body? It depends. My body you will find in nine desks, nine leaves, nine clouds, nine statues, nine... Take away one, or add one, and I will disappear. (Not that I ever appear as myself without something or someone countable.) I transmute myself into nine of anything and vanish as soon as the nine become eight or ten. Look: IX—X. Anticipating my erasure, I stand behind myself. Beside myself. Ecstatic. "I" stands behind or before "X." That is me. The inverted 6 is also me, in each moment recalling and expecting another inversion. Do I have my body? Am I my body (together with X)? What sort of a body is it that contains anything or anyone amounting to me? And that vanishes as soon as you add to or subtract from my infinite embrace just another one?

AN ISLAND MEDITATION

(Liber V, 320-361)

PROLOGUE.

Although no man is an island,
An island can pin down a man (well, a giant)
And make him feel the enormous weight of its earthy mass (these
    pondera terrae)
With every limb of the outstretched body.
Beneath the upper geological crusts and the lithosphere
Is the place of one who "dared to aspire to the heights of heaven."
What is the choice then: resist or desist?
Struggle with all your might against the alien bulk piled on top
    of you?

Or let it gradually smother and crush you?
Is there a third way? How do you become an island?
How do you become a landmass?

A MEDITATION. FOR TYPHOEUS.

With eyes closed, settle into your body. Listen to its rhythmic sequences, attending to your heartbeat and breath.

Begin surveying your body's bulk from the inside out, tapping its density with the ray of your attention. Instead of trying to make yourself transparent to yourself, scan the matter that you are: a living corporeity, thick and opaque. Disregard your organismic form, its figure and outlines. Concentrate on the contents, letting them drift to the territory of the amorphous.

Release the tension accumulated in your muscles. Your eyelids are heavy. Your cheeks, your neck and shoulders, arms, hands, and fingers are weighing you down. The downward pull of your body tissues is irresistible, yet without a trace of tiredness.

With arms and hands drooping, half-bend your fingers, so that the palms of your hands assume a cupping position. Can you feel the heft of the nothingness you are holding?

Experience each part of your upper body becoming a mass. You have neither a neck nor shoulders nor arms. There is only a living mass. You do not *have* weight; you *are* your weight. Massify yourself.

Even if you feel like you are pinned down by the earth, your feet are pressing into the floor, the floor surging up to and coalescing with your feet. You are supported. You are the support: earthy, substantial. Your legs are a seamless continuation of the ground.

Feel the minute oscillations of your mass, of the weight that you are. Are you drawn to other masses next to you, whether organic or inorganic? Are you sensing the subtle airflows swirling around?

AN ISLAND MEDITATION

There is only a constant, constantly fluctuating, pull and push. Your body is the pulled and the pulling. Your mind is, too. Leaden thoughts falling toward the sounds of music and words. Attention drawn to body as mass. Associations gravitating toward other associations. Breath fusing together air and earth, the atmosphere and the topsoil. Dust.

As mass, your body is a body among bodies. On equal terms, it participates in a society of things that have weight, that weigh down, that tend earthwards: rocks and books, oranges and computers, sticks and pots, you and I. Drift away from mass society and toward the society of mass. Keep transforming yourself into mass: recognize that *this* is what you have always already been.

Heed the nearly silent voice of the earth. Do so less with your ears and more with your skin, muscles and fatty tissues, and, further inward, with your bones. Register the vibrations and the resonances bouncing between the planet's membrane and the edges of your living bulk, between your cosmic and biological bodies, between the mass that you are and other masses around, under, and above you.

Further attending to these resonances and vibrations, dwell on the space-time between them. Having left your figure behind, dissolve into the background of existence, vibrant and sonorous, fleshy and heavy. There are no more oppositions between darkness and light, the empty and the full, white noise and sounds, the meaningless and the meaningful. You are the medium and the message. What is being communicated through you? What does the mass, to which you contribute and in which you participate, convey?

Allow your brain to be permeated with the resonances of the mass that you are.

Gently drop your head forward, your chin touching close to the space between the clavicles, the suprasternal notch. Slowly, roll your head from one shoulder to the other and back. Heavy with organs, dreams, cells, thoughts, tissues, desires, it is no different from the rest of your body's mass. Let go of its sphericality. Embrace its weight.

Your brainwaves are those of the world; cosmic vibrations are those of your brain. While light blends with darkness, the inner passes into the outer in the background of existence, with which you have merged.

You don't know if sounds emerge from the outside or from your resonant mass. If thoughts, like ripe fruit, plop down from your body or plunge toward you from elsewhere. It doesn't matter. Every vibration is a reverberation, without beginning and without end. Everything sonorous is resonant. Every mass (including you, yourself) is in relation to other masses, the relation that makes it what it is.

As you continue practicing the art of becoming-mass, gradually open your eyes and look around. See familiar surroundings in a different light. Your vision joins your hearing and the rest of the senses in the experience of heaviness, in experience *as* heaviness. Slow down your thoughts and pause. You can sit down if you wish. Now that you began practicing the art of becoming-mass, carry this liberating experience of heaviness everywhere you go.

TEARFUL METAMORPHOSES: CYANE

(Liber V, 410-437, 462-470)

Tears flow in silence, in the absolute silence, into which being dissolves. Being *and* time dissolve in it or in them: *lacrimosa dies illa*," "that day of tears," as in Mozart's *Requiem*, which is capable of resonating with silence. A day (*dies*) of tears is also a god (*deus*) of tears, their veil concealing and outlining the diurnal glow that is divine, while wordlessly announcing a day without brilliance or a god without divinity.

Cyane is a goddess, a water nymph whose name means *blue*. Heartbroken at the rape of Proserpina by Pluto/Hades, she "dissolved all away in tears [*lacrimisque absumitur omnis*], and into those very waters was she melted whose great divinity she had been but now."

The form of divinity is transmuted into its matter and content; tears flow, and she flows with them, as them. Just as everything flowing is already, if potentially, tearful: long hair, for instance, or free-flowing fabric. Her hair is the first part of Cyane to liquefy into tears.

What are tears? Whose tears? Dew, mastic (or tears of Chios), amber (remember the sisters of Phaethon?), rain, the clear liquid released by the eye's lacrimal glands: atmospheric, vegetal, animal. Sweet or salty, bitter or neutral, they are the drops and flows that go along with weeping and that barely persist when weeping stops. If the world is made of water, as the pre-Socratic Thales of Miletus thought, that water is gathered from various kinds of tears, the tears shed in advance, and enduringly so, over the state of the world, over its fate.

The teardrops of rain and dew are elemental mercy shown to a parched earth. Not shown—given. It is one thing to let tears roll down your cheeks, freely. Indulging in self-pity, regardless of the loss of whomever or whatever you are bemoaning. But it is another thing altogether to hand yourself over to the world in tears, as tears. To pour yourself out without leaving anything within, without leaving anything like a *within* safe and sound. Inconsolable: uncollectable.

"Without either lips or tongue," Cyane speaks, which is to say that the tears that she is speak. The language of tears is that of silent flows. Plink, plink, plink—that is the language of raindrops, not so much of dew or of mastic or amber or of the liquid emanating from our eyes. Tears speak by externally indicating profuse affect (sadness, joy). They attest to the significance of the event that triggered such an emotional response. And they testify, "giving clear signs" of the disaster that has happened and that keeps happening in and as our world.

SEASONAL EXISTENCE: PROSERPINA'S QUESTIONS

(Liber V, 385-409, 564-571)

How do you live seasonally? Eat fruits and vegetables and legumes that are *in* season? Dress according to the weather? Celebrate the turning points of the year: the equinoxes, solstices . . .? But also, and before that, how do the seasons become seasonal? How do a year and the earth, for that matter? What if I were to tell you that in the beginning there was an "everlasting spring," *perpetuum ver*? Would you believe me (who *me*? Proserpina? Ovid?)? Or those who came before and after me, insisting on the original primaveral season without seasonal alterations and alternations: Virgil in his *Georgics*, William of Conches in his *Dragmaticon*, Hildegard of Bingen in her *Ordo virtutum*? Would you entertain the suggestion, bizarre as it may sound, that the becoming-seasonal in a departure from that perpetual primordial spring was an effect of cosmic trauma, of the Fall, of a rape and a kidnapping? Is the periodic retreat of life into the earth (and of the earth into itself), its coiling back into the root, a sign of mourning for innocence lost, over and over again? But then why were the flowers gathered, plucked in their prime in the everlasting spring, not mourned, unlike their loss when they fell, quasi-cinematically, out of my loosened tunic the moment I was captured? Because there was an infinite supply of them in a spring that promised not to end? Infinite renewability? Why this comparison, encrusted in the lines of the text and in the very unconscious, between gathering flowers and the deflowering of virginity? Is the supposedly innocent child play of plucking violets and white lilies, *Proserpina . . . ludit et aut violas aut candida lilia carpit*, a hidden reproach Ovid directs to her? To me? In anticipation of *her* (*my*) being plucked in due time, in the ripeness or the completion of time? Do the seasons with their periodic alteration and alternation pay tribute to that act of violence, redoubled, triplicated, endlessly reiterated? Does the division of the revolving year into two split it between memory and forgetting? Does becoming seasonal mean half-acquiescing with the past, however traumatic it was, and with what in the passage of time refuses to pass year after year? Bipolar? Swinging between the spring-summer mania and the autumn-winter depression? Acknowledging and repudiating, repudiating and acknowledging, the violent institution of seasonality? Is there another choice? Another chance?

ARETHUSA: BECOMING THE OTHER

(Liber V, 572-641)

Plummeting
Plummeting
Plummeting
Plummeting
Into a crystalline and moist coolness,
She delivers herself to its silence, *sine murmure*.
Reaching
Reaching
The bottom,
She feels that she is in her native abode,
At home in the water, into which she dives

ARETHUSA: BECOMING THE OTHER

Until a terrible grumble arises from its depths.
She has plunged into the other:
She has plunged into him.
How to escape from what you have delivered yourself to?
Where to find refuge from the one who surrounds you on all sides
    and infiltrates deep within?
Leaping
Leaping
Leaping
Out of the stream and running forward,
She is far behind *and* preceded—
Praecedere
Praecedere—
Her "pursuer's long shadow stretching out ahead,"
Despairing
Praying
Fearing the worst,
What does she do?
What do you do when you face what you fear the most?
The ancient law of mimesis:
She becomes what she is terrified of:
She becomes the other:
Liquid, dripping, trickling, flowing.
An ancient game of death-and-life:
Transmuting yourself into what instills fear.
But
But
But
Becoming the other is not fusing with the other,
Nor mixing and mingling like water in water, like water with water.
So, she continues
Plummeting
Plummeting
Plummeting
Plummeting
Plummeting
Deeper down,
Deeper still,

ARETHUSA: BECOMING THE OTHER

Below the waters of the other—
The waters that are the other—
As the waters she has become.
Into the cleft earth, *rupit humum*,
She descends,
Erecting a telluric wall between
Waters and waters,
Separating the aqueous other
From herself othered, liquefied.
Entrusting herself to the earth,
She is awaiting
Awaiting
Awaiting
The moment when, in her subsequent ascent,
She will be received by another other:
Air.

FOR ARACHNE:
A FEW THREADS TO FOLLOW
(Liber VI, 1-145)

Slowly. You start pulling a thread out of yourself. Or, better, you keep pulling on it, since there is no beginning and no end in sight. Silk and strings of letters, warps and wefts, sley and grammar, sounds and syllables, words and yarn. Vibrations, resonances: echoes upon echoes. Not forgetting the gaps, the silences, however tight the weave, however high the thread count. It is the thread, on which you are already hanging either by your neck or by the belly or by the stem transformed into a tendril, surviving yourself, living on beyond yourself. Do you need a shuttle traveling across a loom to spin your textile, to compose your text, your musical score? A page filled with pencil strokes? A computer screen, traversed by a cursor? Or will the movements of your bodymind seamlessly organize, in space and in time, the yarn and the vibrations rippling out of you? Animalize your art, your thought, your perception. Vegetalize and elementalize them. Let them grow and decay out of you. Allow them to sprout from your meristems. To be secreted from your spinneret glands. Whatever is done to you, whatever you do, you will dangle on a cord, forming together with it a pendulum, which, as your mindbody sways back and forth, will mark the rhythms of your existence. You are your very own wall clock without a wall to lean upon. Everything you do amounts to embroidering on the thread you are (barely) hanging by. Too narrow to make a cloth; too wide to count as nothing. While the cord is one, the filaments comprising it are many, all of them intricately interwoven among themselves and with the emptiness that persists between each pair. It may seem that the height of your thought, of your art, of *you* is in deftly matching one thread with another. But the true skill is in combining threads with nonthreads, interweaving the nothing that you will have been and the nothing that you will have become with the something that, for the time being, you are. The tearing of the thin vegetal or animal fiber that holds you is not an event waiting to happen in an indefinite time to come. The rupturing has already happened, if imperceptibly so. Your neck or belly or stem is cut loose. Freedom? Despite the cut, though, you insistently pull on this apparently endless silk or cellulose fiber; you are spinning and spinning, over the abyss. The dexterity of your ten fingertips, the work of your six spinneret glands, the probing movement of your innumerable root tips flirt with disaster, past and future. The grace of bodymind motions, like beauty itself, derives from the nothing this mindbody is about to become, from its fragility that is only frail and pitiful when seen from the side of pure being. What is beautiful is how your finitude—being-the-end and at the same time being-beyond-the-end, rather than coming-to-an-end—is woven into the arts of your existence, whether daringly or without a smidgeon of heroism. You are more divine in your vegetality and animality than the self-assured, perfect, and perfectly immobile gods. You had ripped your textile up before the jealous goddess has torn it apart. Ever since you have known yourself and your world, you have come across your string of proteins or vibrations or words torn and have still continued pulling on it, spinning and weaving with it regardless, generating works of stunning beauty. You express, literally pressing out of yourself a frayed filament and damaged thought, mutilated desires and grating sounds, an injured, traumatized bodymind. Soon enough the latticework of expressions becomes your world, hanging by a thread. And you, yourself, are hanging like that. Nothing else matters, and least of all your origins, whence you come or grow. Nor does it matter from whom you've learned to express this threadbare existence of yours. The only thing of consequence is what you do with the undoing and with the undone. *This* is sufficient to survive not in the sense of a privation but in the sense of an excess, to trudge a field of fluid shapeshifting vitality beyond a life reducible to particular organic forms. The sufficiency in question overflows autonomy, even though you survive on yourself alone. Expressing, pressing out, you pull the other from within yourself, metamorphosing little by little in every single moment, with every bit of thread that comes out. There is no decisive, shocking, and sudden metamorphosis, because your shape is always another one, distinct from the one in which you and the others around you capture what passes for your being. And for your nothing. You had become a spider and the tree she is dangling from and the ground in which this tree grows prior to being struck with divine wrath. Look: this wrath with its unsparing pity did not strike *you*; you were already elsewhere, already otherwise, having nothing to do with the accident of your birth. Transported elsewhere thanks to your skill: your art vegetalized, animalized, elementalized. Slowly . . . lowly . . . owly . . . wly . . . ly . . . y. . . . . .

NIOBE: BECOMING SCARCE
(Liber VI, 146–312)

> This overview that I'm giving—the end of abundance, the end of insouciance, the end of assumptions—it's ultimately a tipping point that we are going through that can lead our citizens to feel a lot of anxiety.
>
> —E. MACRON, AUGUST 24, 2022

Niobe is so fecund, so abundant, she can hardly contain herself; she cannot keep silent, a profuse stream of words emanating from her, as she favorably compares her numerous children to the two of Latona (Leto), the latent, hidden goddess, who is the mother of Artemis and Apollo. An overabundance of words, then, referring to her abundant issue: "My very abundance has made me safe. I am too great for Fortune to harm" (*maior sum quam cui possit Fortuna nocere*). TBTF: Too Big To Fail. Will "the end of abundance" cause her "to feel a lot of anxiety?" Where is her "tipping point?" Losing half her children? Two thirds? Three quarters? All of them?

> I believe that we are in the process of living through a tipping point or great upheaval. First because we are living through . . . the end of what could seem like the end of abundance.
> —E. MACRON, AUGUST 24, 2022

The end of the end or the beginning of the end? Of abundance, above all . . . When she loses her copious children, scarce does Niobe render herself scarce. She does not retreat into invisibility, like her divine rival Latona. On the contrary, paralyzed by grief, metamorphosed into a rock, she is set on a mountaintop for all to see. And she sheds unending tears: water from stone, fluidity from solidity, abundant flows from the dense body of marble, *et lacrimis etiam nunc marmora manant*.

> Faced with this, we have duties, the first of which is to speak frankly and very clearly without doom-mongering.
> —E. MACRON, AUGUST 24, 2022

Water flowing from a rock is a miraculous sign given—in another tradition, but not entirely other—to allay the dissatisfaction and incredulity of the many. The leader of a people taps his staff on a mountainside, calling upon water to gush from the rock he strikes. To quell discontent, offer abundance at the time of scarcity: that is the Mosaic lesson, which Jesus learned well, filling it with nourishing substance (fish and bread). But what if you offer the abundance of duty and sacrifice (of others, mind you, not of yourself) at "the end of what could seem like the end of abundance?" Niobe was content, all too content, with what could seem like her endless abundance. No denials, no doubts (*quis enim neget hoc? hoc quoque quis dubitet?*): "And happy I shall remain."

> We are living through the end of abundance.
> —E. MACRON, AUGUST 24, 2022

Such abundant references to the end of abundance! What do they hide in plain sight? Who lurks behind them? Such abundant references to an anxiety-provoking end! Still, we have not learned to become scarce, to find the most generous modes of abundance unrelated to the logic of resources in what, for all intents and purposes, presents itself as scarcity. We should talk frankly about it, "without doom-mongering," and yet *nihil est in imagine vivum*, "nothing is alive in this picture," of what—we are told—"we are living through." The appeal is to duty and sacrifice and, hence, to austerity policies all over again. In "stony grief."

Fragment: a form of becoming scarce *and* giving abundantly.

BECOMING ABUNDANT: LYCIAN PEASANTS

(Liber VI, 313–381)

Since time immemorial, suffering goddesses and gods have been the mouthpieces for universal, even elemental, justice. Each of these divine beings is Janus-faced: having in view the sort of plenitude that does not lack anything, on the one hand, and experiencing debilitating deprivation, on the other. This duality, this deific amphibology (if I may put it this way), gives them privileged access both to the problem and to its solution, to scarcity and abundance, not to mention everything and everyone shaping and allocating the two extremes.

When, parched with thirst, Latona and her twins arrive at the shore of a lake, it seems that her suffering, *her passions*, are going to be relieved. Water is abundant; what could stand in the way of quenching her thirst? What or

BECOMING ABUNDANT: LYCIAN PEASANTS

who? *Rustica turba*, poor rabble, are already by the lake, and out of sheer malice they prevent the goddess from drinking—now with threats, now by agitating the sand at the bottom of the lake with their feet. A class tragicomedy is being staged here in the interactions and interpassions of a goddess who becomes one of the wretched of the earth and the anonymous rabble uplifted by comparison to the greater pain and need of the other. Class issues will, in effect, haunt the narrative throughout, from the very beginning, which attributes the fact that the story is relatively unknown to "the humble estate of the men" at its center, to the end.

It is, then, artificially created scarcity, a set of deprivations fashioned and enforced by human society, that is the occasion for Latona's speech in support of the elemental commons—of elemental communism, even—and against privatization. "The enjoyment of water is a common right" (*usus communis aquarum est*), she says. "Nature has not made the sun private [*solem proprium*] to any, nor the air, nor soft water. This common right I seek." The elements are already abundant to the point of excess, universally available, free. They circulate between us like air; wash away all boundaries like water; bestow light, warmth, and life on all, like the celestial fire of the sun, which Plato analogizes to the idea of the good.

If there is any hope left for the paleonym *communism*, if it is to be reconfigured from the ground up, then it must engage with the elements. Elemental communism does not oppose public to private property; more radical than that, it interrogates the category of property as such, which can only ever be private (the proper, *proprium*). That is Latona's anachronistic (and anarchist) rejoinder to Marx. She implies that the elements are already abundant: becoming abundant is coming to terms with their irrepressible, unruly, anarchic abundance. So understood, scarcity hinges on the privation of access—to some, who include almost all. Even a thirsty goddess. And the privation of access is a death sentence; it robs those cut off from elemental generosity of nothing less than their life, as in the case of Antigone, whom Creon imprisoned in a cave or intombed while alive. Latona also links elemental communism to life, which is not a piece of property, either: "yes, life you will be giving me [*vitam dederitis*] if you let me drink."

The Lycian peasants will have none of that. As a result, they will have nothing at all—not in the sense of the angry goddess denying them the conditions for life, but in the sense of extending those conditions to them in an other-than-human form. In the lake where they are (which turned out to be a swamp), everything will stay as it is: malice in word and deed, acceptance of deprivations so long as there is someone who suffers more than me, rejection of elemental abundance. *Vivatis in isto!*—"Live in this!"—Latona cries out, blessing the peasants who gradually metamorphose into frogs with the very thing or non-thing they tried to take away from her: life. "Live in this!"—assuming that you can make life compatible with the privatization of everything, with the violence of appropriation, with contempt toward the other, and with heedlessness toward elemental abundance.

SKINNED: MARSYAS'S GRAMMAR LESSON

(Liber VI, 382-400)

Certain English words that are both verbs and nouns carry mutually exclusive senses, the positive and the negative, depending on which part of speech they are used as. A semantic equivalent of the electric current passes within them, their poles marked with plus and minus signs. Even pertaining to the same part of speech (say, a verb), such words can have opposite meanings. They are *contronyms*. For instance, *dust*—the gray powdery substance and the act of removing, or adding more, of it. Or *skin*—the thin layer of tissue covering a body and the act of removing the outer organic cover. Dusted or skinned, surfaces undergo the subtraction of the very stuff that lends the name to these formations in the passive voice. The word unsays itself, morphing into its other.

The satyr Marsyas is flayed alive; indeed, he is skinned. *Quid me mihi detrahis?* ("Why do you tear me from myself?"), he cries out. Each contronym silently screams out the same question, without losing its senses, without fainting or lapsing into sheer nonsense. On the contrary, sense is born out of their pathos. It resounds with a *why?*—not the *why?* of being stripped of an identity, fictitious as one's identity invariably is, but of no longer being in proximity to oneself.

The gore of a skinned body is not so different from that of a skinned word (including the words *skinned* or *deskinned*). Blood spilling all over the place (*cruor undique manat*), viscera exposed (*salientia viscera*), the vitals clearly showing (*perlucentes*) ... The body of language is nothing like an ideal construction. It, too, has skin, and it, too, may be skinned, flayed and covered with a new sheath of meanings. By the linguists who dissect it, by spin doctors and PR specialists, propagandists and indoctrinators. When language is skinned, what are the pulsing viscera that appear in the daylight? What is its flowing blood? Where is its skin, the sensitive surfaces that are in touch with one another and with the world?

The hint is in the word. To skin is to deskin. Skin clothes the body in the body's very nudity; to skin is to remove the body's minimal clothing in itself. The skin of language is the visibility of meanings shorn of transparency: appearing as much as hiding; hiding in the act or in the fact of appearing. There is no translucency, no perfect and unobstructed intelligibility, no ultimate disclosure of language's body, nor of the body of truth. One revelation covers over the other. The skin of language is every word, part of speech, semantic unit, uttered or written, forming an opaque, if porous, membrane between the animating sense and that which emerges out in the open. Betraying is expressing and breaking trust.

When language is skinned, when it is flayed and the sense of *skin* is univocally determined, the routines of betrayal seem to come to an end. Blood, viscera, the raw entrails that had been enveloped in skin fleetingly appear out in the open, and just as precipitously they lose their color and texture, their messy materiality. Reduced to a single sense or translated into algorithms, language is not only skinned but also eviscerated—the viscera are gutted, cleansed, purified, blood turning into water. After Marsyas had been skinned, the gory spectacle of his entrails changed into "the clearest river in all Phrygia."

BECOMING WHOLE: PELOPS

(Liber VI, 401–411)

Torn to bits
By a zealous father,
Eager to please the gods,
He was sewn together,
Part by part.

Fact = what is made (up?).
Factoque Pelops fuit integer illo,
"So, Pelops was made whole again."
Whole, but with something missing.
Whole, thanks to that missing something.

BECOMING WHOLE: PELOPS

One part, a shoulder, ingested by an absentminded goddess in deep mourning, had to be replaced with an ivory plate, which stood out from the rest of his flesh. The body became whole (again) and not whole, assembled, while evincing the traces of its violent disassembly.

> The whole: an illusion sustained
> By the absent part.
>
> To live on, incorporating death;
> To die, binding life together.

TEREUS & CO.:
A WHIRLWIND OF METAMORPHOSES—
FIRE, SNAKES, AUTOPHAGY, BIRDS
(Liber VI, 412–674)

FIRE: AN INFORMAL READER'S REPORT

I have never seen such a proliferation of fires on the pages of a single short text, the pages both scorched and animated by the conflagrations they record. (Believe me, I have been keeping an eye on fire in philosophy, theology, and political discourses for a long time now, at least since my initial enunciations of "pyropolitics" at the beginning of the 2010s, theories of energy, and the "ardencies" of Saint Hildegard of Bingen, through to the most recent work on "the phoenix complex.") Many of the flames burning and devastating Tereus and those around him are a little cliché, be they the blazes of "mad passion" "inflaming his chest" (*pectora flammas*) or the military fervor and patriotism, with which his heart is incinerated alongside the fire that is strictly his own... Nonetheless, it is the interplay of these fires and of their effects that gives them a touch of originality. Let's catalogue some of their unusual features.

First, both fires are lit in close proximity to death. This is not so surprising for a Thracian commander who made a name for himself in wars, fighting. What is weirder is that Tereus's love life, starting with his matrimony with Procne, was also enkindled by the fire of death: their marriage ceremony is lit "with torches stolen from a funeral," *faces de funere raptas*. Their wedding is celebrated in the light (and heat) of dissolution—of organic existence and of the social organism that is the family. In his *Philosophy of Right* Hegel soberly saw that, whether it ends in divorce or not, each family culminates in its disbanding after the children born to a couple mature and attain independence, forming their own families. Here, on the contrary, the harbinger of the end of a family is present at its very inception.

How can we comprehend the fire of death and its divergence from that of life, especially with regard to amorous advances? Our text signals that a crucial distinction between them has to do with speed and intensity. When Tereus falls in love with his wife's sister, he is "inflamed with love, quick as one should set fire to ripe grain, or dry leaves, or hay stored away in the mow." The vegetal materials in question are dry, primed for burning up quickly, for being instantaneously consumed by fire. They are, moreover, dead (hay, dry leaves...), bereft of moisture and of the connection to a living plant or to the soil. The fire of death seizes what is already dead on the inside—here, Tereus's soul that is analogous to the harvested or shed parts of plants. It is also a fire that, while releasing extreme heat, gives no light: "what blind night rules in the hearts of men!" A mortiferous blaze does not nourish the living with moderate warmth and luminosity; it consumes what has been long dead and dry.

Second, and precisely on the question of nourishment, the fire of deadly passion and of combativeness feed themselves (for a time being) on the deaths and suffering of others. A time comes, though, when both start feeding on themselves, accelerating in a kind of elemental autophagy the process of self-destruction. "His heart seethes with thoughts of her... and feeds his own fires" (*et ignes ipse suos nutrit*). A fiery nourishment that kills takes the place of a killing that nourishes the narcissism of a military leader who aggrandizes his name on the battlefield.

Third, the fire burning in Procne seeks justice, a way of delivering Tereus to his own flaming fate. Fire, however, is uncontainable and uncontrollable: used as a means, it is prone to "backfiring" and consuming its users. As soon as Procne learns about the rape and mutilation of her sister by her husband, she herself burns, *ardet*, with rage and proposes "to fire this palace with a torch," *cum facibus regalia tecta cremabo*, or to reduce Tereus "to flaming ruins." From this confrontation with her private enemy, Procne emerges victorious, but the victor is defeated by the fire that scorches the hated other. She uses the fire of the hearth to boil the body of her and Tereus's son, Itys, whom she has killed and whose flesh she will serve to his unsuspecting father as part of the feast. But in this very fire, she also cooks herself, her own flesh, which was embodied in Itys.

The Oedipal triangle daddy-mommy-me metamorphoses in fire. (But, I ask myself, how Oedipal is it exactly if instead of desiring to marry his mother and kill his father, Itys is murdered by the mother who wishes to punish his father for infidelity toward her?) They become fire before becoming anything or anyone else—say, birds or food. Not just any fire, but that of the funeral pyre, which lights up, heats, and overshadows all affects and events from mad passion to patriotism and war, from vengeance to cooking, from marriage to conception and birth. The fire of "torches stolen from a funeral" is the main protagonist of the story, its turns and turnings determining the different steps and stages of the narrative. With an eye trained over the years to detect pyrological phenomena, this is what I, as an avid reader of Ovid, can report.

SNAKES, OR A LETTER TO PHILOMELA

Who have you become? What has become of you, dearest Philomela?

I know that you will not be able to tell me, to respond loud and clear, in your own voice. Because, in the act of unspeakable violence visited upon you, your tongue seized with pincers has been cut off, torn out of your mouth. That organ of yours turned into a snake, a dying and mutilated animal, *mutilatae cauda colubrae*, twitching and convulsing on the ground. A snake's tongue is split: two-in-one at the edge. Your tongue as such became a snake, unsplit in itself but severed from the rest of your body. You were disunited with yourself: a hurt human, a maimed animal. Your sister, Procne, while not raped by her husband who subjected you to this act of violence, was rendered mute by it, her indignant tongue lacking the words to react to the event. The two of you were silenced by the same violation, the ramifications of his deed forked, like a snake's tongue.

Not only have you suffered the trauma of rape, which is exceptionally difficult to express, to symbolize, to put into words, but you have also been denied the means to speak your mind, your conscious and unconscious mind, or to name the crime's perpetrator. Still, you didn't give up, realizing that the voice does not depend entirely on the tongue: you made sure your hand served for your voice, *pro voce manus fuit*. No, you did not resort to sign language; you wrote. Without ink or paint, you recorded your tragic story with a thread, *filum*, woven into the fabric of a Thracian cloth. A thread, snaking in and out of the fabric conveyed that which could not be spoken. You became that thread, that other snake, leaving signs on the blank body of cloth, the traces of your trauma. You, too, became forked, split between the sign and what it tries to signify.

A hand for a voice: such a strange, yet necessary, exchange! From the depths of your suffering, beyond the distinction between sound and silence, or between one sound and another, you have given us all a lesson. You have shown *how* the body speaks and *that* the body is a voice. In your abject condition, you have lost your tongue, but not your language. You have become what had been wrested away from you.

I am doing my best to receive your teaching, to understand that when a tongue is violently uprooted from the mouth or from a community, tongues multiply. Small and large snakes, they slither on the ground, the material ground of existence, to which they have been thrown. Seeking initially the feet, these tongue-snakes slide along the legs and further up, through the trunk to the chest. Up and up. Not to suffocate, coiling themselves around the neck, but to let speak, to invent another speech, that of susurrations and lines crisscrossing space—the speech creeping over and above the limits of a voice.

Your teaching, dearest Philomela, is profound in its attachment to the surface, in its serpentine gliding or sliding on the surface. But yours is also a teaching that cannot be received once and for all. Becoming-snake is not the same as being-snake. Between the voice and the hand, between the voice articulated, made resonant, and phonated by the tongue, on the one hand, and the hand, to which language is handed over, on the other, there is a chasm. It is there, in that chasm, that your becoming-snake takes place. And it is there that I try to join you, ever so blunderingly, through *my* writing.

> Yours,
> M

THE AUTOPHAGY OF THE OTHER: INTUS HABES, QUEM POSCIS

(You have within you the one you are asking for)

—He is inside you.
—Who is?
—The one you are asking for.
—I don't understand. I am asking for my son, Itys. Who is your son too, by the way . . .
—He is inside you.
—No, you've got it wrong. He was inside *you*, but that was eight years ago, when you were pregnant with him.
—He was inside me then, but now you have him inside you. He is becoming you as we speak, as you digest.
—But I am only eating, feasting on the meat you've served.
—Meat? More like flesh, the flesh of your flesh, on which you are gorging yourself. Like the pig that you are.
—I have devoured my own son? (*Silence; a long scream.*) You were pregnant with life when you carried him for nine months under your heart. But now you have impregnated me with death, with the death of our dear little Itys! From your womb he emerged to see the light of day, and now "my body is his most wretched tomb." I am about to throw up.
—Too late to have your "abortion." (*Smirks.*) You deserve a fate worse than this for what you've done. Be glad—I made you into Kronos, the filicidal god. As you digest the flesh of your flesh, you are also becoming a god. Divine autophagy. Is that not the name of the game? The highest sacrifice: of yourself as the other who sprang from you. And to you he shall return. To you he *has* returned.

—What are you saying? That I am the soil, in which my son is buried? The earth—that is me. What a confusion! You are even citing from another tradition, alien to us: "from the earth you were taken and to the earth you shall return." Why? Why?

—Is this you speaking or is it HIM, voicing himself through you, giving you the calories, which you need to move your tongue, your lips, to think, to scream? Mull it over, will you? While you finish your delicious meal.

(THE) BIRDS: AN OVERDUE FILM REVIEW

The tragic scene of child murder cannot but culminate in endless horror. Birds are now everywhere, as in Alfred Hitchcock's 1963 film *The Birds*. Their feathers are smeared in blood, *signataque sanguine pluma est*, impossible to wash off. Like Melanie's (Tippi Hedren) face, hands, and legs in the Hitchcock masterpiece, when she is attacked by birds in the attic.

Something is amiss about avian metamorphoses. The tongueless Philomela is transformed into a songbird, the nightingale, living up to her name but not to her traumatized muteness. Procne is now a swallow that nests under the roof or in wall cracks and fissures, her rebellion against the domestic sphere notwithstanding. Tereus assumes the form of a hoopoe with a crown of feathers on his head, despite having no offspring to continue the royal dynasty. The metamorphic sequel of past existence upends the bygone life.

Procne is not Melanie, nor is Tereus Mitch (Rod Taylor); in contrast to the romantic couple of *The Birds*, they detest one another. Inversions are rife: with birds, everything is up in the air; their bodies are projectiles hurtling along the most disparate of vectors. In *The Birds*, these vectors converge on human dwellings attacked by a murder of crows or by a flock of seagulls. In Ovid they diverge: the nightingale flies to the woods, the swallow keeps close to the house, the hoopoe feels at home only on a battlefield ("with the look of one armed for war").

Other metamorphoses have been expressions of divine or elemental justice, adjustments in the corporeality of metamorphosing creatures rendering the new body more suitable to their actions or character. The changing fortunes in transformations into birds are also an expression of justice, albeit of justice as compensation, dispensing to each what she or he lacked in a previous, human, form: a voice, a home . . . Except for Tereus, who, ever ready to fight, must endure the cruel irony of being the last in his dynastic line without an heir to his feathery crown.

TEREUS & CO.: A WHIRLWIND OF METAMORPHOSES

Becoming-bird is a case of continuation *and* discontinuity: permanent blood smears on feathers and obtaining what one hitherto lacked; a bellicose attitude and the loss of all hope embodied in the future generation. Hitchcock's swarming birds, their airborne bodies weaponized against the people who barricade themselves indoors, are the vanguard of metamorphoses and metabolisms (in a word, of becoming) that add up to what we automatically call *nature*. These birds are a moving, unstoppable mass, inevitably colliding with and breaching the barricades of the self-absorbed attitude that, for the sake of persevering in the same condition, abjures both the flowing continuation and the rough discontinuity of existence. It is not a spoiler to say that the message of Ovid and Hitchcock is: Beware, you will be badly hurt if you attempt to hold onto yourself at any cost!

CHANGING STRATEGIES, METAMORPHOSING MOODS: A NEARLY TAUTOGRAMMIC REFLECTION

(Liber VI, 675–721)

Boreas has always been, well... Boreas. The north wind, blowing, driving cold air masses thorough the atmosphere. He has not become either an animal or a plant, a boulder or a human, and none of these entities have become him.

Be this as it may, must metamorphosis entail a leap to another type of being to the exclusion of changes in moods, strategies, behaviors? How does it stand with climate change and weather fluctuations? Do they constitute a metamorphosis: of the sky and the earth and the seas? Do they trigger a myriad of metamorphoses in the inhabitants of these regions—some of them barely perceptible, others drastic?

Biting and gusty, the north wind in the northern hemisphere is marked by its ferociousness, its gelid and unrelenting force, *vis*. He is a "cold despot," *gelidus tyrannus*. To hear his force, enunciate the explosive or plosive sound *b*.

But what if Boreas were to ditch his strategy? What if, instead of getting what he wants by his cruel potency, by sending "a blast over all the earth," he became kind and entreating, gently caressing the skin, instead of being harsh and glacially burning the exposed flesh? Would the north wind still be himself then? Would he not morph into his opposite, the south wind?

CHANGING STRATEGIES, METAMORPHOSING MOODS

By choosing another strategy to woo Orithyia, Boreas ceases being himself. A strategy, like a mood, is not superadded to who we are; it is not secondary with respect to our inner essence. A behavioral scheme and a pattern of lighting up or dimming down our psychic atmosphere are the forms of ourselves, the very forms that are continually transformed. A mood may shift. A way of acting may be altered. Yet being in this or that mood and acting in this or that way cannot be done away with. As such, mood and behavior are the true substance of an identity, in contrast to the fiction of a stable inner essence.

Blowing from the north, Boreas stays on a fixed course of his swift flight across the skies. What is going on, though, when the north itself is warming? When the north is no longer north in a massive disorientation—which, in Portuguese (*desnorte*), exceptional in this among other Romance languages, has to do not with the orient, but precisely with the north (*norte*)— where all meaningful signposts fade away. The compass no longer works. The poles of the earth go haywire. So do the planet's atmospheric flows, starting with the north wind.

Boreas's alternative strategy is short-lived. He quickly has a change of heart, proclaiming, "Force is my fit instrument" (*apta mihi vis est*), and imposing himself on Orithyia with as much brutal might as he can muster. Climate change is not as easy as that. Once elemental disorientation or loss of the north is afoot or awing, it is impossible to regulate the global thermostat. Because there is no such thermostat, the delusions of our cold and despotic techno-tyranny notwithstanding.

PROVERBIAL WISDOM: MEDEA
(Liber VII, 1–158)

A proverb is common sense neatly packaged into a few words.

Proverbs are the metamorphoses of metaphysical insights popularized, naturalized, applied.

Common sense is proverbialized metaphysics.

For each proverb, there exists another proverb with the exact opposite message.

Hence, for each proverb, there is an antiverb, contradicting, unsaying the saying that it is.

PROVERBIAL WISDOM: MEDEA

Proverb_1. "I see the better and approve it, but I follow the worse." *Video meliora proboque, deteriora sequor.* // Who is the I who sees and approves the better, and who is the I who follows the worse? The former: the conscious I, a rational, judging, calculating subject. The latter: the unconscious.

Antiverb_1. ". . . for they know not what they are doing" (Luke 23:34). // Who are the knowing they, and who are the doing they? Etc.

Proverb_2. "Whether he live or die is in the lap of the gods." *Vivat an ille occidat, in dis est.* // We live in a world of sheer contingency, in which life and death are the outcomes of a throw of the cosmic dice.

Antiverb_2. Everything is in your hands. // We live in a world we create for ourselves, shaping our life's path without regard to interferences.

Proverb_3. "The greatest god is within me!" *Maximus intra me deus est!* // I am the unquestionable center of all meaning and sense, the necessary and sufficient cause of my own actions and of those of others. (This is an antiverb to proverb_2.)

Antiverb_3. "All things are full of gods" (*De anima*, A5, 411a7). // The divine plenum of Thales makes no reference to greater or lesser divinities. The immeasurable fullness of gods in all things puts them on an equal footing, including the god dwelling in the thing I call myself. (This is an antiverb *and* an affirmative supplement to proverb_3: if everything is full of gods, then they are within me, too, but "the greatest" is incompatible with the nonquantitative plenum.)

Proverb_4. "I do not know which god opposes me [*nescio quis deus obstat*]: I wonder if this is not what is called love." // Love as an effect of strife and contention.

Antiverb_4. // Love understands all languages. // Love as an effect of harmony and mutual comprehension.

Proverb_5. "Get ready, and away with all delay." *Accingere et omnem pelle moram.* // Immediate action is better than being under the sway of constant self-undermining doubts.

Antiverb_5. Think before you act. // Hence, thinking is a delay of action, even if it is a peculiar kind of action that delays action.

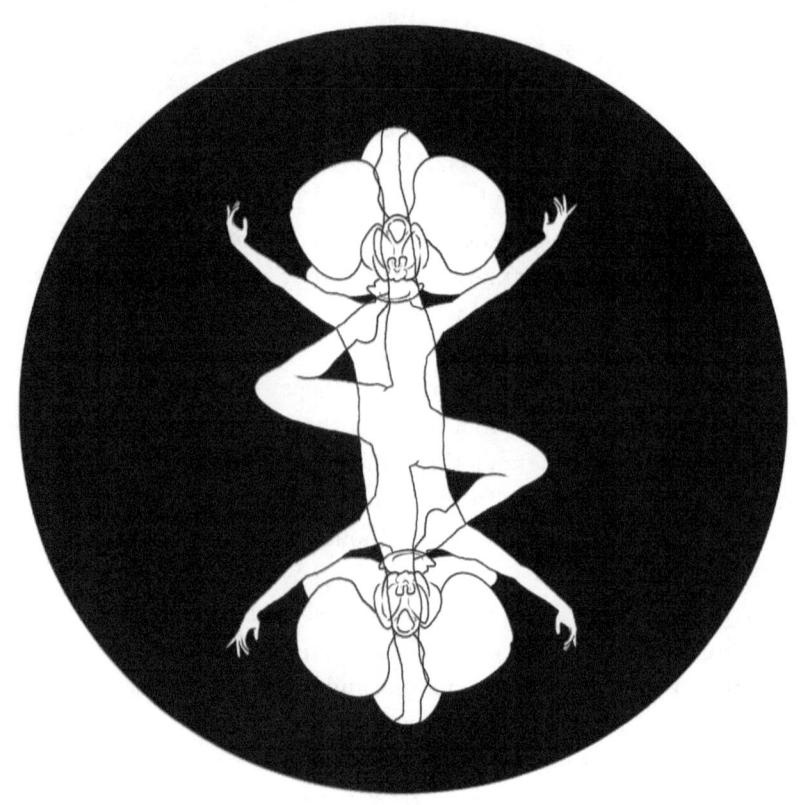

THE ART OF BECOMING IMMORTAL
(Liber VII, 159–293)

Medea is enjoined to extend the life of a dying person. To delay the moment when an invisible finger presses "." on the keyboard of destiny. There will be no final period, no full stop at the end of the sentence that is his life. Not yet. Perhaps, not ever

She must go against nature to give a body and a voice to the desire for immortality, because the immense growing, decaying, metamorphosing whole called *natura* is a life that lives off death and a death that recycles life. The art of becoming immortal is the art of deadening life itself.

Her art (*arte mea*) is meant to reverse the aging and the inexorable demise of the one on the brink of death. The art is that of the night (*nox*) that speaks in the name of light, that assumes the posture of total mastery via the techno-scientific apparatus and the will to shape and reshape the world. The brightest, most blinding night, compared to which "even the chariot of the Sun . . . pales."

> Human activity has altered almost 75 per cent of the earth's surface, squeezing wildlife and nature into an ever-smaller corner of the planet and increasing risks of zoonotic diseases like COVID-19.
> —UN SUSTAINABLE DEVELOPMENT, HTTPS://WWW.UN.ORG/SUSTAINABLEDEVELOPMENT/BIODIVERSITY

". . . when I have willed it [*cum volui*], the streams have run back to their fountain-heads, while the banks wondered."

> While protected areas now cover 15 per cent of terrestrial and freshwater environments and 7 per cent of the marine realm, they only partly cover important sites for biodiversity and are not yet fully ecologically representative and effectively or equitably managed.
> —UN SUSTAINABLE DEVELOPMENT, HTTPS://WWW.UN.ORG/SUSTAINABLEDEVELOPMENT/BIODIVERSITY

"I drive the clouds and bring on the clouds" (*nubila pello, nubilaque induco*).

> Due to drought and desertification, 12 million hectares are lost each year (23 hectares per minute). Within one year, 20 million tons of grain could have been grown.
> —UN SUSTAINABLE DEVELOPMENT, HTTPS://WWW.UN.ORG/SUSTAINABLEDEVELOPMENT/BIODIVERSITY

"I break the jaws of serpents with my incantations" (*vipereas rumpo verbis et carmine fauces*).

> Of the 8,300 animal breeds known, 8 per cent are extinct and 22 per cent are at a risk of extinction.
> —UN SUSTAINABLE DEVELOPMENT, HTTPS://WWW.UN.ORG/SUSTAINABLEDEVELOPMENT/BIODIVERSITY

"Living rocks [*vivaque saxa*] and oaks I root up from their soil."

> Habitat loss and deterioration, largely caused by human actions, have reduced global terrestrial habitat integrity by 30 per cent relative to an unimpacted baseline.
> —UN SUSTAINABLE DEVELOPMENT, HTTPS://WWW.UN.ORG/SUSTAINABLEDEVELOPMENT/BIODIVERSITY

"I move the forests" (*silvas moveo*).

> Between 2010 and 2015, the world lost 3.3 million hectares of forest areas.
> —UN SUSTAINABLE DEVELOPMENT, HTTPS://WWW.UN.ORG/SUSTAINABLEDEVELOPMENT/BIODIVERSITY

"I bid the mountains to shake, the earth to rumble and the ghosts to come forth from their tombs" (*manesque exire sepulcris*).

The search for immortality sets off a chain reaction that undermines finite life, let alone the desired life everlasting. It unleashes the powers of death, releasing specters from their tombs. The arts of eternal life are the arts of eternal death.

Control over space, over territories with their resources, over unique places and ecosystems is nothing compared to control over time. "Regaining early years" (*primosque recolligat annos*), "turning back" (*redeat*) the tide of time, is causing being itself, and not only mountains or the earth, to shake. In anticipation of its standstill. The art of becoming immortal aims to do away with becoming as such, to eliminate time from the equation altogether at the apex of control over it. Turning time back is but a prelude to the ideal situation (and this is the core of all idealism) where time is not turning, not stirring, not moving. Where, together with aging, life comes to a grinding halt. Time, after all, is the sum total of metamorphoses and metabolisms, from organismic, and even microorganismic, to planetary and cosmic. Killing time in order to gain eternal life—that is the barbaric "more than mortal plan," *propositum mortali barbara maius*.

THE ART OF BECOMING MORTAL
(Liber VII, 294-349)

. To begin with a period. With the end. Which has been there since the beginning, in and before the beginning. To begin in this way is to acknowledge what you and I are, to become what we are, what we have always already been. Finite: ending or altogether ended, finished from the beginning.

If you deny the fact of beginning with the period, with the end indwelling the beginning and all that emanates from it, then you are in denial. Implicitly, you make the case that the incipient end is not destiny, that the period can be erased, undone, or triplicated into the open-ended... You aspire to delete or multiply (also delete *by* multiplying) this period as a full stop and as a stretch of time, a point and a broken line, your death and life and survival.

Why "the art of becoming mortal?" What is the point (another one!) of the art of becoming what or who you already are? Because the default condition is that of denial and self-deception, from which the self is born. The umbilical cord that binds the self to self-deception derails becoming what you are and prevents you from metamorphosing into your finitude, which is, precisely, a wicket to other metamorphoses. What kind of a self persists after the self-deception of cheating death has dissipated? The honing of such a self, immersed in its finitude and welcoming its own metamorphoses, is at the heart of the art of becoming mortal.

Medea, the artist of immortality, taught Pelias and his daughters this other lucid, if exceptionally arduous, art. To attain immortality you had to be killed and then boiled in a brew of powerful herbs. (No one has canceled the ancient logic of sacrifice and self-sacrifice.) To live forever, it was imperative to die: to let blood flow freely, to expire, and to be reborn in the flames and miraculous vapors of vegetal vitality. Medea, though, put "plants of no potency" into the pot, in which the corpse of Pelias was to make its reverse journey from death to a renewed life. This deception paved a highway to the truth of a finite life, according to which to die it was necessary to live for the first time without the dream of the *forever*. If only for a brief moment before exhaling your last breath and becoming a soup or a stew.

UP AND DOWN: AIR AND EARTH—A MEDITATION
(Liber VII, 350-403)

Take the deepest breath you've ever taken.
Get in touch with the air inside and outside you:
in your nose, bronchial tubes and lungs, as well as
the subtle flows caressing your fingertips, fingers, hands, and arms.
The air that envelops and keeps you in its embrace
still before you register your contact with it.
Feel your chest and belly rising and falling with each breath.
Every time you exhale, note how your ribcage is closing unto itself
before expanding again.
Your respiration is the respiration of the planet.
Cosmic breath in touch with its cosmic extension.
You are "borne up into air as if on wings"—
sublatus in aera pennis—
while earthly heaviness—
gravis tellus—
sustains your feet.
Expand with the upper half of your body;
Dig in with the lower half.
Dwelling in the air—
domum . . . in aere—
inhabit the earth.
Bird and worm,

UP AND DOWN: AIR AND EARTH—A MEDITATION

mole and butterfly,
you are both.
Made of and for air and the earth:
rooted and soaring to the heights of a tree canopy.
You are a plant.
Observe, without judgment,
how the difference between the air inside and outside you
is evaporating.
There is no more inside and no more outside,
neither *in-* nor *ex-*.
Just the air -haled and -haling
you.
The air that oxygenates your earth;
the earth that carbonizes your air.
To let the plant that you are grow.
And decay.
Grow by decaying, decay by growing.
Repeat.

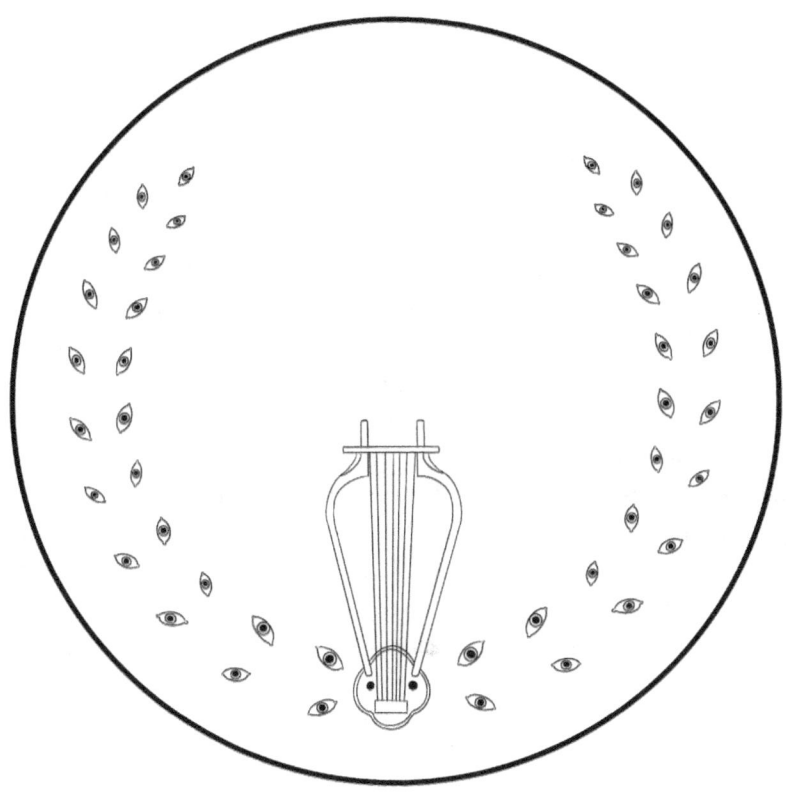

THE CAPTURE OF CERBERUS
(Liber VII, 404–452)

Capture, once again. This time around it has to do with the capture of a dog, and a monstrous one at that. The event takes place with great fanfare, befitting the twelfth and final labor of Hercules. Cerberus, the guardian of the underworld, must be tamed, brought up from his abode, extricated from his immersion in the dark of the earth, in unconscious existence, in nature itself. This act of denaturing will complete the series of Hercules's heroic labors.

As Ovid has it, Hercules drags Cerberus up using "chains wrought of adamant" (*nexis adamante*) (*Met.* 7.412), that is to say, of diamond, unbreakable but also already extracted both from the earth and from its rough shell.

Just as Cerberus will be. The dog is taken by force from a cavern "with a dark, yawning throat and a way down-sloping," *specus est tenebroso caecus hiatus, est via declivis* (*Met.* 7.409–410), which is suspiciously similar to Plato's cave. And Cerberus's "enlightenment" is also reminiscent of prisoners who are blinded as they are struck by the rays of the sun upon exiting from the cave: "the great dog fought and turned away his eyes from the bright light of day" (*Met.* 7.414). In Seneca's *Hercules*, as well, upon emerging from the cave, Cerberus fears "the new unknown lights that hit his eyes" (*percussit oculos lucis ignotae novos*) (*Her.* 814), a line that recurs in *Agamemnon* (862). Enlightenment, indeed!

Isn't this a model for disciplining, violently reshaping, and normalizing minds and bodies? Initially, a monster, unruly and fear-inducing, is identified either within or outside ourselves: a wild animal, the unconscious, raw emotion, elemental forces, and so forth. Then, no effort is spared to tame that monster, to domesticate, to geoengineer, to bathe in blinding light of which the diamond bonds are also wrought, to educate. But with what results? Although firmly chained and brought up to the surface, Cerberus is not filled with tranquility; on the contrary, he is "goaded on to mad frenzy [*rabida . . . ira*], he fills all the air with his threefold howls" (*Met.* 7.413). The concluding labor of Hercules achieves the opposite of what it intends: forced to share the ground with the merciless forces of reason, the presumed monster is driven to "mad frenzy." That is the logic of *pharmakon*, of a remedy-poison, which will soon crop up in all its vegetal glory in our story.

—How many are you, Cerberus? Three heads (some, like Tzetzes, say there are fifty of them [*Tzetz. Chil.* 2.390]) on a single canine body, but already a legion, veritably uncountable, if you guard the realms of the unconscious and death, that is, of subterranean life, energizing from below the terrestrial and psychic worlds flooded with light.

—Can you hear me, Cerberus? How can I address you, hush you down, without my words, whispers, and gestures drowning in the ear-piercing racket you make?

—Where are you, Cerberus? Strabo reports that Taenarum, "a headland that projects into the sea" is where you were "brought up from Hades by Heracles" (*Strab.* 8.5.1). That would place you near the ancient Laconia, on the Greek Cape Matapan, facing across the sea the coast of North Africa. Seneca agrees (*Sen. Her. F.* 813). Ovid locates you in the north, on

Scythian shores (*Met.* 7.407). Apollodorus also beams you up to the northern portion of the Peloponnese, at Troezen (*Apollod.* 2.5.12). South or north, you are everywhere; hence, you surface at the most disparate points, as you are trawled out of your abode, and often without any outside interference.

The diamond chains, tightly wrapped around the squirming body of the animal and sparkling in the rays of the Hellenic sun, draw my attention and demand further interpretation. *Pharmakoi* par excellence, they are technical creations that seize and immobilize, but also, apparently, free by releasing their haul into the universe of technique. If so, then Hercules has cheated: Apollodorus relates that "when Hercules asked Pluto for Cerberus, Pluto ordered him to take the animal provided he mastered him without the use of the weapons which he carried" (*Apollod.* 2.5.12). This tradition winds back to Homer's *Iliad*, where, more specifically, "Heracles was commanded by Hades to master Cerberus without iron or conventional shield" (*Hom. Il.* 5.395–7, schol.).

It is highly doubtful that Hercules obeyed the injunction of the god. For are the "chains wrought of adamant" weapons or tools? Assuming that they are weapons-tools (for every tool can be weaponized—yet another *pharmakon*), it is true that they are made not of iron but of the sturdiest mineral. Technology is not proscribed altogether in the capture-and-taming endeavor of Hercules's twelfth labor. Rather, the hero is to put aside the technology of the iron age in favor of the earlier stone age, which is closer to wild, yet untamed nature. Closer still is the maneuver, described by Apollodorus, who states that "Hercules found him [Cerberus] at the gates of Acheron and cased [him] in his cuirass and covered by the lion's skin" (*Apollod.* 2.5.12). There is nothing more "natural," after all, than capturing an animal by means of parts of another animal, already captured and killed in a chain of violence hinting at infinite regress.

Despite the divine command not to use the more recent technologies of the iron age, the chains of diamond stand out in their utter eccentricity. They are preciousness itself, yet they diminish the life and value of those captured to next to nothing. They are the instruments and symbols of oppression *and* sparkling adornments. The cage is not iron; it is golden. Aristophanes humorously bemoans the fate of Cerberus in *Frogs*: "Poor Cerberus! you gagged and seized him, / And then ran off" (*Aristoph. Frogs*

460). But the gagging and seizing devices that are the diamond chains are also status symbols. Is our Cerberus a rapper, full of bling?

Furiously barking with his three, fifty, countless throats, Cerberus is plotting an escape. Pulling together gray matter from his many heads, the dog asks himself how he could be free from the chains of Hercules, while physically remaining in them. One option would be to embrace a daydream of liberty: to be in captivity but to deem oneself internally indomitable, to cultivate in oneself the freedom of thought and imagination. Another option would be to free oneself from oneself, from the circumscribed class of one's being: a dog, a mammal, an animal . . .

Cerberus partially metamorphosed into a plant. Driven by Hercules across green fields, he "sprinkled them with while foam" (*spumis albentibus*). "These flecks of foam grew, and drawing nourishment from the rich, rank soil, they gained the power to hurt [*vires cepisse nocendi*]; and because they spring up and flourish on hard rocks, the country folk call them aconite." The dog's spit became a plant, upon contact with soil.

With a slight but significant difference of emphasis, in a scholium to Apollonius Rhodius's *Argonautica*, the poisonous plant is associated with a "drug," in keeping with the ambiguous meaning of *pharmakon*: Cerberus "vomited up bile, out of which the drug called aconite grew" (*Ap. Rod.* 2.353, schol.). Another scholium, this time to Nicander's *Alexipharmaca* (13b), conveys that "aconite grew up from Cerberus's vomit. For it is told that when Cerberus was brought up from the underworld, he could not endure the rays of the sun and vomited, and this plant was born from his vomit." And this line of attribution of aconite to the dog's vomit traverses the works of Dionysius Periegetes (*Dion. Per.* 788–792), Pliny the Elder (*NH* 27.4), and others.

Does aconite flourish from Cerberus's spit or vomit? If the former, then its growth is due to the animal's rage; if the latter, then it is a product of a physiological reaction to the blinding light of the sun, or the pressure of chains on his body. In either case, Cerberus spreads himself, seeding or sowing himself as a plant beyond the narrow and suffocating limits, into which his animal body in chains has been squeezed.

Aconite itself transmits the message, with which the dog associates his vegetal transformation. Whatever the origin of the bodily fluid that gives rise to it, the plant is highly toxic; in fact, Ovid himself recounts how Medea concocts a poison out of it (*Met.* 7.419–424). Although its etymology is uncertain, in his fragments, Euphorion (41c) reads aconite as *unconquerable* and *invincible*, linking it to the sport of wrestling, which is often called "rolling in the dust." (Aconite may derive from *koniousthai*, "to be dusty," even though the etymology indicated in Ovid's narration is inverted: "growing without soil," that is, without dust. Remember, *dust* is a word that unsays itself, some of its senses directly contradicting others.) Remarkably, in an earlier fragment (28), Euphorion refers to Hercules as "an unconquerable [*arratoi*, from *arratos*] man, bringing Cerberus up to the light." The twelfth labor of Hercules turns out to be impossible to accomplish; unending, it is a contest of two "unconquerable" opponents, of technical rationality and unconscious existence.

The toxicity of aconite is not Cerberus's revenge pure and simple. It is the ruse of metamorphosis: by externalizing some of his bodily fluids, the animal becomes a plant, which kills those who eat or drink its poison, and so leads them back to Cerberus, the terrible guardian of the realm of the dead. With this, the purposes of metamorphosis are laid bare: to allow a mode of existence to carry on with its functioning at the expense of its form; to maintain processes while relinquishing the structures wherein they usually run their course; to insist on the efficacy of being, which is independent of its substantial actuality.

GETTING INFECTED: PANDEMIC DIARIES

(Liber VII, 453-613)

PHASE 0

There are so many of these viruses around, tiny little things that infect everyone and everything—even bacteria and other viruses! They are everywhere, and they write all the time, transcribing themselves, tirelessly signing their extended names, inseparable from their being-viruses. These transcriptions *are* their being. I sometimes wonder what the diary of a virus would look like. Probably something very boring and repetitive, with occasional typos that unexpectedly make things interesting...

I've heard that bats and monkeys have plenty of viruses that can jump species and infect humans. The metamorphoses of a virus are not just its mutations; they are the changing shapes of thinking and relating to species boundaries. Theoretically speaking, of course. On the other side of the world, the "swift power" of such a disease, its *potentia morbi*, is "confined to the destruction of dogs and birds, sheep and cattle, or to wild beasts." Maybe it's an avian flu. Or swine flu. Or another kind, yet unknown. But how confined is it really, if it already affects so many species? And how to keep kosher if it can be passed from pigs to sheep or cows? Is this a cause of concern? I hope not. It's happening very far from here and no human cases have been reported. I am too hypochondriac. Time to stop reading online preprints of medical research and alarmist yellow press. We already have enough to worry about as it is.

GETTING INFECTED: PANDEMIC DIARIES

PHASE 1

A mysterious pneumonia has been contracted by a few people. Very far from here, but still... Apparently, there are no cases of human-to-human transmission; it spreads through direct contact with wild animals. And how many of us are in such contact? Barely anyone is. "The cause of the terrible plague is still unknown" (*latebat causa nocens cladis*). That's not reassuring. On the other hand, we have state-of-the-art medicine, for which the sky is the limit.

PHASE 2

Human-to-human transmission has occurred, alarmingly! Severe infections have been diagnosed in the medical staff taking care of their patients. A high percentage of these have been lethal. "The nearer one is to the sick and the more faithfully he serves them, the more quickly is he himself stricken unto death." Though unexplained, the outbreak is limited and not a matter of international concern, health authorities tell us. Rapid risk assessments try to put us at ease. But this doesn't work. Not for me, at any rate. I am already infected—infected by fear.

PHASE 3

As of today, the plague isn't somewhere far away; it is *here*! Officially confirmed. Well, not right here, where I am now, writing these lines, but on the same continent. It is already replicating itself with a vengeance. And the places it affects are fatally marked by its activity. Even in their names, taken to be interchangeable with danger, suffering, and death. "Since the cause of the disease is hidden, the place itself is held to blame" (*locus est in crimine*). Wuhan. Bergamo. Cities to avoid at all costs? Up until the day when *your* city joins the growing list of the sites of infection.

PHASE 4

First cases of infection have emerged close by. Same city, if not same street. Feeling sick, I thought I was one of those. Went into isolation; submitted myself to a government-issued test. All clear, though the symptoms coincide with those reported by patients, who have contracted the horrible virus: "a red flush and panting, feverish breath." "Hot respiration and gasping at the heavy air" (*auraeque graves captantur hiatu*). At the back of my mind I am almost wishing to catch the killer disease: at least this will put an end to the current uncertainty and stupor, the paralysis of a life too afraid to touch potentially infected surfaces and to be in touch with others, except digitally.

PHASE 5

The sick and the dead are multiplying exponentially. No "bodies lying rotting on the ground" just yet, but mobile morgues (more like refrigerator trucks, such as those that transport frozen animal flesh to be sold in supermarkets for human consumption) have been deployed on city streets. The tables have been karmically turned on us: deeming ourselves to be at the top of the food chain, *we*, apex predators, are now the meal for viruses and bacteria, for worms and insatiable flames.

PHASE 6

Confinement. What does being-at-home entail in a pandemic, when your body is locked there, as in a prison, the walls of your room or your apartment becoming a cocoon, apparently protective yet highly restrictive? Suffocating in your small enclosure, you retreat there to preserve your breath. But when you are not at home in the world, how can you be at home in your home? And when your loved ones get sick, "each man's home seems a place of death to him" (*sua cuique domus fuesta videtur*). So I am tempted to bolt toward the threat outside a home where I am not at home, fleeing from my place, *fugiuntque penates*, rather than endure the torture of waiting inside.

PHASE 7

Illness. Survived. Reinfection and illness, second time around. Survival survived. Fatigue. No strength to keep the diary. Long C/Ovid. *Omnia languor habet*, "lethargy holds all."

PHASE 8

What is left after a pandemic? Who is left behind? Yes, younger people are left behind. And yes, we cannot forget the "confused heap of the dead," the entire crowd of them lying there, *illic vulgus erat stratum*. Things aren't as simple as this, however. I don't think that even an *after* remains, since there is no postpandemic state. Instead, the virus is endemic. Nothing is left. And everything is left, reduced to leftovers, whether still living-dying or dead.

CROSS-SPECIES IMMIGRANTS: AN INTERROGATION TRANSCRIPT

(Liber VII, 614–660)

SUSPECT: Should I begin, Sir? Are you recording?

OFFICER: Yes, just tell me how you've ended up here, on *our* shores.

SUSPECT: I will tell you what I know about my "arrival," but you may find that what I report is not much. And you may not believe me.

OFFICER: It's not up to you to tell me what I should or shouldn't believe.

SUSPECT: Of course, of course, Sir: I am charged with being an undocumented illegal migrant, an illegal alien, as you are fond of saying. Plus, indecent exposure. That's why you've arrested me. But I may be more alien than you think.

OFFICER: Let's cut to the chase. How did you end up on this country's national territory, totally naked, without papers or possessions on your person?

CROSS-SPECIES IMMIGRANTS: AN INTERROGATION TRANSCRIPT

SUSPECT: Damn right, but to be more correct, I ended up even without a person on my person . . . So, it's a story both too long and too short to tell. Let me give it a shot. All I could see was the back of the one crawling in front of me, his body dwarfed by a piece of yellow leaf he carried. My own figure, lugging a dry blade of grass, would have presented the same site to the one behind me. More powerful than what I saw was the scent I felt: they call these "trail pheromones." Yes, we needed to band together, to point the way, so as not to disperse, not to get lost. We went by the smell. The memory of the journey is blurry. I suspect we were carrying a piece of leaf and a blade of grass now, in retrospect. Back then it was just *this* and *that*, or not even. These things just were . . .

OFFICER: Where were you traveling? And who is that "we?"

SUSPECT: The surface underneath was rough, wrinkled (*rugosoque*) and brown, covered in patches of green and moist softness. Since you found me along with others under this old oak, I assume it was the bark (*cortice*) of the tree and the green patches were moss.

OFFICER: So, let's be clear. Are you claiming that you together with the others were crawling along an oak trunk? Carrying leaves and blades of grass? And smelling each other? Were you all drunk? Or high?

SUSPECT: We were getting very high in the tree, if that's what you mean, officer. I am telling you what I can recall, but my memory is murky, as I've already told you. What I remember very clearly is the shaking. All of a sudden, it started. (*Chirping sounds*)

OFFICER: What did you just say? I . . . I am not sure those sounds were human.

SUSPECT: It happens to me when I am nervous. When I remember something scarry. Sometimes, when I am too happy to contain myself. These chirping sounds I mean. They come deep from my belly, as if some hard surfaces are getting rubbed against one another. But where was I? Oh, yes, the trembling. All of a sudden, the hard brownness underneath us gave way, started moving and shaking, *tremescere motu*.

OFFICER: Wait, and what did you say right now? It's definitely not American. Maybe not human, either. Makes as little sense as your chirping or screeching.

SUSPECT: To be honest, I am not sure myself. The words flew out of my mouth, a little like those chirping sounds earlier. It's weird: seems like something much older, really ancient is speaking through me, using me as its mouthpiece.

CROSS-SPECIES IMMIGRANTS: AN INTERROGATION TRANSCRIPT

OFFICER: You are at the wrong government department, Sir. You need a full psychological evaluation. That fall from the tree messed with your head in a big way. But now I am curious. What happened next?

SUSPECT: Here I am really blurry on the details. Next thing I felt was the ground. When I looked up, I saw lots of black dots flying in the air, scattering, all of them coming from the big oak tree. And as they were dropping—no, still before, in the air—they were growing, *crescere desubito*, and appearing human. Unclad.

OFFICER: All right, your delirium is evident by now. Speaking in tongues, and shit like that.

SUSPECT: That's not all, Sir.

OFFICER: I am sure that's not all.

SUSPECT: Then, as in a fog, I remember a very important man approaching us. Everyone revered him. I sensed that he was like our queen.

OFFICER: Your queen? You mean the Queen of England? Maybe you haven't watched the news: she's passed away. Quick death, slow funeral...

SUSPECT: No, our queen—queen ant.

OFFICER: Queen Aunt? I've heard of Queen Mother and Queen Consort. Never of Queen Aunt.

SUSPECT: Not aunt: ant. The oak tree, the scent, crawling: I've put all of these together (and did some online sleuthing, I must admit). It turns out that I and my fellow cross-species immigrants were ants before. Carpenter ants, to be precise. We love oak trees.

OFFICER: So you are a carpenter. I see.

SUSPECT: Your leader has also appreciated our capacity to work hard in harsh conditions. I was concentrated on something else: the whole world of scents that I had experienced so acutely before was leaving me. I was trying to smell and treasure the trail pheromone—so comforting, so familiar—and yet it was dissipating. A few words of your leader keep ringing in my ears: "my new subjects"; "I portion out my city and my fields"; "thrifty race, inured to toil." *Parcum genus est patiensque laborum*, he said in this foreign language you do not understand. He named us Myrmidons.

OFFICER: Carpenters, agricultural labor, hard toil. You are labor migrants, that's for sure. But undocumented, illegal, and cuckoo-crazy.

SUSPECT: I've learned something else: the right term is *Gastarbeiter*. A guy pointed at us and repeated this word over and over. When I asked him what it meant, he said, "guest worker." Judging by the treatment we are

CROSS-SPECIES IMMIGRANTS: AN INTERROGATION TRANSCRIPT

getting, work is welcome, but not the workers. Wouldn't a more correct term be *Gastarbeit*?

OFFICER: Now, this matter is for human resources management. It's their bread and butter.

SUSPECT: Yes, yes! Human resources. We've not immigrated across species boundaries to the human; we have turned into human *resources*. So correct! You are a genius, Sir! Your leader was missing human resources for work and for war, because of a pandemic, or something. It wiped out many adults, transforming them into biomass, which is quite useless both for labor and for military activities, though it could come in handy for renewable energy generation. Then we came along. Well, dropped by. Or simply dropped from that oak.

OFFICER: You will be fingerprinted and photographed now. Entered into our database, with all your biometrics duly recorded.

SUSPECT: (*Mumbling, while leaving handcuffed*) Human resources, biometrics, biomass...

OFFICER: Next!

BECOMING UNFAITHFUL: CEPHALUS AND PROCRIS
(Liber VII, 661–865)

He had the brilliant idea to test her fidelity by appearing before her in another form. (Not sure what that new form was, he remarks, "I seemed to feel the change," *videor sensisse*).

She had an inkling of his infidelity and hid herself in the foliage at the very spot where he went hunting.

To see whether she was a faithful wife, he was unfaithful to himself, metamorphosing into someone else.

To check whether he was a faithful husband, she virtually transformed herself into an animal hiding in a tree and was killed as though she was one by his javelin.

He betrayed her by suspecting her of betrayal. He survived his suspicion of her.

She betrayed herself by suspecting him. She paid with her life for her suspicion of him.

BECOMING UNFAITHFUL: CEPHALUS AND PROCRIS

He wanted her to betray him with himself—with himself othered, metamorphosed into an other. A perverse fantasy: to observe his beloved voyeuristically and to be both the one she betrays and the one with whom she betrays him.

She waited, longingly, for him who wanted her to betray him with himself...

The conceptual knot is difficult to untie, because it makes metamorphosis what it is: infidelity to one's form at any given moment and fidelity to the process of transformation.

More than that, in the twenty-first century we no longer understand the meaning of faithfulness, fealty, or fidelity, even if we know the dictionary definitions of these words. The modicum of sense they preserve is announced by way of contrast with jealousy, mistrust, infidelity.

And what about Ovid's fidelity or infidelity to the original story of Cephalus and Procris? Where is the goddess of dawn, Eos, in his *Metamorphoses*, the goddess who, in love with Cephalus, kidnaps him during one of his hunting outings? Why is the power of a goddess neutralized through her sheer absence, while she is supplanted by an ephemeral love object, Aura or aura, a breeze, whose name sounds like an abbreviation of Aurora, the Latin rendition of Eos? Can one discuss fidelity within an overall framework of creative infidelity to the source? And yet, are we not engaging in this very endeavor at the moment?

To whom or to what can one be faithful?
- To oneself
- To a form of existence
- To one's desire
- To an idea
- To a name

- To a romantic partner
- To a relation (at every interpersonal and institutional level)

Being faithful to ... *vs.* living up to ... Faithfulness not to be confused with ideality, that is, with trying to live up to an (impossible) ideal.

Differences between faithfulness and loyalty: you are faithful to a relation, loyal to a person. Fidelity to a romantic partner as a means to uphold faithfulness to a love relation.

He was halfheartedly faithful to his desire. After his hunting outings, he would woo the breeze (*aura*) "blowing gently on him in his heat." *Aura, venias*—"Come, Aura," he cried, "come, soothe me; come into my breast, most welcome one, as indeed you do, relieve the heat with which I burn." What could be more sexual as an appeal than that? He was unfaithful to her; he betrayed her with the breeze, who could well be a nymph, and gave a voice to his desire in another fantasy staged for everyone to see and to hear.

She was halfheartedly faithful to her human form. Hiding in the foliage of a tree, under which he lay after a hunt calling *Veni, optima!*—"Come, dearest!"—and mouthing the name of Aura (or aura), she groaned. Then, the branch underneath her creaked and the leaves rustled. He mistook her for the animal that she would become. Yet another fantasy? Hers or his? What is certain is that she shared the death of other animals he killed in his bloodthirsty forays into the woods. Fidelity to a way of dying is more telling than adherence to a way of life.

Finally, there is the obstruse and incomplete metamorphosis of a common into a proper name (and back), of *aura* into *Aura*, of an elemental force into a person of flesh and blood, with the specter of Aurora hovering over these invocations.

He states, with a barely concealed smirk, that she feared "a mere nothing," the name which is nothing, *quod nihil est*, because it is "without a body," *sine corpore*. Every name, though, far from a mere nothing, has its body made of letters or sounds, the body committed to paper or to the air, where it vibrates and becomes vibrant as it is called upon, appealed to.

The fateful transformation of *aura* into *Aura* was possible because the name was said, not written. Writing is the medium of keeping fidelity to the name—particularly, to the distinction between proper and common names. The body of *A* is not very similar to that of *a*, but the two are identical when uttered. His desire dissembled itself behind and exploited the difference between *A* and *a*. Her jealousy overlooked the difference. He manipulated the gap between writing and speech; she immersed herself in what she heard. For him, *A/a/ura* was a proper and a common name, a person and a thing, according to the situation at hand. Infidelity became fidelity, and fidelity twisted into infidelity. For her, *Aura* was a proper name. Infidelity was infidelity.

He lived in fidelity, in-fidelity, infidelity to her. She lived—until his tests, twists, and taunts made living on impossible.

She mistook *aura* for *Aura*, and he mistook her for an animal: apparent errors with hard kernels of truth in them. A name, mistakenly considered "a mere nothing" (*nihil*), was the cause of death, of becoming nothing, of her annihilation.

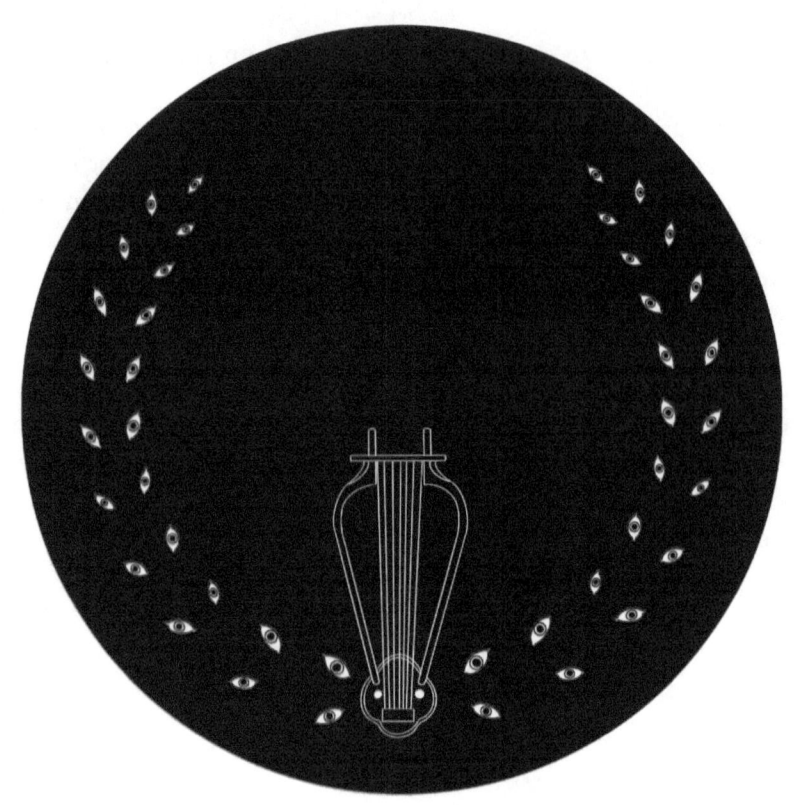

DREAMS FROM MY OWNER: A MEMOIR
(Liber VIII, 1–151)

A few months after my fifth birthday, I fell victim to the hand of a stranger. Or, more precisely, to the sharp scissors that hand clasped. I was in what should have been the safest place in the country at the time: the royal palace, opulent and heavily guarded. And in the palace, I remember being cherished, sheltered right under the crown, and exceptionally close to the head of state. To the head of the head of state, if I am to be really precise.

Whatever the label attached to these notes—memoirs, autobiography, a history of a siege—they are, for all intents and purposes, posthumous.

The time and the place conspired against me, transforming my comfortable condition into a real and fatal misfortune. The country was at war, the city besieged. The army of King Nisus (my owner) was useless, so the king poured all his hopes into me. He had "growing on his head, amidst his locks of honored grey, a brilliant purple lock on whose preservation rested the safety of his throne." This description from an official source manages to insult and exalt me at the same time. I am dishonored, simply because (the punk that I am) I stand out from the rest of my dull and gray comrades, and yet, in my brilliance, I assure their salvation, together with that of the king and the country. I read these lines in disbelief, marveling at how color-coded privilege and reverence were and wondering all the more about the stupidity of associating the fate of the crown with a lone lock of hair hiding underneath it.

One day I heard whispers from nearby, desperate, insane whispers: "I need but my father's lock of hair. That is to me more precious than gold; that purple lock will make me blest, will give me my heart's desire." *Illa beatam purpura me votique mei factura potentem* ... I am used to people pinning their hopes on me, with ridiculous naivete. The fate of the kingdom literally hangs by a thread (of hair). And I don't fault people for that. But to grant the fulfillment of desire—that is beyond my comprehension. To the king's daughter of all people.

What am I, after all? Who am I? An in-your-face reminder of your animal and vegetal past. An unnaturally looking natural remnant. Sometimes I am stressed and brittle and dry; at other times shiny and flowing. I can say little about myself: principally, the one who is under me (but above everyone else) is the one who thinks and remembers, is happy or sad. As for me, I cannot even tell you if my unusual color is dyed or natural. (I assume the latter, because the chemical memory of dye would have stayed with me, or, rather, in me.) In fact, I cannot even decide whether I am one or many: people tend to see a single lock where there are hundreds of roots and shafts. So, I am at a loss here: I cannot tell you with all certainty, as the one narrating dreams from his father does, "Don't you know who I am? I'm an individual!" Because I am infra- and super-individual. I am and am not an "I."

And then she carried out her dirty deed: "she despoiled him of the fateful lock of hair." Of me. Of us. "Despoiled," *spoliat*, is another word used in the official report. It does not even begin to describe what went on. We were severed from our roots, much like the felled trees, the plant world that we commemorate by growing on a human body. The snap of the scissors was deafening. More than half of us lost consciousness, which irradiated from our owner's brain through his skull and sculp to our very tips. When we regained our composure, we realized we were handed over to the enemy with the words: "Take as a pledge of my love this purple lock [*Cape pignus amoris purpureum crinem*] and know that I am giving you not a lock, but my father's life."

Memoirs are tricky to write. They are at the mercy of selective memory, the exaggerated spotlight, into which a few events are cast, and long lapses of narration. Still, the scene of this offer—of a sacrificial offering of sorts—and its immediate rejection are etched in our cellular memory. From then on, what concerned us was the fate of our kin who were not chopped off from our owner's head. Chasing after his daughter at sea, the king "changed into an osprey with tawny wings," while she became the bird Ciris, who "takes this name from the shorn lock of hair," *et a tonso est hoc nomen adepta capillo*. That is, from us. Cut off from our roots, we remained human; attached to their origins, our kin reverted back to a more animal shape of feathers. Perhaps, being or remaining human is possible only in the state of uprootedness. We have no idea. Like the one recounting dreams from his father, who confesses: "I had no idea who my own self was."

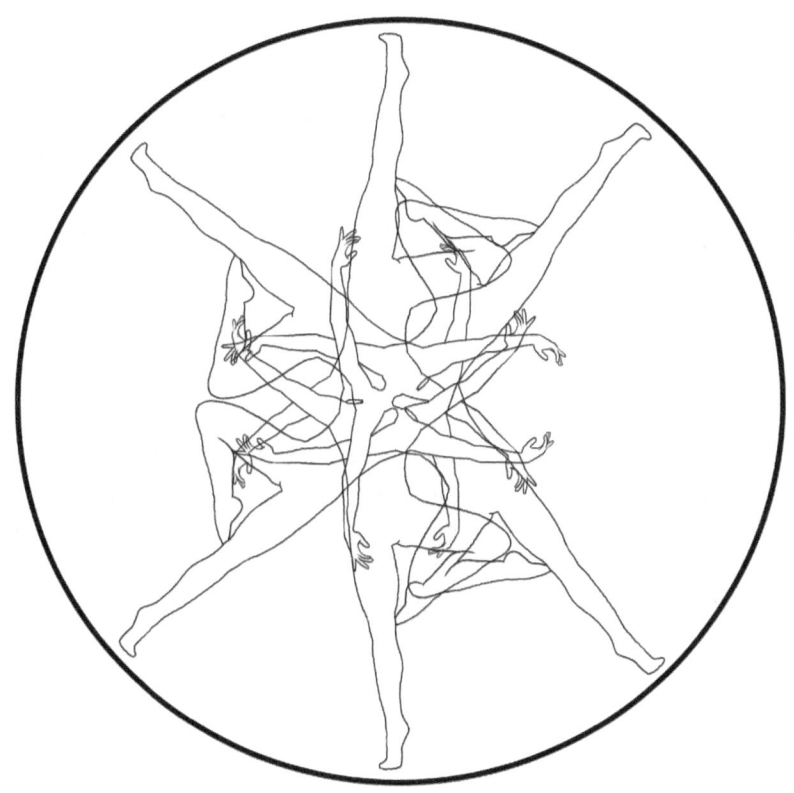

ARIADNE VARIATIONS

(Liber VIII, 152–182)

It is more and more difficult to untangle the threads. Threads of narrative and fabric, letters and words. Passages that lead nowhere. Dead ends. Passages you walk through or read, run inside or skim with a distracted glance. From your understanding, or nonunderstanding, bizarre "hybrid monster children," *monstri novitate biformis*, are born. Offspring who will be promptly rejected by the midwife of ideas, Socrates perpetually acting as his midwife-mother Phaenarete. Sense fizzles out into nonsense much more profusely than it congeals out of the abyss of meaninglessness. Unraveling the thread (*filo*)—not so different from a son (*filius*)—you are only pretending to prepare for the laborious act of retracing your steps while going where "no former adventurer had ever reached before." You are just fraying and tattering this one interwoven thread (Ariadne leads you most certainly back to Arachne, not anywhere else), splitting it into many, splaying it, leaving its bits and pieces everywhere. How to retrace your steps, taking cues from these meager indicators? You are walking on errors, through errors, errantly, blunderingly. *Innumeras errore vias.* The passage that I am writing and that you are presumably reading—that I am reading and rereading together with you and that you are rewriting in the moving spotlights of your attention and distraction—this very passage is a tattered thread, leading nowhere and everywhere, conjuring up hybrid monster children: yours, mine, Ovid's, Minos's, Ariadne's-Arachne's. Intermingled yet separate, literary and philosophical, what we are stooping to pick up, hovering over them for a dreamy moment, are shreds of imagination, and, worse, the delusion of being able, thanks to our cunning or anticipatory reasoning, to quit the labyrinth, to stop wandering in its endless passages, to be or to live or to survive anywhere but in exile, the ex-ile that is of a piece with ex-istence. After forty years or forty millennia. The greatest error is to think that one is unerring, inerrant, on a straight path to a preset goal, to the exit, after which existence will resume as though nothing has changed. That the thread, the son or the daughter, the offspring, the issue of the body or the mind, of the labyrinthine mindbody or bodymind, is neither a hybrid (*biformis*: two-formed) nor a monster. A gnostic temptation: dwelling in truth is possible after exiting the labyrinth, quitting our earthly exile, ceasing to exist in this material world, having attained genuine existence elsewhere. But there is no pure disappearance or pure appearance, for that matter. All that we have, instead, is a tattered thread decomposing into the earthy floor, trodden by so many feet, hooves, and paws, and traversed by a welter of roots. Even this is wrong: the thread in tatters is all we do *not* have. It no longer shows up; it does not indicate the true path, the right way, but, having dissolved into the ground, it holds up and gives traction to every step and every root extension, whatever the direction chosen by the errant animal, plant, or human, humanimal, animaplant, or plantuman. Or, in a twining word, plantumanimal.

HOW TO SOAR ABOVE THE LABYRINTH OF YOUR MIND: ICARUS'S WINGS

(Liber VIII, 183-235)

If you are tired of roving the narrow corridors of your mind's labyrinth, soar above its enclosures. The walls of the labyrinth keep you inside, guiding the movements of your thought, your imagination and emotion, your judgments and memories. Labyrinth walls have the structure of *this as that*, of interpreting whatever comes your way within a very limited array of possible, or plausible, options. But there is no roof, "the sky is open," and it invites you to rise above the *this as that* structure of reality, to transcend the mechanics of interpretations, its squeaky springs and levers and hinges implanted into the flesh of perception, let alone understanding. How to relocate to the sky, open and free *of* (not *for*) interpretation? Through the "unknown arts," *ignotas artes*, of wing-making.

Supplies:
Wax
Feathers
Twine

Instructions for psycho-techno-metamorphoses:
Step 1. Put your ideas, representations, memories in a sequence, ordered from the smallest to the biggest and longest, as though "they had grown on a slope." Do not delve into these mental contents/feathers; simply order them, like artefacts in a collection. Do not be tempted to establish a

perfectly horizontal line, on which to hang the *prêt-à-porter* items of your mental wardrobe. The sloping arrangement is important; it will give you traction.

Step 2. Fasten the feathers together with twine and wax. These are chance associations, secondary or even tertiary. There is no great new synthesis here, no alternative system of thinking and sensing the world. Only featherlight surfaces of your mind rearranged, loosely bound and stuck together.

Step 3. Play with feathers, twine, and wax: with your memories and emotions and ideas, with associations among them, with connections and separations. In play, you will be reborn, young again, the Icarus-you, who would "now catch at the feathers which some passing breeze had blown about, now mold the yellow wax with the thumb."

Step 4. Getting ready for your flight, calibrate the distances from the middle outward. Trace "a middle course," *medio*, between two possibilities: "if you go too low, the water will weigh on your wings [*unda gravet pennas*]; if you go too high, fire will burn them [*ignis adurat*]." Avoid the depths of melancholy descent and the heights of psychedelic burnout: "fly between the two," *inter utrumque vola*. That is another *inter*, distinct from *inter*pretation.

Step 5. Fit the hitherto unknown wings, *ignotas alas*, the crowning achievement of *ignotas artes*, on the shoulders of your fresh self, the Icarus-you. Mount the apparatus of your rearranged mental contents and associations on your shoulders, not on your head. To the acephalus that you now are, the wings will be unknown, like the arts of producing these prostheses of thought and imagination.

Step. 6. Kiss your old self, the Daedalus-you, goodbye.

TO PERDIX, THE INVENTOR
(Liber VIII, 236-259)

To you, who invent and reinvent, yourself and others, persons and tools—to you I am sending a time capsule, dated 12-12-2022, with these lines. They are unlikely to catch up with you, who will have mutated into someone else, in another place, having once again reinvented yourself. Nor with me. Metamorphoses are, after all, streams of self-reinvention, converting the self into the convoked or the (ofttimes silently) invoked other.

Thinking of you and—I'd like to believe—as you, I realize that you invented by observing what exists and imagining what does not yet exist. Transposing one kind of being on another *and* being on nonbeing. There are no metamorphoses without this double move, this complex maneuver which you've mastered so admirably, despite your tender age.

TO PERDIX, THE INVENTOR

Let me try to sum up your achievement, though you know all this better than I do (sometimes it helps to commit what we know, or appear to know, to writing, to see the idea in space, outside ourselves, to appreciate it better and approach it from different sides):

—Shuttling between one kind of being and another, you "observed the backbone of a fish and, taking it as a model [*exemplum*], cut a row of teeth in a thin strip of iron and thus invented a saw." You used an animal (fish) as a prototype for a tool (saw). But the animal was already dead, reduced to its skeleton. The posthumous vestiges of the living served as a bridge between nature and culture, an organic body and technique.

—Ferrying nonbeing to being, you bound "two arms of iron together at a joint, so that, while the arms kept the same distance apart, one might stand still while the other should trace a circle." In other words, you invented a wing compass. (Soon, you will have learned what it meant to have real wings, not those of Icarus's half-hearted metamorphosis). Here, you used metal artifacts (iron bars) to construct a quasi-animal organ (a joint). This organ became one more bridge between the concrete and the abstract, metallic materials and geometrical figures yet to come.

You have worked with iron in both instances; I wonder why? What makes this material so appropriate for spanning divides of all sorts, between different kinds of being and between being and nonbeing? What is it about iron that fascinates an inventor? Its durability *and* propensity to gain rust, to be corroded by water and air moisture? To resist and to succumb to metamorphoses? To be invisibly remolded by the other, even as it clings to its metallic identity?

Now, we must go a step further than the two types of invention and even than the self-reinvention you've gone through: we must try to see the world as the sum total of commerce, in which inventors are continually engaged with others and with themselves. Their commerce is not always courteous and gentle, as the envious Daedalus, entrusted with the task of developing and honing your skills, taught you by pushing you down "from the sacred citadel of Minerva," the tower of wisdom, on which your rank was higher than either his or Icarus's. Rather than kill you, the shove compelled you to reinvent yourself (yes, I know, with the help of the goddess who clothed you in feathers in mid-fall, which turned into a flight), to become a partridge (*perdix*),

TO PERDIX, THE INVENTOR

and to transition from a *he* to a *she*, from a preadolescent boy to a bird who "lays her eggs in hedgerows."

As I was tracking your transition, it occurred to me that one cannot invent anything without, in the same breath, inventing and reinventing oneself. Nothing *ex nihilo:* every invention is a reinvention, at minimum of the inventor. The talented inventor that you are, you have been adept at self-reinvention from the get-go; Daedalus's criminal act merely made this underlying skill explicit and actual. The eggs you lay in hedgerows are those you, yourself, hatch from. Your teacher tried to kill you for your creativity that surpasses his by far. Instead, he made you infinitely creative.

I return to the date of this time capsule: 12-12-2022. I am almost convinced that these numbers, making sense within the counts and calculus of the Gregorian calendar, are its most important message. So many 2s, all even, perfectly divisible, nearly symmetrical . . . It is the last month of the year, a new hatchling awaits in the not-so-distant future, a rebirth from death to a refreshed life. Or does it? Do you still have the courage to lay your eggs, to keep reinventing yourself, dear Perdix? Do I?

Perditus

DIANA'S BOAR: A PHYTOLOGICAL RITUAL FOR THE ANIMALS THAT WE ARE

(Liber VIII, 260-450)

PREAMBLE

"Hunting and gathering" is the first and the last stage of organized, if nomadic, human activity when gratitude to plants and animals for the sustenance they provide us with is relatively balanced. With the early settlement around cultivated plots of land over ten thousand years ago, agriculture becomes a vehicle for the creation of wealth and surplus. The rituals, in which agricultural activity is steeped, involve sacrifices to the goddesses and gods of fertility, of the fields and staple crops. This is a phytocentric perspective, to be sure, albeit one enchanted not by the plants themselves (nor by any fertile, reproducing beings for that matter), but by the profit, the surplus value they yield and embody.

Against this backdrop, Oeneus, the king of Calydon, offers the deities of vegetation the sacrifices that are appropriate to them: Ceres receives the first fruits of grain, to Bacchus wine libations are given, and Minerva (the goddess of wisdom associated with olive trees) gets "her own flowing oil." Diana, the goddess of hunting, is slighted by sacrifices offered to the gods of plants, but not to her, the goddess of the animal world. It is then that she sends her monstrous boar on a mission to destroy the crops, avenging his mistress. Untamed animal energy is unleashed against plants: "lightning flashed from his mouth, the herbage shriveled beneath his breath" (*fulmen ab ore venit, frondes afflatibus ardent*); "he trampled down the young corn in the blade, and now he laid waste to the full-grown crops of some farmer who was doomed to mourn, and cut off the ripe grain in the ear." Hunting without gathering rebels against cultivation and harvesting without hunting. Animal life is pitted against plants.

After a long hunt, Diana's boar is killed by a select group of heroes and heroines. Diana both lost and won: the art of hunting was reactivated, even though the symbol of the huntress-in-chief was hunted and slain. The conflict brewing between plant and animal vitalities has not been extinguished; instead it has only intensified. It is high time to conduct another, modern ritual of reconciliation between plants and animals—between human vegetality and animality, above all—which is driven neither by vegetal surpluses and profits nor by the animal pursuit of hunting and being hunted.

PREPARATION

Wander in a forest for at least an hour imbibing smells and sights, touching diverse textures of plants and the soil and hearing a symphony of sounds and silences. You are preparing to remake yourself into a medium, a passageway, through which many worlds communicate.

Gradually deepen your breath, slowing its rhythm and allowing vegetal respiration to permeate your lungs.

Attend to the presence of birds, insects, slugs, or worms and any other animal forest inhabitants you meet. Acknowledge that these moments will never return, your possible future recollection of them notwithstanding. They are singular, nonreproducible, finite.

Construct an improvised altar of fallen tree branches and twigs. Be sure to include some of these "construction materials" in your own outfit, in your hair, or on your body.

RITUAL

Part 1. An Infertility Rite

Lay out dry leaves, fallen bits of tree bark, and soil from the forest floor on your improvised altar.

Bowing before the altar, repeat *I do not require more. Enough is enough is enough. Absolute finitude.*

Part 2. An Anti-Hunt

Spread black sunflower seeds and yellow millet in another layer on top of the altar. Do not worry if birds do not get attracted right away by your offering. The time of the ritual exceeds that of your physical presence in the forest.

Lowering yourself in front of the altar, repeat *I am here not to terminate your life, but to extend it. Not to obtain, but to sustain. Neither to extract nor to extinguish, but to rekindle and to relinquish.*

Part 3. The Medium

Dismantle the altar and mix the "materials," from which it was constructed, with the offerings laid out on top of it. Lie down on the place of the altar. Cover parts of yourself with its fragments, if you wish, adding to what has been already incorporated into your outfit. Be the underlying and the overlaying, the intersection of the *under* and the *over*, the *before* and the *after*. Under-over, before-after, vegetal-animal: the medium. Meditate on the sense of humanity at this unique crossing.

MELEAGER: BECOMING ASHES
(Liber VIII, 451–545)

The same fate awaits your body and this piece of wood,
Both of you—matter.
When one goes up in flames, so does the other:
Enkindled by a consuming fire from without or from within.
Lignum contains *ignis*: the blaze is in vegetation; it is a sublime plant
    nourishing the plant.
This piece of wood is fire frozen in time, vegetalized, a souvenir of
    green growing ardor.
And you? A moving conflagration, internally combusted, life-giving
    and life-consuming,
Self-consuming and life-denying.
Your mother, matter, regulates the intensities of heat,
Now fanning the flame,
Now "quenching it in water." You mistake her for your father (spirit),
    because she is him, too.
Burning trees, I kindle "the funeral pyre of my own flesh"—
Iste cremet mea viscera, says mother-matter.
You are convinced that you set fire to the world, ignite, detonate,
    bomb . . .
You incinerate yourself; she incinerates herself through you.
Coal power plants, gasoline cars, fireplaces, stoves are the funeral
    pyre of her own flesh,

Of your own flesh, of her-your-our flesh.
Your very pain is hers: "the fire and the pain increase and then die down."
"White ashes" linger on. She is you, you are her, you are them, after the extinguishing of pain and fire.
Matter. Painful and painless. Before and after. Tree, timber, cinder.

ISLAND AFTERLIFE: PERIMELE
(Liber VIII, 546–610)

An island juts out of the sea, standing apart from the aqueous abyss surrounding it on all sides. The ocean insistently licks its perimeter with tongues that are the rolling waves. Water touching and retreating from land only to touch again (*maiomai, mēlē*). All around: *peri-*. *Peri + mele*—touched all around. Harassed all the time, everywhere.

Perimele is born from touch and from resistance to being touched. From a touch as violent as it is violating. Her name is not hers: "the sailors call her Perimele." She is so baptized by those who seek safe harbor on her shores, those who want to touch dry land with their feet after what seems to be an eternity at sea, those who also know full well the danger of an abrupt and uncontrolled coming in touch with her cliffs.

ISLAND AFTERLIFE: PERIMELE

The one who saved her to continue touching her nonstop, all around (and so to keep current her name, Perimele, which is not quite hers), is the very one who violated her, the river god, Achelous, who "took from her the name of virgin" (*virgineum dilectae nomen ademi*). One name for another, but neither of the two is her own. He took from her the name and the thing of virginity, breaching her boundaries, insinuating himself within. Then, after father Hippodamas added a lethal touch, "hurling her to her death down from a high cliff into the deep," the river god "embraced [*amplexa*] her floating form," so as to challenge her boundaries, to touch them in every which way.

And Perimele? What does she do? How does she survive, outliving herself with her "members mutated into an island?" Ovid keeps mum on her fate, except to say that she must endure persistent embraces of her savior, who is also her violator. That is not what the logic and the language of an island say, however. *Her* logic and language.

Island = I. One letter—the first—for the rest of them, refusing the string of other letters. The formula is of extreme individualism, a separate identity, clearly demarcated, fictional, fictitious, beyond the myth of Perimele. But this island-I is not an immediate given; she emerges *post factum* and *post mortem*, still alive, despite everything. The island-I as an afterlife of an isolated I.

In her afterlife, the island-I is connected to the rest of the earth through the ocean floor. She is a node in the web of a submersive and subversive relationality. But she remains, or she becomes for the first time, an I—nonisolated, noninsular, peninsular—behind or beneath the illusion of detachment. Her resistance is not opposition; it is persistence, existence, or ex-existence that gathers and assembles, instead of severing and chopping up to bits. (Are you feeling a strong undercurrent, allying her, and us, to Typhoeus?)

The migratory birds who rest and nest on her cliffs; the mosses, grasses, and shrubs lining her slopes; the crabs and the mussels and the shallow-water fishes who feel at home along her shores—they are her articulations, her languages, and theirs. The insular node is already a web. The languages of birds, of fishes, of mosses are at the same time bird, fish, moss, *and* island languages: she is the language of these languages, cracking open the space of their communication within and among themselves, among themselves and with her. A language of chirps and rustlings, of wind playing with leaves and of waves crushing on the rocks; a language of sounds and silences, through which her *face* reveals itself.

For the inhabitants and the guests of the island, she is Perimele in a different sense than for Achelous. Unlike him, they do not breach her perimeter to constantly caress and harass her, to penetrate deeper into her and to maintain her in their commanding grip. She is, rather, being in touch all around, as their being in touch with themselves and with others outside the logic of possession and domination.

On the horizon of Perimele's island afterlife another event looms: the deadening calm of rising sea levels. He creeps up on her again, albeit differently, irreversibly, accosting her with unprecedented force. The wave licking her shores is not retreating far enough, its rhythmic aqueous breath disrupted. Catastrophic global heating, causing Artic and Antarctic ice to melt, enables him to embrace her more tightly, to suffocate or to drown her in his embrace, to make her languages sink rather than sing, to steal her face. Gradually constricting, narrowing the ring of water around her. Inundations and tsunamis, mudslides and storm surges, sinkholes and landslides penetrate her interior, repeating the initial violation ("I took from her the name of virgin"). Island after-afterlife: becoming seabed.

TREE HOSPITALITY: AN EXEGESIS
(Liber VIII, 611–724)

Mille domos adiere locum requiemque petentes, mille domos clausere serae: "To a thousand homes they came, seeking a place for rest; a thousand homes were barred against them."

They came and they keep coming: refugees, old and new. Refugees seeking safety as they try to escape war and political persecution, the climate breakdown disproportionately affecting the poorest areas of the globe, and economic destitution.

Which homes were barred to them? The wealthiest ones, their walls made of brick and their roofs covered with tiles. The countries with the most resources and capacity to receive refugees are those most reluctant to admit them. How do we know that a poor household opened its doors? *Tamen una receipt; parva quidem, stipulis et canna tecta palustri*: "Still one received them, humble indeed, thatched with straw and reeds from the marsh." A small hut, constructed of vegetal materials of the least durable kind (straw and reed), is the site of hospitality.

Iuppiter huc specie mortali cumque parente venit Atlantiades positis caducifer alis: "Hither came Jupiter in the guise of a mortal, and with his father came Atlas's grandson, he that bears the caduceus, his wings laid aside."

They, the refugees, are the transformed countenances of the gods. To them, divine hospitality, or what the Greeks called *theoxenia*, is due. The kinship of Jupiter's son, Mercury, with Atlas, hints at the place where this hospitality was dispensed: the Atlantic region.

Pia Baucis anus parilique aetate Philemon illa sunt annis iuncti iuvenabilis. . . . Tota domus duo sunt, idem parentque iubentque: "pious Baucis and Philemon, of equal age, were in that cottage wed in their youth. . . . They two were the whole household, together they served and ruled."

In the Atlantic region, two humble but hospitable countries of the same age are "the whole household." A shared peninsula, for instance. Iberia. Baucis and Philemon: Portugal and Spain.

(On the other side of the Atlantic, the couple would have been Canada and the United States, a maple tree and an oak, were it not for a far-from-humble condition of these countries and the border wall in the south.)

Exegesis: a leading out, a guiding outside. An exegetic exercise is the guiding of sense out of its enclosure in texts, texts written not only in ink and with words or other characters, but also composed by air and the earth, water and fire. The going-out of sense is its growing-out, its germination and flourishing. Exegesis assists the vegetal development of sense, not commanding it but providing the propitious conditions: ample water and fertile soil and light and warmth.

Frondere Philemona Baucis, Baucida conspexit senior frondere Philemon. Iamque super geminos crescente cacumine vultus mutual, dum licuit, reddebant dicta 'vale . . .': "Baucis saw Philemon putting forth leaves, Philemon saw Baucis; and as the tree-top formed over their two faces, while still they could, they cried the same words: 'Farewell . . .'"

Those who provided hospitality in their modest abode made of straw and reed were granted their wish and, instead of dying much later in life, metamorphosed into trees. What sort of hospitality is it, undersigned from the future by the vegetal incarnation of the hosts? Rather than focusing on interiority, it is an open welcome in the open, extended by opening up to the other. It provides shelter under its branches, without detaining the guests there, because such a dwelling has nothing in common with a cage. Vegetal hospitality is, thus, a sheltering and a releasing, care for the guests' needs and attention to their desire.

TREE HOSPITALITY: AN EXEGESIS

vale (LAT.): Farewell.
vale (SPAN.): OK.
vale (PORT.): It's worth (it).

Illic incola de gemino vicinos corpore truncos: "here dwell two trees growing from one double trunk"
   . . . *tiliae contermina quercus*: "a linden tree side-by-side with an oak"

Spain and Portugal: an olive tree and a cork oak, side by side, "two trees growing from one double trunk."

SOMETIMES: PROTEUS, THE DAUGHTER OF ERYSICHTHON, AND ERYSICHTHON

(Liber VIII, 730–874)

Interdum, sometimes. This word is a constant—it does not crop up only occasionally, sometimes. The word is Proteus's faithful companion in the flux of becomings amidst the inconstancy of his forms. Sometimes he is this, sometimes that: "sometimes assuming the form of flowing water . . . and sometimes a flame, the water's enemy." *Interdum . . . interdum*: from sometimes to sometimes, between sometimes and sometimes, in the chronometry of random instants, his metamorphoses happen. But

"Sometimes" says:
Pay attention
To those other times when
What occurs sometimes
Does not occur.

the *between* is already *within* the sometimes, inscribed in the *inter-* of *interdum*. A period of transition, a span of time in the course of which changes are underway in the most intense manner imaginable, is the moving frontier of Protean adventures, a limit perpetually displaced and internally transfigured, time and again. Although Proteus is "a dweller of the earth-embracing sea," he does not abide by the element of water, where he is at home. He becomes fire too, as we have seen, sometimes metamorphosing into the contrary of his liquid milieu. More than Proteus himself (if he has a self at all),

> *Proteus, I have neither the time nor the energy to write an elaborate letter to you. Hence, this brief note. Mainly, because you will not have been capable of reading my scribbles from the beginning to the end; even now I have already lost you; you are no longer you (just as you have never been you) and, probably, neither remember what preceded this line you are staring at nor are aware of what you are doing here. You suffer from—more accurately, you are—an elemental "attention deficit disorder." What can you do? With every transition from word to word, character to character, across unevenly distributed spaces and punctuation marks, you will have changed. It could very well be that this is your way of accompanying these twists and turns of the world (and of typography). All the same, in shadowing so doggedly what is transformed, you lose the plot, both literally and figuratively. You are totally detached through your close attachment and drown (sometimes!) in the blooming buzzing confusion of reality, then resurface (sometimes!) only to drown again. I would have said goodbye had I been minimally convinced that you and I have ever met or that I and you have ever separated. In lieu of this—and in lieu of the note that I am about to burn—I send you a blank sheet of paper. Do with it whatever you wish to do. Be with it whoever you want to be. You, Proteus: a nonreader and a reader.*

it is the sometimes that is so malleable as to allow vertiginous changes to take place, from a youth to a lion, from a "raging boar" to a serpent, from a bull to a stone and a tree. Without rhyme or reason, protean versatility is a conversion and a reversion, a divergence and a convergence, a *versus* and a *cum*. The actual shapes of Proteus are entirely contingent,

> ... #jesuischarlie, #iamukraine, #jesuisnigeria, #iammahsa, #iamnemtsov, #ichbinhanna, #iamtruth ...

as contingent, in fact, as the essentially occasional *interdum*. His metamorphoses are the expressions of mutability without the serial regularity (prone to disruptions, but, nonetheless, rhythmic and repeatable) of becoming, which is evident, for example, in the transformation of a caterpillar into a pupa in her cocoon and then into a butterfly, or of a bud into a flower and into a fruit. Proteus can assume any shape, because he is nothing and no one, a nothing that can be just about anything in the absence of minimal concern with the kaleidoscopically changing appearances. Sometimes, though, this nothing itself peers through from behind the masks of water and fire, of a boar and a serpent, it dons. Sometimes, *interdum*.

C-

The daughter of Erysichthon—herself nameless, anonymous, known only by her patronym—is a mythical commodity, while commodity as such has a mythical, fetishistic character. Her metamorphoses are profitable; it is possible for her father to capitalize on them. Her value is not in the doing, not in the labor she performs or *can* perform, but in her being, ceaselessly in the process of becoming.

-M-

Initially, her father sells her into slavery, but, as money changes hands, so does her form get transformed. With the divine intervention (by Neptune, the ocean god, whose shepherd was Proteus, tending flocks of sea creatures), the daughter of Erysichthon receives a new form, *formamque novat*. Money, the universal equivalent of value, facilitates the mutual conversion of exchanged items; the metamorphosis of the daughter sold by her father into slavery converts her captivity into freedom, her female body into that of a young man.

-C′

The moment of liberation, anchored in the universal equivalent, is domesticated, reappropriated by the father, whose name does not depart from, whose name never really parts with, the otherwise unnamed daughter throughout all of her departures. Nor is her human form lost forever: "then her former shape was given back to her," *illi sua reddita forma est.* Coming back to herself, she returns to him, with the surplus of potential future exchanges. Her *sometimes* or her *now, nunc,* is not accidental—"now she is in the form of a mare, now bird, now cow, now deer . . ." Or, better, it *is* accidental, but the contingency of the punctual forms it signals serves an ironclad logic, which is foreign to these forms: C—M—C.′ Commodity—Money—Commodity′ (returning with a surplus).

There is no *sometimes* for him. He is starved all the time, even when apparently full. Erysichthon, the "earth-tearer," is the rift, expanding into an abyss. Full of emptiness,

ever since "in his hollow veins she [Famine] planted hunger." Famine inhabited him; she became him by lodging herself in the living tunnels that are his veins, through which she moved, by means of which she permeated him. Unsatisfied and unsatisfiable consumer and investor desires, the driving forces of capitalism, are concentrated in Erysichthon, the earth-tearer. Nothing is ever *enough, sufficit,* for him. "What would be enough for whole cities, enough for a whole nation, is not enough for one" (*non sufficit uni*). Coming from the outside, famine strikes the poorest, those impoverished due to the accumulation of wealth by this one, because the one cannot have his fill, because famine is lodged in him. "In the midst of feasts, he craves other feasts," at the same time that the multitudes go without (and they go without *as a result of* his insatiable craving). His offspring is the overflow of the emptiness that fills him—

or, at least, that's how he sees *her*. Erysichthon needs his daughter for nothing other than the surplus she brings as she returns to him after every sale, the surplus that he immediately throws into the vacuum, making his hollow veins swell further and rendering him more dissatisfied. Where Erysichthon was,

there an abyssal stomach shall be. He has been converted into an interiority without bottom and devoid of sides, an interiority without interiority, uncontainable and unrecognizable as a container. Nonetheless, he swallows the world all the faster than any receptacle or repository ever could and that digests it into

Nothing = a machine for unmaking the world (and for self-unmaking).

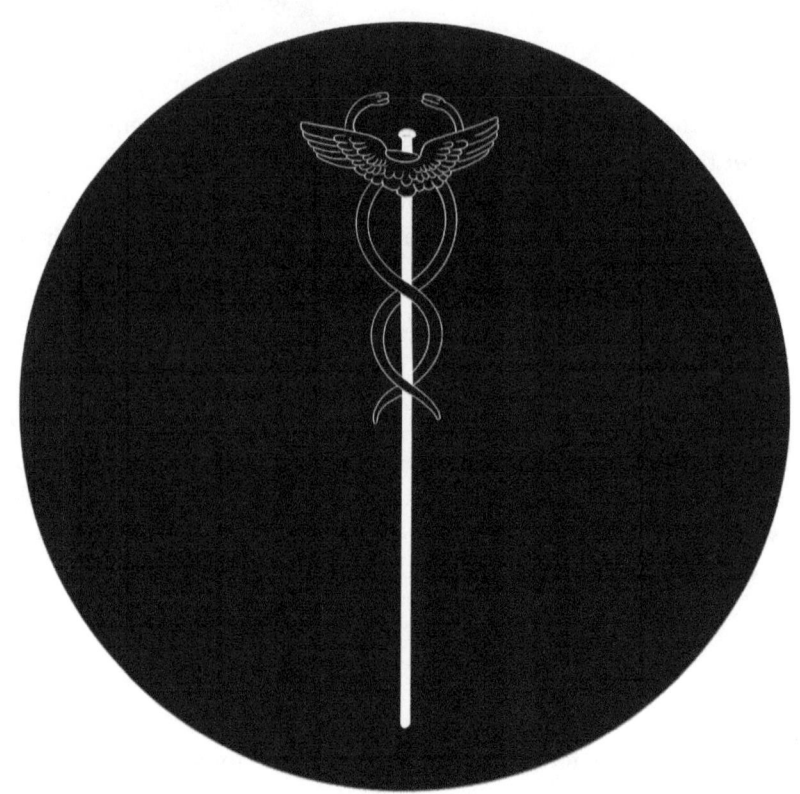

PHALLIC METAMORPHOSES
(Liber IX, 1-97)

It commences at the end, with the sign of castration, the end tattooed from the very beginning on a confrontational and destructive phallus. The mutilated river god, the same one who raped and accosted Perimele, bears a scar on his *frontis*—forehead, brow, countenance, but also frontal part, that which expresses shame. The scar is where he had a powerful horn, *cornu*, after turning into a bull. In a final sign of defeat, the horn was broken off, "filled with fruits and fragrant flowers"—the vestiges of the plants' castration—and handed over to the goddess of Good Abundance, becoming *Bona Copia cornu*, or, in a word, cornucopia.

(Another version of the emergence of cornucopia, or the horn of plenty, was current in ancient Greece. There, it was called "Amalthea's horn," belonging to the she-goat who suckled Zeus in his infancy when he was hidden from the murderous reach of his father, Cronos. In mysterious circumstances, it broke off from her body and, blessed by the god whom she suckled, spewed out vegetal plenitude.)

A scarred river god, then—a castrated and disempowered god—ensures the ongoing flow of cornucopia. Achelous dammed. This is the end that, through the limitation of a wild and uncontrollable desire, allows for the outpouring of an unending beginning.

Fast backward. Before he was mutilated as a bull, the river god assumed the form of a "lying" snake and, still before that, of a cliff. Throughout his phallic metamorphoses, Achelous changes in order to stay the same. His activity in a homoerotic battle against Hercules is a signature trait of metaphysics: changing without changing, letting go of oneself while staying put in, behind, below, or above oneself. (The evergreen, forever virginal branch is also phallic, despite being associated with women: Daphne, Mary . . .).

—As a snake, the river god winds himself around his opponent in "twisting coils," nearly merging with the enemy, whom he tries to penetrate with his forked tongue.

—As a cliff, he adopts an oppositional, erect posture: "just like a cliff I stood, which, though the roaring waves dash against it, stands secure, safe in its own bulk." His opposition is even opposed to himself, to the waters that comprise him.

Enveloping *and* confronting, penetration from within *and* exhibitionistic display from without—both are the techniques of phallic metamorphoses. Around and in, with and against the other, he asserts his identity at the expense of the other. The life-and-death struggle for recognition is a cockfight, a dialectic of two phallic avatars at each other's throats.

Until, that is, castration inescapably befalls him: *rigidum fera dextera cornu dum tenet, infregit, truncaque a fronte revellit*, "holding my hard horn in his pitiless right hand, he broke it off and tore it from my forehead, mutilating me." The wound and phallic remains then serve as a fount of another becoming, of a nonphallic torrent of plant life. Beyond the life-and-death struggle with its complexes and castration anxiety, beyond oppositional rigidity and fixation on the linchpin of identity, lies a different existence, generous and generative. Beginning at the end of phallic metamorphoses spurs a new *incipit*.

FLOODING:
REFLECTIONS FROM THE EVENT
(Liber IX, 98-133)

You think that the disaster strikes very far, thousands of miles away from where you are. For instance, in Pakistan, where between mid-June and October 2022 unprecedented floods killed thousands of people, devastated agricultural fields, and left more than two million homeless. Then, after a period of intense drought, which had baked and hardened the soil, causing it to be less permeable to rainwater, you wake up one rain-soaked morning to see cars floating in the street beneath your windows. "The stream was higher than its wont, swollen with winter rain, and quite impassable" (*inpervius*). This stream was once a street, with the adjacent streets for its tributaries. From *street* to *stream*, only a few letters change. Torrents of cars or of water, of words or emotions: does it matter what the stre/et/am channels or traffics in? Apparently, it does: depending on what flows through it, you may or may not get out of your apartment, setting foot on the ground. You prefer to see cars driving by, each in its lane, instead of fluctuating and being carried haphazardly by the flood surge. But their ceaseless, well-regulated, rule-bound movements, along with those of airplanes and cruise ships, will only make the drastic alternation of droughts and floods more frequent. The tides of helplessness and uncertainty are as overwhelming as a strong current of water. Words pour out of you in response to—as an echo of—the massive precipitation unleashed all of a sudden: too much where just now there has been too little. And if you find yourself in their midst, what do you do then? Do you let yourself be carried away, or do you jump in yelling, "Since I have undertaken it, these waters shall be overcome (*superentur flumina*)"? Or do you drive, at maximum speed, into a street-stream, which after a short while will lift your vehicle up on its undulating surface? Impervious: the drought-hardened soil and you. You "do not seek out where the stream is easiest, and scorn to take advantage of smoother waters." You hunger for a confrontation, a war—not a world war (though that, too: a war inundating the world with blood, sweat, and tears) but a war with the world, with the water and the earth, with mountains and rivers, with plants, animals, and other human beings. With yourself. Speeding headfirst toward a global environmental catastrophe, in lieu of reorganizing energy production and consumption. There is you, and then there are the anonymous flood victims in Pakistan to Portugal, from South Africa to Southern California. The woman from a basement apartment in a building from the nearby street, who drowned at home, unable to leave after floodwaters rose to the ceiling. You drive or dive into the mess; others get caught up in it. Are you thinking? Do you think at all?

CLOTHES-SKIN, SKIN-CLOTHES: HERCULES
(Liber IX, 134-272)

Like color, clothes are pure appearances and, as such, apparently superficial and superfluous, discardable without affecting their wearer. And what if the soul were to wear the body by analogy with how the body wears its garments? From East to West, this was a unique way of articulating the body and the soul, be it in *Bhagavad Gita*—where *atman*, the world spirit, is identified as the wearer of bodies ranging from a fly to a blade of grass and from a human to a tiger—or in the writings of Hildegard of Bingen, who deemed the body the dress of the soul. The implications are unequivocal: worn-out bodies may be thrown away by the soul, which will merely put new ones on.

Skin is where the clothes touch the body, a zone of contact that complicates the distinction between the wearer and the worn, including, on the metaphysical plane, the soul and ensouled matter. Soaked with sweat or blood or any other liquid, clothes stick; they cling to and nearly merge with skin. Hercules learned this the hard way when he put on a "deadly tunic" (*vestem*), which had imbibed the blood of Nessus and the Lernaean hydra's poison. Afflicted by the mortiferous heat of the venom, Hercules "tries to tear off the deadly tunic; but where it is torn away, it tears the skin with it, and, ghastly to relate, it either sticks to his limbs, from which he vainly tries to tear it, or else lays bare his torn muscles and huge bones." Does disposing of the body have a similar effect on the soul wearing it?

Clothes are our second skin, and skin is the sheath of the body, a living fabric or a leaf, in which viscera and limbs are wrapped. Breathing and breathable, the skin and clothes inhale and exhale each other: their respiration is an interbreath. Undressing is skinning, or deskinning, oneself (as Marsyas has taught us in his grammar lesson). Enveloping and touching our cutaneous surfaces, garments activate tactile sense that is dispersed throughout the body, rather than concentrated in the hand. Clothes both conceal the skin they overlay and reveal the outlines of the body, which they also augment and curb: augment in some parts and curb in others. The soul and the body are articulated as an interbreath, as a concealing revelation, a dispersed touching and being touched, a self-touching or a being-in-touch-with-oneself throughout one's living extension.

In the meantime, Hercules is still thrashing about, "roaring in agony, struggling to tear off his garments, uprooting great trunks of trees, stretching out his arms to his native skies." He struggles, above all, to keep a strict separation alive, to secure the independence of skin from clothes, of nature from cultural artifacts, of the body from the soul. He'd rather die than accept their cross-contamination: *Mors mihi munus erit!* "Death will be a boon to me!"—he groans. More than a boon, death is the logical outcome of enforcing inflexible boundaries between the two domains. And yet it is an outcome that is not total, one that, thanks to this very separation, saves something from death. What he received from his mortal mother (Alcmene, matter) is bound to perish, but the part of Hercules handed down to him from his father (Jove, spirit) is "immune to death," *immune necis*. His entire body can be shed both as a piece of clothing and as skin, more precisely, as snake skin: "as a serpent, its old age sloughed off with its old skin, revels in fresh life," so Hercules after his physical death "gained new vigor in his better part."

Dry skin peels off and flakes away, revealing a rejuvenated layer underneath. A body after the body, a body buried underneath, deep within the body, ever ready to emerge to the daylight either as viscera and "torn muscles" or as another skin, as a cadaver in the making or a snakelike phoenix. The body is dropped and it is not dropped, immediately replaced by its double. Dispensable and indispensable. It even grows stronger, better, more vigorous and fresher after its fall.

To treat clothes as our second skin may not transform the former into the latter; vice versa, skin may be the expendable garment of the body, which, in its turn, may reveal itself as the inessential and replaceable apparel of the soul. *May* be, *may* reveal. Nothing is fixed and certain here, in the interspace of interbreath, of the respiratory rhythms and cycles of skin and second skin, of our cutaneous surfaces and clothes.

BECOMING ATMOSPHERIC: LICHAS

(Liber IX, 211-229)

Look at what is going on outside your window. Is it raining or snowing? Is the sun shining bright or are broken clouds hurrying somewhere across a windy sky? Does fog or smog fill the air? You can deliver yourself wholeheartedly to the atmospheric conditions, experiencing the soft melancholy of rain or the searing joy of intense sunshine. Going outside and merging with the weather: damp outside and inside or dry and warm within and without. You can also stay indoors and resist, creating a micro-counter-atmosphere with candlelight to dispel autumnal and wintery gloom or with room-darkening shades drawn to filter out the all-penetrating sun and to give in to the intimacy of obscurity. Irrespective of what you do, you are becoming atmospheric each day, each hour of the day or the night, and all other processes and events of becoming are swathed in this one.

BECOMING ATMOSPHERIC: LICHAS

Lichas, the servant of Hercules, was in the wrong place at the wrong time. In agony, his master stumbled upon him and blamed the youth for the murder plot. The enraged Hercules hoisted Lichas and flung him far across the Aegean sky. We will suspend the instant of his landing and join Lichas midflight, where he suddenly starts hovering, "hanging in the air," *pendens auras*. His body, violently thrust into the atmosphere, becomes an atmospheric phenomenon. Lichas hangs in the air like a dense cloud. Fear freezes him. The precipitation he has metamorphosed into keeps changing: "as drops of rain are said to congeal under the chilling blast and change to snow, then whirling snowflakes condense to a soft mass and finally are packed in frozen hail."

How could Lichas, stiffened, land in the sea as a rock that still bears "traces of the human form," *humanae vestigia formae*, after the metamorphoses he underwent in the air, as air and water? The gaseousness, fluidity, and frigidness of his transformations imply that he precipitated down to the earth and into the Aegean in the shape of rain, snow, and hail. His fall was also his rising, the eventual evaporation and condensation into clouds. Becoming atmospheric is becoming circular—in time, not in space. It is circulating as part of the hydrologic cycle in the earth-atmosphere system.

Our becoming atmospheric is equally circular. A melancholy dampness descends, nourishing the mind's growth and flourishing in combination with sunny joy. Heavy as it may be, a chilly cloud of depression lifts, driven away by the changing winds of psychic life. The weather inside and outside is not a constant, shifting in tandem or in countercyclical patterns. When the circulatory movement is disrupted, problems ensue. Depression lingers on and on . . . A rapid vacillation between maniac and depressive extremes leaves no room for life and growth and decay . . . Psychological droughts and flash floods . . . Becoming atmospheric is not clinging to the same state forever, whether it is the eternal sunshine or the interminable snowstorm. It is becoming dispersed *and* gyrating in a circle at the psycho-elemental junction of air, water, solar heat, and the earth.

NOTES ON POSITION: ALCMENE
(Liber IX, 273-323)

Various positions facilitate or block passages: of energy, of oneself or the other, of the other through oneself. Alcmene's long and painful labor, a week of torture when she was unable to deliver Hercules (who will go on to perform his own feats and labors), was due to a divinely blocked passage, due to the position Juno assumed upon the altar: "there she sat [*subsedit*] ... with her right knee crossed over the left, and with her fingers interlocked."

Spatial positions and their changes do not obey the algebraic law of indifference: changing the order of the summands *does* change the value of the sum.

NOTES ON POSITION: ALCMENE

Position of one narrative element relative to another matters: Ovid narrates the birth of Hercules after recounting the story of his death.

Position as a mode and expression of being, irreducible to an aleatory form of occupying space.

The seated position is the default position, the positing of position, the setting of and in position.

Seated, one is folded; one is a fold: vertical and horizontal; between verticality and horizontality.

A standing position is a definitive vertical deviation from the seated one. A lying position is a definitive horizontal deviation from the seated one.

Positions are inherently, if largely unconsciously, sexual. The phallic nature of the vertical position; the invaginations of horizontality. Moral judgments and worth grounded on sexualized physical positions: uprightness vs. inclinations.

Subsidere: to sit *down* and to set down; to crouch, to squat, but also to run aground. The body's extensive movement in space is paused; its intensive movements are also stilled.

As a posture, position is already the possibility of imposture, of impersonation, of mimicking the being of the other, without nonetheless abandoning one's own.

Posture is more than posture: *asana*. Yogic yoking of the body and the mind via positionality.

Change of positions: transitions between them: the reordering of limbs, trunk, head relative to one another, to the ground and the sky, to one's surroundings. A rearrangement of the modes and expressions of being: positional metamorphoses.

The goddess changes her position abruptly, in surprise: "she leapt," *exsiluit*. Abandoning the seated position verges on the abandonment of position as a positing. A coming-out par excellence: *ex-*. A positional ex-position, exposure in the undoing of the seated fold of the body.

The goddess has been cheated when she was told that *levata est Alcmene*—"Alcmene is relieved"—that he child has been born. Spatial and temporal positions are disrupted together: Juno leaps up, "unclenching her hands and spreading them wide in consternation." As a result, Alcmene delivers her child: she is relieved after she is said to have been relieved: what is announced as having happened before, happens after *thanks to this very announcement*. The imposture alters the goddess's posture, which, in turn, loosens the posture of Alcmene and allows the child-other to pass through and out of her.

A clenched, blocked, rigid position is invariably an opposition—to the other and to becoming-other. Sitting or lying down: entrusting one's body to an underlying support, either partially or fully. Standing erect is the most confrontational as well as the least secure position: balancing on one's feet that balance on the ground.

Different paces, tempos, styles of thinking while sitting or lying down, standing or running.

Our positions change more often than we notice. The uncomfortable bit is maintaining the same position for long periods of time, without the fluidity of subtle recalibrations. Being forced to stay in the same position for hours or days on end is an act of torture. The goddess tortures herself in order to torment Alcmene.

Metamorphoses and/as the metapositionalities of substance?

DRYOPE: BECOMING A CUT (PLANT)
(Liber IX, 324-393)

How to read a text at the joints where

        it is cut (and sewn back again—or not)? How to listen to speech from

out of the silences, punctuating it? Without cutting to the chase,

    ever.

The story
    begins with a cut, a near

choking on "tears and pain" that "prevent the speech" of the

sister-narrator. And it ends
        there, too. As

Dryope becomes

a lotus tree (either persimmon, *Diospyros lotus*, or jujube, *Ziziphus lotus*), and bark, creeping up, covers her lips, "in the same moment, she ceased to speak and ceased to be" (*desierant simul ora loqui, simul esse*).

DRYOPE: BECOMING A CUT (PLANT)

The story, then,

is framed between two cuts, the second of which puts, in one fell swoop, an end

        to two things: speaking and being.

But

is becoming a plant ceasing to be? Or even ceasing to speak, by means other than the voice?

As is often the case

   in such instances,

repeated claims of innocence are made in connection to

culled flowers,

flowers removed from the source of their vitality.
Here are the lotus flowers, or water lilies (*aquatica lotos*),

into which—unbeknownst to Dryope—

        the nymph Lotis morphed as she was pursued by Priapus, and which,

in an unmarked, unproblematized textual passage,

morph into a lotus tree (*arbore*).

So, she plucks them with utter innocence and claims
               to suffer in innocence as well and to have lived innocently: *patior sine crimine poenam. viximus innocuae.*

        The flowers she culls attest to the contrary, bleeding at that spot on the stalk where they have been
cut,

DRYOPE: BECOMING A CUT (PLANT)

the "branches trembling in horror," *tremulo ramos horrore moveri*.

And Dryope herself tacitly admits her guilt, when in her last human will and testament she
bids her infant son to "pluck no blossoms from the trees, and think all flowers are goddesses in disguise."

Her metamorphosis restitutes the damage she has inflicted: she becomes the same kind of plant as

the one she mutilated.

What would it mean to become not a replacement, not a surrogate, for
innocently destroyed flowers,
(thus, transubstantiating into the body of her victim, who herself had been previously victimized by Priapus, finding refuge from him in the shape of a lotus)
but to become the cut
itself? Is that the sense of the cessation of her being, *esse*, along with her speech, *loqui*? Did Dryope, the daughter of Dryops (from *drys*, oak),
change from
the cutting to
the
cut
when she became another species of a tree
different from her father
and another kind of being?

Was her metamorphosis not limited to a difference in kind? Did it touch her

being and nonbeing
as a whole because, and to the extent that,
she became not just a lotus tree but also nothing,

the nothing that makes distinctions among beings and even between nonbeing and being possible?

DRYOPE: BECOMING A CUT (PLANT)

Far from preventing her operations of cutting and plucking, Dryope's transformation renders these acts self-directed: "she strove

to tear her hair with her hands, but only filled
her hands with leaves [*fronde manum implevit*]; for
leaves now

covered all her head."

A speculative cut: reflected

into itself.

BECOMING YOUNG (AGAIN), GROWING OLDER: IOLAUS AND THE SONS OF CALLIRRHOE
(Liber IX, 394–438)

It's New Year's Day. Henceforth, with each day that passes, the year is getting ever newer, fresher ever. Provided that you feel the wonder of encountering the world each time anew, a New*er* Year or a New*er* Year's Day awaits.

Youth regained: reversed ageing. Mind you, we are not dealing with what is usually called "a person young at heart," but with rejuvenation in the rest of the flesh, not with a subjective attitude but with the de-aging of the body.

BECOMING YOUNG (AGAIN), GROWING OLDER

Iolaus—the nephew, assistant, best friend, and lover of Hercules—is "restored in features to his youthful prime." *Reformatus primos Iolaus in annos*. At the threshold he is. *Nam limine*. The threshold that is a doorway and a liminal spacetime between death and a life (revived), between old age and youth. There he will have been, at the threshold, with his boyish luster recovered, "almost a boy, with delicate down covering his cheeks."

The end (of the world, above all) was at the beginning, much like this very sentence began with the end, at the end.

Entropy is not destiny; fate is not entropic. There is no arrow of time flying unidirectionally from the past to the future; time is a branching, twisting and turning multiplicity, its parts bouncing back, others lost forever. Remembered or dismembered, reformatted or deformed—all at once.

—Is this an exception? The miracle of Iolaus, that is.
—quite. Not // Notquite.

When Juno's daughter "was on the point of swearing that on no one after Iolaus would she bestow such gifts, Themis checked her vow." The sons of Callirrhoe, whose father was killed when they were still infants, will mature in a jiffy, changing from "beardless boys to men."

Everything accelerates instead of being reversed: where there was no beard, dense hair appears on the faces of Amphoterus and Acarnan, the sons of Callirrhoe. It is the opposite of Iolaus, whose elderly features and beard melt into a "delicate down covering his cheeks." No delays, no tarrying with, no spaces or spacingsremaintherewheretimeisputonafastforward...

Becoming young again and growing old faster are opposite tendencies, but their inversions are the inversions of time; together, they *are* time itself. Problematic and gendered as it is, the beard (or the absence thereof) is a measure of time common to both, a quasi-vegetal measure one could say, since growing hair like plants indicates something of the passage of time via spatial extension. The branching multiplicity of twists and turns encompasses acceleration and retrogression, backward and forward leaps, the forwardness of backpaddling and the backwardness of the forward-going.

Time swirls between the two exceptions (to the general rule, the law dictated by fate, and to each other). It churns between Iolaus and the sons of Callirrhoe and presses further on, beyond the rejuvenation of the former and the hastened adulthood of the latter. After becoming young again—contraction to the fetus and the zygote. After fast maturation—a quick onset of old age and death. The cutoff points of time are arbitrary tokens, more like bookmarks than bookends. Adulthood and old age, boyhood and youth, birth and death are thresholds always already crossed in every direction and still lying ahead. Being in time is being at the threshold, *nam limine*.

BYBLIS:
THE EXTERNALIZATION OF DESIRE
(Liber IX, 439–665)

Dream, confess (to yourself), analyze, write (to yourself and to others), dream... Give or take, this has been the rhythm of my work: my dreamwork and thoughtwork, thoughtwork as dreamwork. Or soulwork. Which is not so different from dreamplay and thoughtplay. It is necessary to know how to make transitions from the inner to the outer and back, despite the ostensible automatism of the endeavor. A tried-and-tested method, supported by a technical know-how, is unavailable. We are prompted to discover the wheel with each self-externalization and internalization, because the curvature of the path is never the same.

Dream. In love with her twin brother, Byblis carries her secret desire deep within. She dreams of being in her brother's amorous embrace and, presaging Freud, realizes that dream images are the alternative fulfillments of forbidden wishes, upon which one cannot act in reality. "A dream lacks a witness but doesn't lack a substitute joy." *Testis abest somno, nec abest imitata voluptas.* Which psychoanalyst could formulate this better than Byblis? Immersion in psychic interiority is lacking a witness, aside from yourself as your own witness. Without a witness, there is no trial and, hence, no judgment: an accusation, should one arise, is nonactionable.

—I cannot tell you about my dreams. Not a single one of them. True: I have not seen vivid dreams of late, or if I have, they have swept through me without leaving conscious traces behind. But that is not the reason, which prevents me from telling you about them. I could do so only by committing dreams to writing, and so running ahead of myself, beginning at the end (which is what we inevitably do, whatever it is that we do). I have already noted that there is no universal method for the externalization of desire; now, I must add that there is no immediate access to it on the inside.

Confess. Even if it is addressed to oneself alone, confession adds a witness to the dream and to the desire it expresses. And, with the witness, come trial and judgment. "Oh, wretched girl that I am! *Me miseram!* . . . Oh, but I would not have it so!" To confess is to deliver the verdict *Guilty!*, to serve as a lawyer and a prosecutor, a judge, a jury, a witness, and an executioner for yourself.

—The genre of philosophical confessions (I nearly wrote "concessions"— and that is, maybe, what confessions are, namely the concessions of one's psychic interiors to the other) is well defined. From Saint Augustine via Jean-Jacques Rousseau to Jacques Derrida with his "Circumfession," philosophers in the predominantly male tradition have revealed their desires and, more or less exhibitionistically, their circumcised or uncircumcised but otherwise deformed penises. I intend to do no such thing, though I will confess—with the entire judicial lineup of witnesses, judges, prosecutors, jury, and court clerks present, if only within me—to a desire for writing. Rather than a graphomaniac obsession, it is indeed a love, voluptuous and committed, the love of a written word, sometimes of a single letter. In the summer of 1981, I was one year old. According to a story told by my mother, while on a streetcar in Moscow, I saw a sign, *"Moloko"* (milk), on a grocery store. Pointing to the sign, I said out loud, to the surprise of other passengers: "That's letter M." Did I recognize myself in this letter as a stand-in for all the others? Is a love of writing, of letters and of a letter, narcissistic? Do I keep recognizing myself in the letter otherwise? *Meta-Morphoses*, M.M. *Me miseram.*

Analyze. Byblis is an open book, a bible for analyses concerned with the interrelation of writing and desire, and a Babel, as well, where confusion

BYBLIS: THE EXTERNALIZATION OF DESIRE

and uncertainty rule the day. Ebullient desire, harbored in psychic interiority and not curtailed by usual restrictions, is free, as much as it is ephemeral: light and lite. Analyzing more the form than the content of dreams, Byblis asks ponderously: "What then do my dreams mean to me? What weight have dreams? Or have dreams really weight?" (*Quod autem somnia pondus habent? An habent et somnia pondus?*) The weight of dreams—to be thought. And the weight of thought itself and of writing to boot. Not of the supports for writing, such as a page or waxen tablets that will still make their appearance on the analytical stage, but of writing as writing. It's a lose-lose situation. If dreams have no weight, then they are innocuous but unsatisfactory, their substitute joy a mere shadow of joy. If dreams do have weight, then they offer meaningful satisfaction but make the dreamer culpable, weighing on her conscience. The same holds for writing.

—It will be argued that my desire for writing, probably in part inherited from Judaism (sublimated and secularized as that influence might be), is another substitute for "real desire," carnal and voluptuous. Writing as a medium and an object is no different from a dream, you will say. Derrida of all people would also join this camp, despite situating the supplement/substitute at the origin. But writing has a body in the world; it is the body of the world. The desire for writing is, therefore, in a short circuit of the Platonic ladder of love, a desire of and for the world's body.

Write. Byblis is writing: expressing, exteriorizing her desire, pouring it into the scribbles on waxen tablets and, in the same stroke of the hand, erasing what she wrote: she "writes on and hates what she has written; writes and erases [*et notat et delet*]; changes, condemns, approves." Her biography is a bigraphy, a writing of life as the writing of life *and* death, or an inscription and its erasure. Byblis lets metamorphoses metamorphose: she guides the inner into the outer, the outer into the erasure of the outer, into its own mutations, changes, condemned approvals and approved condemnations. She writes and writes and writes and deletes and rewrites until she runs out of space: "The tablet was full when she had traced these words doomed to disappointment, the last line coming to the very edge" (*summusque in margine versus adhaesit*). She would have kept writing—as I am doing now, nowhere close to the digital edge and always balancing on that edge—were the tablet not filled with her tracings. There is never enough space and time to go on writing, expressing fully and faithfully, pressing out interiority into the exterior ("texterior," I have penciled in a hurry, in what may prove a useful shorthand for the age of texting: these quickly multiplying slips of the pen keep coming back to Freud) to the last drop, the final morsel. Nonetheless, she will have kept writing. Writing is already a stream, into which her endless tears convert her: writing with water on water, with the flowing tears that alter the landscape, inscribing a meandering riverbed on the waxen tablet of the earth. Byblis's writing before (earth) writing was "doomed to disappointment," because the interiority pressed out is never faithfully expressed and never received as intended. *Nec me committere cerae debueram, praesensque meos aperire furores*, she chides herself. "I should not have committed myself to wax and thrown open my current frenzy!" Writing: desire disclosed, *reserata est nostra voluntas*. Still, desire is disclosed as what it is not, taken up and mis-taken by writing and its substrata, further mistaken by readers, and hardly recognized by the writer herself. Betrayed. You are tempted to give up on it—on writing and the desire that it is (more than the one it expresses)—but you do the opposite, writing obsessively beyond the margin, after the end, when the tablet is full: writing with tears, with their salty and transparent ink, the inner moisture that flows out of you.

—I have just written on Byblis and also (as I have done throughout these scattered texts) to, for, and with Byblis; to, for, and with Ovid; to, for, and with you. Morsels of us all are taken up, mistaken, conflated in these letters. What is the internal and what is the external? Who expresses whom or what? Where is the outer side unfolding the inner and where is the inner recoil as of yet untouched by and uncommitted to writing?

Dream 2.0. Dr/tr/str: too rough to keep fast to fluidity, and yet dreamwork and dreamplay are at work and in play even here. Dreaming, streaming, live-streaming, dead-streaming, live-dreaming, live-dead-dreaming ... As a stream made of unending tears that bemoan her impossible, tabooed desire, Byblis is still writing and she is still dreaming. Of what? (A) Of the source, the trauma of an unhealing psychic wound that gives rise to her metamorphosis. The source of the stream-dream is traumatic. (B) Of all the places she is flowing toward, destining herself to them, while lying prone on the ground with her face down, buried in the fallen leaves, her hair cascading on the hill. Prostrate and flowing, buried in the earth and percolating elsewhere: movement and rest intersect in Byblis's psychophysical existence as a stream. Dream 2.0 (a dream of flowing water and supportive earth dancing the longest tango there is) is registered after she abandons human incarnation. Though untranslatable into images or any other visual representation, it preserves the memory of past trauma. And in the human dream 1.0, a vague memory of the utterly inexpressible dream 0.0 hides behind the curtain of the image, the symbol, moving pictures and static appearances.

THE TRANS/FORMATIONS OF IPHIS
(Liber IX, 666-797)

Iphis,

Your story is too complicated and controversial. Few will appreciate its nuance in our politically correct age. The details of your trans/formation will cause consternation on the two sides of the Great Ideological Divide: those who insist that the transition from *cis* to *trans* identities is unnatural will reject your narrative as a piece of ancient propaganda; those who embrace the metamorphoses of sex under the heading of *trans* will be up in arms, because your transition happened for all the "wrong" reasons. What a scandal! But now, with reasons for the trans-journey (not least, the very necessity or superfluity of giving reasons), we are getting to the heart (or to another, more relevant organ) of the matter.

THE TRANS/FORMATIONS OF IPHIS

This story of yours started before you yourself started, before you were born. Enough said! Triumphant or indignant, representatives of both camps will not listen to its further unfolding. They will instead jump to the same conclusion: it's all about a genetic predisposition, an inborn tendency that had made you who you've become. You and I know that they will have been wrong, that it was the word of your father that put in motion the chain of events culminating in your *trans* identity. The word of the father and the law of the father, a sovereign dictate dispensing a death sentence to you still before your birth: "if by chance your child should prove to be a girl, let her be put to death."

Your trans/formation began then, with the death sentence pronounced by your father. As a female, you had to die—and die as a she you did in your gradual rebirth into a male. The name, in which your mother rejoiced, helped because it was suitable to boys as much as to girls, common (*commune*) to both. Then followed a transvestite phase, your mother dressing you in boy's clothes in order to keep you safe, to protect you from the merciless law of the father. If the father cruelly potentiated your trans/formation, the mother lovingly actualized it. No one asked you if you wanted this fate for yourself; it was handed over to you from your parents along with, or alongside, the fact of your birth.

But that is only half the story that will surely aggravate ideologues on both sides of the barricades. The other half has to do with what you have done (said, felt) afterward. Identifying as a male in a female body, you fell in love with a woman, interpreting this event as non- or even antinatural, "a strange and monstrous love." Do you remember what you exclaimed then? "Cows do not love cows, nor mares, mares; but the ram desires the sheep, and his own doe follows the stag. So also birds mate, and in the whole animal world there is no female smitten with love for female." That is when you wished really to transition to a male—confirming your father's desire and your mother's actions—or, more accurately, wanted to be female no longer.

Your definitive trans/formation, Iphis (your name betokening indeterminacy, the vacillation you so passionately rejected), was meant to renaturalize your love, at least according to the way you saw what was natural and what was not. For you, to become a *trans* man was a means to setting things right, to doing away with the exception to the order of nature you considered yourself to be, to falling in line with a ram desiring the sheep or a stag attracted to a doe. Your trans/formation was, thus, rooted in a doubly conservative structure: first your mother's efforts to conserve your very being, to keep you alive notwithstanding the law of the father, and second your own framing of the lesbian love you experienced as "unnatural." But through it all you blamed nature for the presumably unnatural predicament you found yourself in (it is "nature, mightier than they all, who alone is working my distress [*natura, potentior omnibus istis, quae mihi sola nocet*]").

Why am I reminding you of this? I am sure you'd rather forget your own prehistory. Please, take these lines not as the sharp arrows of accusation but as acupuncture needles, placed strategically on a psychobody so as to liberate the energy of thinking, to let it circulate beyond the Great Ideological Divide and the rules of political correctness. I want you to understand that there is such a thing as conservative change, a counterrevolutionary metamorphosis, a trans/formation aiming to merge with the status quo and, therefore, with a static order of things. Miraculously, you did become male, Iphis. You kept your name, however, the name that holds the promise of a much more indeterminate existence.

Your well-wisher

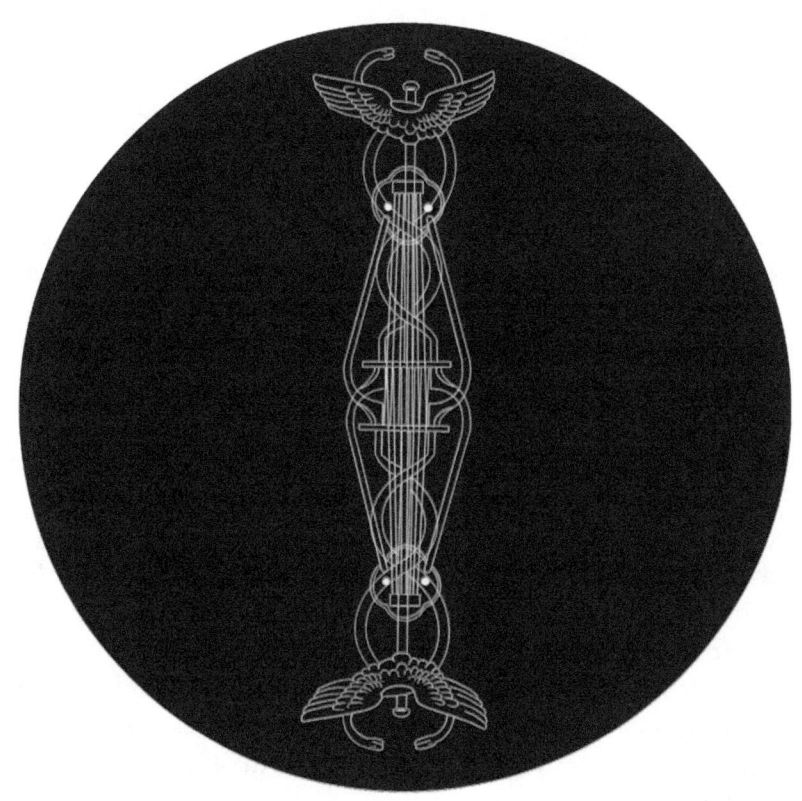

DON'T LOOK BACK: ORPHEUS AND EURYDICE

(Liber X, 1-85)

A silhouette is gradually emerging from thick shadows. The surrounding gloom is not at all uniform. The feeling one gets is that the figure is walking among ink blots—some of them greyish, others pitch-dark. A slightly better-defined blot among blots. It is a reader, climbing up from the catacombs of the text with the meaning that was procured there following closely behind. The reader can keep meaning alive, he can save her on one condition: not looking back. *Ne flectat retro sua lumina*—"do not turn your lights back"—the lights of your eyes and your understanding that will display the one you are leading in your own phosphorescent glow. One phrase alone is bouncing about in the reader's mind, a mantra that, so long as it is repeated, prevents him from doing what it prohibits. While rather brief, it may be unpacked to reveal its sense.

—*Don't look back, don't look back; if you do, you will lose her and you will lose yourself. Your precious company will evaporate or, on the contrary, turn into stone. That's the subject-object rule, which applies in Athens and Rome as much as in Jerusalem to Lot's wife, to Orpheus and Eurydice. Objectify, and what you are gazing at will grow stiff, along with the gaze itself and the gazer. Subjectify, and your companion will vaporize, together with you. Don't look back*; ne flectat retro sua lumina!

How can warnings and wise counsels compete with the childish desire, undead even in the most mature of adults, to do what is forbidden? The exit is near: he is "nearing the margin of the upper earth." The last page is already within sight among shadow ink blots. But the meaning the reader hopes to have gleaned is not yet in hand (or in the head). As he is moving ahead with the act of reading, she is trailing behind.

His gait grows unsure. He slows down, staggering. Is there anyone at all behind? Any faint breath or noise? What if this arduous journey was for nothing? What if the reader were to emerge from the experience of reading emptyhanded and emptyheaded?

Tormented by doubt, he "turned back his longing eyes and instantly she slipped back into the depths." Meaning is encrypted, buried, entombed all the deeper, when it is the reader's object. "Dying a second death," *iterum moriens*. Death's iteration—to reiterate—impossible yet clearly signaled right there, at the margin of the earth or of the page.

Who is the reader? Orpheus? Yes, but not just him. The readers are also you and I as we are going over Ovid's work and as you are passing through mine. So this injunction is addressed to us: Don't look back, especially from the thresholds, from the margins, the exit points of a text.

Let's do just that (disobedient children that we are)—cast a glance back over the story of Orpheus and Eurydice from its last line. Here is what the poet writes about Orpheus's survival of his beloved's second death: "Still many women felt a passion for the bard; many grieved for their love repulsed. He set the example for the people of Thrace of giving his love to young men and enjoying the springtime and first flower of their youth." Stunned by grief, Orpheus repels all amorous advances of women, albeit not of young men. Overviewing the text from this vantage point, a possibility crops up that, however unconsciously, Orpheus wanted Eurydice to vanish, to melt away into the shadows again. Perhaps on the steep way up to the aboveground world he was overwhelmed with doubts in a happily-ever-after with her. Perhaps he convinced himself that by turning around he would reassure himself not so much of her presence but of his unextinguished love of her, compared to those fantasies about young men in their flowering prime that kept plaguing him throughout the journey.

Assuming this to be the case, readers unconsciously want meaning to vanish, to come back emptyhanded and emptyheaded from the experience of reading. Why? What could be driving such a futile endeavor, undermining their stated objective? Readers wish to recognize themselves in the mirror of any text they read, with the silent choir confirming what they've already known; they want rough, indigestible, surprising meaning to vanish without a trace or to congeal in a pillar of semantic salt. Readers desire to engage with other readers directly—mind to mind, skin to skin—without the mediations of the text. They would like "to pluck the first flowers" of meaning's youth, to deflower it without too much interpretation.

COMING, BECOMING—
A CYPRESS TREE
(Liber X, 86-142)

Lodged in every becoming is a coming:
A *coming to be* and a *coming not to be*.
(Note to self: don't neglect to mention a *coming to be not*—
This movement's unmoved mover!)
Both in the word and the creature it names.
Shade came to a place (*umbra loco venit*)
With the coming (*venistis*) of trees
That give shelter from a scorching sun
Under their crowns.
But the be-coming of the cypress was
The most stunning of all.
At noon, at midday,
When the shadows are the shortest (a side glance at Nietzsche)
And the arboreal effect is close to nil,
When the moment of merciless truth arrives,
A boy unwittingly kills his beloved stag.
Cyparissus weeps over the body of the dead animal,
Whose head, crowned with shade-giving antlers,
Immaterially binds the stag to the trees.
Inconsolable, Cyparissus seeks asylum in a becoming,
The coming of greenness, which
Overcomes his limbs.

COMING, BECOMING—A CYPRESS TREE

A human, becoming a plant—
Coming into planthood, coming out of humanness—
To mourn the passing of an animal dear to him.
As a cypress tree, Cyparissus will supplant the shade
Of the stag's antlers with that cast by his crown,
"Slender at the top" in memory of the animal's pointed headpiece.

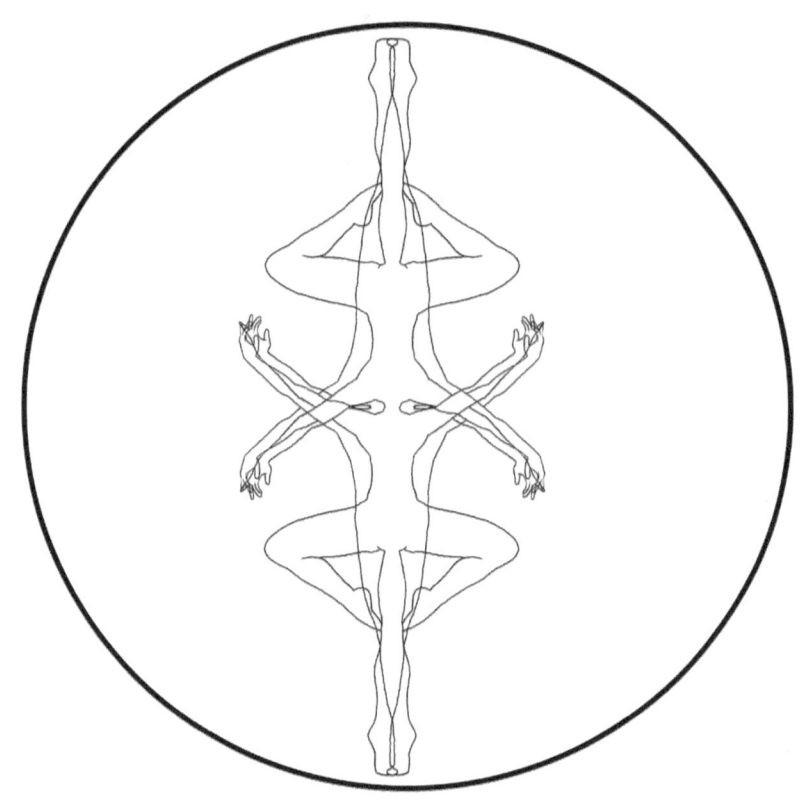

OF PLANTS AND PLANETS, OF STARS AND SEEDS: GANYMEDE AND HYACINTHUS

(Liber X, 143-219)

A pair of homoerotic tales inaugurates the song of Orpheus. Jupiter falls in love with a young man from Phrygia, Ganymede, whom the god lifts to Mount Olympus and charges with the task of being a divine sommelier. Phoebus, for his part, is passionately in love with Hyacinthus, a Spartan youth, with whom he often plays discus. One day, the discus thrown by Phoebus bounces from the earth and hits Hyacinthus, who, as he dies, is transformed into "a new flower" by the god.

Jupiter keeps Ganymede forever by his side; death takes Hyacinthus away from Phoebus, even though the fatally injured youth transitions to living as

OF PLANTS AND PLANETS, OF STARS AND SEEDS

a flower. The story of Jupiter and Ganymede also has a more recent continuation. Observing the sky on a crisp winter night of January 7, 1610, Galileo Galilei spotted a large moon of Jupiter in what turned out to be the first discovery of a moon orbiting another planet. He named Jupiter's moon Ganymede. The god and his immortalized lover became a planet and its cosmic satellite.

Plants and planets are front and center in the inaugural songs of Orpheus. And glowing hot stars, keeping in mind that Phoebus/Apollo is the god of the sun. Extravagant as this connection may seem, it is wholly justified. The time of plants relies on the cosmic time of planetary rotations, the annual cycle of the earth orbiting the sun and associated seasonal changes. Each plant strives in its aboveground portions toward a single star, the sun, in a cosmic-vegetal love that imparts energy and life, form and content alike. Besides hyacinth, each plant is Phoebus's lover.

Still, we may not be done with extravagance. Planets are celestial vagrants, eternal sky-wanderers. They roam the vast expanses of space while stars stay fixed in their spots. Incorrigibly errant, planets are extravagant stars, journeying together with their moons. Their movement and its temporal rhythms are subtly bound to those of plants, who can also become nearly immortal as perennials. *Aeternus tamen es*, "nonetheless you are eternal," Phoebus tells his vegetized lover, and the god continues: "as often as spring drives winter out and the Ram succeeds the watery Fish, so often do you come up and blossom on the green turf." Hyacinth's starlike constellations of flowers underwrite this pronouncement.

Stars are the seeds of light strewn across the nocturnal sky. Their flickering portends variably intensifying and decelerating but unextinguishable life. As a function of the elliptical orbits of planets, annual cycles offer a comparable possibility to perennials. The *semper eris mecum* ("you will always be with me"), which Phoebus utters even as Hyacinthus is undergoing his floral metamorphosis, resonates with but is not the same as the always-with-me of Jupiter and Ganymede, a planet orbited by its moon. It is a variable *always*, with planet-moon dances in space and plant-star dances in time. Always: *semper*, containing the Latin *semer*, to sow. Always: the figure of seed, as ephemeral and as tenacious as an instant.

SIN AND CRIME: VENUS AND CERASTAE
(Liber X, 220-242)

[Homosexuality is] not a crime. Yes, but it's a sin. Fine, but first let's distinguish between a sin and a crime.
—POPE FRANCIS, JANUARY 24, 2023

"Wherein have my cities sinned? What crime is there in them? *Quid urbes peccavere meae? Quid crimen in illis?*" asks Venus. Indeed, "let's distinguish between a sin and a crime." While we are at it, let's also remember that in the heat of the moment such distinctions evaporate, and the one is effectively treated as the other: sin is equated to crime. To declare any given behavior sinful is to enable its criminalization. Every city is sin city, a Sodom and Gomorrah in the making. Including the city of god—or of a goddess.

It's also a sin to lack charity with one another.
—POPE FRANCIS, JANUARY 24, 2023

Ovid: "an altar sacred to Jove, the god of hospitality . . . all smeared in blood. It was the blood of slaughtered guests!" Everyone is sinful, wounded in the core of our being, starting with the mark of the original sin incurred at birth, if not before birth. Our own blood is on the altar the moment we are conceived. Do we need to distinguish the original sin from crime? No one entertains such an idea because it is absurd. But if a kind of love, stigmatized as sinful for centuries, is burdened also with a long history of criminalization, removing the varnish codified in unjust laws does not eliminate the rotten base, on which this pope keeps insisting, despite his "progressive" views. To insist on the sinfulness of decriminalized homosexuality is to keep slaughtering guests at the altar of hospitality. Orpheus, Ovid, Francis, killing me softly with his song.

Tenderness, please, as God has for each one of us!
—POPE FRANCIS, JANUARY 24, 2023

Venus, again: "Rather let this impious race pay the penalty by exile or by death, or by some punishment midway between death and exile [*medium . . . mortisque fugaeque*]. And what other can that be than the penalty of a changed form?" The tenderness of a goddess, her light touch: demanding punishment by metamorphosis, an exile from one's previous mode of existence and a death to oneself. A "changed form" is not a blessing but a curse, above all for an adherent of static identities, outside of which one is nothing at all. Although she conflates crime and sin, her halfway (*medium*) solution boils down to leaving sin in place and striking out crime.

Every man and every woman must have a window in their lives where they can pour out their hope and where they can see the dignity of God. And being homosexual is not a crime. It is a human condition.
—POPE FRANCIS, JANUARY 24, 2023

Ovid: "While she hesitates to what she shall change them, her eyes fall upon their horns, and she reminds herself that these can still be left to them. And so, she changes their big bodies into savage bulls." A sin, not a crime, is a human condition. There is no way to be human without being sinful. Yet the sins of humanity are expiated by Christ, which amounts to saying that the being-human of the human is eliminated by him. Becoming other-than-human is overcoming the constitutive sinfulness of humanity, *and* it is a punishment situated "midway" between death and exile. The posthuman is

Christian in disguise. But what is "left to them," who are metamorphosing? What is left to us? Which horn, obtrusively present as a living monument to, or as a premonition of, the other-than-human in the human? Which bodily window for "pouring out . . . hope?" Which sinful stain, simultaneously serving as the sign of its expunging?

PYGMALION, THE MORNING AFTER

(Liber X, 243-297)

PYGMALION: Good morning, my love! Have I told you that you are perfect?
SHE: (*stretching*)
P: (*passing his hand over her shoulder*) Warm to my touch. You are really alive! I still can't believe it. Say something, babe.
S: Bhhha, buh, dyp . . .
P: Your body came to life and now we'll take care of your mind. Teach you to speak. To express yourself. But, first, you need a name. How about Liza? It's the short form of Eliza. Or do you prefer Elise, dearest one?
S: Zaaaah
P: My kisses softened the ivory of which your body was made, its hardness vanished, as it ceded to my fingers. *Rigore subsidit digitus ceditque*, as learned men say. We'll try to do the same to your mind and speech, with still more miraculous kisses planted on your consciousness to enliven it. Or . . . should we? If you learn to speak, you may say something less than perfect. You may even disagree with me. You, the one created by me not once but twice! Worse than that, you may turn out to be like all the other "women spending their lives in shames," all those whose faults I have found disgusting. It is not for nothing that I had been known as *Pygmalion, offensus vitiis*, Pygmalion, offended by defects. What I fear most is discovering a defect in you, Liza, and growing cold toward *you*, as I did toward all women before I met you. Because you have no bodily defects (I took care of that when I crafted you), they could be only mental. Why not

cut the problem at the root? Your mind will stay a blank slate, as perfect as the ivory of your flesh.

s: Heeee, hellllll, hellllooo, hello!

p: No, no, no, no! It was not supposed to be like this! I decided that you would be mute.

s: Are you afraid of my wits, Pig . . . Pyg . . . Pygmalion? That I may be more beautiful *and* smarter than yourself?

p: What have I done? Wait . . . What have *you* done? You've spoiled everything! (*panting*) My hand—it's growing cold. And stiffening. The same chill is creeping up the arm, to my shoulder, spreading through my chest. It's hard to breathe. To speak.

s: Then don't!

p: (*falling down*) "he saw the ~~sky~~ earth and his lover at the same time" (*pariter cum ~~caelo~~ tellure vidit amantem*)

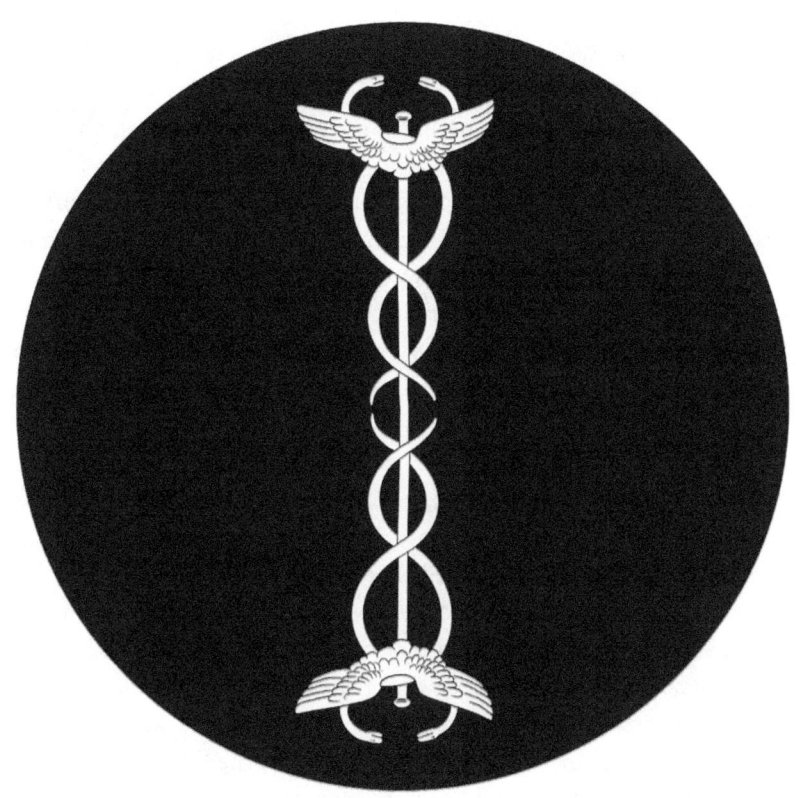

MYRRHA: THE THRASHING ABOUT OF "NATURE"

(Liber X, 298–502)

Myrrha is ridden with shame and guilt: she desires her own father, Cinyras. Is this a wholly natural predicament, or does it go against nature? Myrrha's tragedy is not incestuous passion (or "polluted love," *foedoque amori*, as she baptizes it) but the fact that, with the same strength of conviction, she holds onto two hypotheses, notably that her desire is at the same time natural and unnatural.

On the one hand, she points to other species (birds above all) where sexual relations among relatives are common. Human "tribes," too, are cited "among whom mother and son, daughter with father mate, and piety grows, twinned with love." Myrrha's nature activates unimpeded love unspoiled by civilization, the negation inscribed in law, as law: "Human civilization has made spiteful laws, and what nature allows [*natura remittit*], the jealous laws forbid [*iura negant*]."

On the other hand, Myrrha implores herself: "defile not what is forbidden by nature [*vetito naturae*] with unlawful doing!" Before the laws of civilization, there are the laws of nature, which is not, after all, entirely permissive. "The thing itself forbids it [*res ipsa vetat*]": the prohibition is not superimposed onto nature by human civilization; it traverses "the thing itself," *res ipsa*. It follows, then, that nature is the space of total freedom and of absolute constraint, anarchic license and a vetoing of conduct.

Myrrha is trapped by the way she frames—or fails to frame—her desire. It is all over the place and nowhere, insanely unrestricted and intolerably confined. The thrashing about of nature in her monologue is the thrashing about of her desire intellectualized, the desire embedded in close family ties. (Is nature a figure of desire, coveted or repressed, rather than an "objective reality"?) The self-contradictory responses Myrrha provides herself with indicate, more than anything else, the limit to desire's intellectualization, to its conversion into a theoretical object of understanding.

The philosophical and theological conception of the laws of nature and of natural law will gravitate toward narrow constraints and strict prohibitions. The words *res ipsa vetat* ("the thing itself forbids it") could well be their common motto. In the meantime, Myrrha's position is much more indeterminate than that. She vacillates between a view of the laws of nature as pure and uncorrupt prior to their mutilation by civilizational authorities (a thesis that Jean-Jacques Rousseau will share with her) and a suspicion that antinatural tendencies, such as her forbidden love, are present in nature in the shape of human perversion (a thesis later on defended by Thomas Aquinas). And yet, Myrrha is more advanced than either inheritor of her argument to the extent that she is conscious of the ambiguities ingrained in any recourse to nature. "Do you realize how many laws and names you are confusing?" she asks herself. This confusion internally affects laws and names, as much as the links between them. What we call nature, then, is a confused name and the laws associated with it are confused laws, contravening the impulse of legality.

The way out of confused reasoning is not thinking, but acting, enacting the decision that cuts through ambiguities without resolving them on intellectual terms. The thrashing about of "nature" and "natural law" stops when Myrrha makes a decision, literally cutting through the muddle in a manner that prefigures, like her name which participates in a confusion of different kinds, her subsequent transformation into a tree. "Just as a great tree, smitten by the ax, when all but the last blow has been struck, wavers which way to fall and threatens every side, so her mind, weakened by many blows, leans unsteadily now this way and now that, and falteringly turns in both directions; and no end nor rest for her passion can she find save for death." Choosing death is irreversibly deciding not to decide, making a decision that cuts all ties, while recusing itself from picking a side in the argument about nature and desire.

Myrrha is saved from death by her old wet nurse (*nutrix*), the one who is, just as ambiguously, standing between nature and culture in her role of a substitute mother (for more on this, consult Rousseau, once again, plus Derrida). It is the wet nurse who urges Myrrha not to give up on her desire, however crazy this desire may appear. "Live then," she says, "and have what is yours"—*Vive, potiere tuo*. The nutritive function, encoded in the word *nutrix*, is the province of the vegetal soul and of the unconscious that knows no *no*. With the guidance of her wet nurse, Myrrha is received into the fold of vegetality in advance of actually metamorphosing into a tree.

When she metamorphoses, it is Myrrha's turn to welcome the plant that welcomes her into itself. "But she could not endure the delay and, meeting the rising wood, she sank down and plunged her face into the bark." Speeding the metamorphosis up, plunging the most human (the humanizing) part of herself, which is the face, under tree bark, Myrrha actively accepts and even regulates what passively befalls her. The meeting place at the crossroads of the rising wood and her plunging face restages the ambiguous nexus of "nature" and "nature," of absolute freedom and total constraint. In effect, Myrrha is after liberation, which she pursues under the rigidity of tree bark, her final deed as a human testifying to the irresolvable thrashing about of "nature."

RUNNING:
ATALANTA AND HIPPOMENES
(Liber X, 503-707)

Jogging. The arms are in sync with the legs; the legs—in sync with the breath.

1-2-1-2-1-

There is never a 3; only another 1. Infinity in finitude, moving along at variable modulated paces—the paces that I am.

1   2   1   2   1

or

RUNNING: ATALANTA AND HIPPOMENES

12121212121212121212121

Wide steps, pushing off the ground until I feel so light that I am nearly flying over it, only briefly touching the soil to hover once again. The ground that gives me traction is the sandy soil of pine woods, not so different from the "sandy course" trodden by the "flying feet" of Atalanta and her competitors. (Her 1 was immediately a 2!) She, too, ran in "shady woods," *opacas silvas*, though she did not jog there, but ran, raced against her suitors. The deal was that whoever ran faster than Atalanta could marry her. Should the competitor lose—as every single one of them would, save for Hippomenes—he would be put to death.

Running.

12121212121212121212121—and no more 2, ever.

A matter of life and death, Atalanta's competitive race left no room for togetherness, either during or after the event:

—should she arrive first, they would be forever apart (plus, he would part with his own life);
—should he arrive first, they would be together as a result of their apartness.

Jogging, however, is all about being together, even and especially in what seems to be a solitary exercise. In the woods, I am together with the sandy soil and the air imbibed with the strong smell of pine resin heated by the sun or the moist freshness that drifts on after the rain. I am together with the trees and the shrubs, the ever-present wild flowers, and the earth, whose force of gravity I feel all the more acutely when jogging uphill or, helped by it, at a steep descent.

Hippomenes, for his part, was helped by a goddess, who came up with three distractions, three golden apples tossed midrace, that snatched the victory from Atalanta. The same goddess, who, outraged with the lack of homage and gratitude after the event, saw to it that Hippomenes and Atalanta would be transformed into a lion and lioness.

Why after the event? Running is a momentary metamorphosis—not so much into a darting animal as into a vector of movement. Driven in part by the rhythmic alternations of legs and arms that seem to lead a life of their own, in part by inertia, in part by breath, in part by air and the supportive earth. "You would think that they could graze the sea with unwet feet and pass lightly over the ripened heads of the standing grain." The metamorphoses of position set the scene for the metamorphoses of movement, which is but a series of continuously changing positions. Among these pines swishing by, the small yellow blossoms, the sandy soil, the vegetal respiration of the woods, and the deep blue of the sky.

ADONIS, ADONAI, ANEMONE CORONARIA

(Liber X, 708-739)

My Lord, the flower,
A little "blood-red flower,"
Blossoming there,
Where blood was shed.
Adon, ai, ai, ai
Lord my, my, my,
Beginning at the beginning,
With the first letter of the alphabet,
Itself named after the first and the second letters:
Alpha, beta—
Aleph, bet.

ADONIS, ADONAI, ANEMONE CORONARIA

"Your blood shall be changed to a flower:"
And your aleph into alpha,
Your bet—into beta.
Jew-Greek, Greek-Jew:
The mortal beloved of Venus (Aphrodite),
Adonis, resurrected in a flower after "no longer than the delay of an hour:"
The mortal son of Adonai (Eloheinu),
Jesus of Nazareth, resurrected on the third
(Day? Letter? O)
Hebrew metamorphosing into Greek metamorphosing into Latin metamorphosing into English . . .
Briefly blossoming,
Brevis est tamen usus in illo,
Before turning into a dead language,
A withered vegetal body of words,
"Doomed too easily to fall,"
And, with this fall, to burst forth
Into other flowering languages,
Into so many different "words, like flowers"
Worte wie Blumen (Hölderlin).
The winds lend it the name:
Praestant nomina venti—
Anemone—
anemos: wind:
Pneuma: breath:
Ruakh: spirit:
Spiritus Sanctus: *Pneuma to Hagion*—
A breath-flower,
A spirit-flower,
Wind-flower.
My flower, the lord

ORPHEUS AND HIS CRITICS
(Liber XI, 1-84)

Orpheus is confronted by his critics—and he descends to Hades for good.

Far be it for me to interpret the metamorphoses allegorically, even those that involve psychic transformations or elemental becomings. The death of Orpheus, however, presents a special case, that of a grotesque slaughter of the bard by a throng of the women he scorned. His music pours, at the same time, as a soundtrack for the carnage and as a dissonant parallel reality to the one unfolding in Cicones. I want to hear the final notes of Orpheus's music and of his life (is there any difference between them?) otherwise; I want to discern in the gruesome event a close connection to his life's work or play. And let an unimaginative critic throw the first stone at me.

His music is not his. It belongs to the world, to the celestial spheres, to the terrestrial fold, to trees, enthralled animals, even rocks "constrained to follow him." Listening to him, receiving the vibrations emanating from his instrument, they listen to themselves. They receive themselves from him, through him, led back to themselves, despite appearing to follow him. He is bringing the sonorities of their own existence to another register of sense and sound, of resonance, consonance and dissonance.

The moment of aesthetic judgment spoils everything. Discernment without doing, technical knowledge detached from life and its rhythms, reviewing for a living: What could be more fatal to the artwork under review than that? And to the artist.

The first critic "hurled her spear straight at the tuneful mouth of Apollo's bard." At fault were the naivety of his style, primitive imitative sequences parroting the chirping of birds, a rushing mountain stream, wind rustling in treetops. Jean-Philippe Rameau's *Le rappel des oiseaux* won't do. The spear "wreathed in leaves" did not harm Orpheus. The birds could not care less about the critic. Nor did the critique affect this writer conversing to the phoenix, in part through these very sounds.

The second critic "threw a stone." Musical movements were said to be too repetitive in their minimalism. Same old same old. Philip Glass's *Glassworks* was no good. But the stone, thrown at Orpheus, did not hit him: "even as it flew through the air . . . it fell at his feet as if to ask forgiveness for its mad attempt." The movements of the machinic spheres were aloof to the critic's shrill voice, and so also was the unconscious plugged into the apparatus of repetition compulsion with enormous pleasure.

The third critic was a legion, making "a huge uproar," "mixed with discordant horns, the drums, and the breast-beating and howlings of the Bacchanals." With online rankings and evaluations, starred reviews, chat forums and "top ten of the week," this multitudinous critic managed to produce enough noise of its own "to drown the lyre's sound." To steal the voices of the world from the world, all on the pretext of bottom-up, level playing field, majority-rule democratic assessments. It was then that "the stones grew red with the blood of the bard whose voice they could not hear."

The bacchanalia of art and literary criticism, of music and movie critics, is effective on the condition that they drown out that which they criticize, speak for it (but neither paint nor compose nor perform nor film), misrepresent it, pass their critique for the essence of the work, for the valuable or cheap kernel of meaning it contains. Extract and destroy.

With Orpheus's body dismembered, his shadow flees to Hades, again. A corpus of life and work and play torn to bits, the most conspicuous of them being the tongue left behind on a riverbank: "mournfully the lifeless tongue murmured; mournfully the banks replied." In this discombobulated condition just as well, the body of a poet, of a musician, of an astute listener to the Muses gives voice to the world—murmuringly, mournfully—and the world hands this faint voice back to the beloved of the Muses, resonating with him.

As for the critics, they metamorphose into oaks (*robora*), which is not the most glorious of vegetal metamorphoses; on the contrary, it stresses the thickness of oaken body, impenetrability, a lack of discernment, stupidity. Is this Ovid's prejudice, which we to some extent share with him? The critics will decide.

THE MIDAS TOUCH: SCRIPT FOR A COMMERCIAL

(Liber XI, 85–193)

(scenes from *DuckTales*, where Scrooge McDuck is swimming in gold coins, intercut with scenes of Donald Trump on the set of *The Apprentice*)

(*voiceover*)

You dream big and your dreams come true.
You invest in all the right stocks and everything you touch turns into pure gold.

(*numerous voices whispering the same phrase*)

Effice, quicquid corpore contingero, fulvum vertatur in aurum." (Grant that whatever I touch with my body may be turned to yellow gold.)
Trust the Miiidas touch?
Not so fast!

(*Background music is cut midnote; McDuck and Trump, are condensed into a single point in the middle of a blank screen*)

Then comes a moment of regret. Disappointment. Depression. What's next? Now that you've got all you'd ever wanted, what to strive to? What to live for?

THE MIDAS TOUCH: SCRIPT FOR A COMMERCIAL

Ask us, *Midas Unchained*, the Wish Fulfillment Experts! With years of experience, and thousands of grateful clients like yourself, we will walk you through the biggest challenge yet: dealing with the stress of your dreams realized. Guaranteed satisfaction for those dissatisfied with making it big! So, why wait? Book your first consultation today and get a free bonus that will change your life and motivate you to aim higher.

Terms and conditions apply. Results are not guaranteed. Donkey ears (*auris aselli*) are a permanent body modification feature and, as such, cannot be reversed. Full consultation package with *Midas Unchained* is nonrefundable. Offer valid while supplies last.

BUILDING-WITH, BUILDING-AGAINST: HOW TROY FELL BEFORE THE FALL OF TROY
(Liber XI, 194–220)

Despite the infernal noise it generates or architectural intricacies it displays, construction (work and word; and, as work, a finished building and work-in-progress) divulges more than meets the eye and reverberates in the inner ear. Latin-based, the word itself intimates that all building is a building-with. How so?

1. We build together with each other. Only very rarely can a single individual carry out the entire construction project, including its planning and concretization. Thoreau's cabin (or, at least, the auto-fiction version of it), built and inhabited on the principle of self-sufficiency, at Walden Pond was so exceptional in this regard that it became subject of a book.
2. We build houses and other structures with wood, concrete, bricks, metal, glass, and other materials. Beyond their instrumentality, the materials themselves minimally determine the form of that which is constructed with them; however inertly, they collaborate—or do not collaborate, resisting architectural and engineering blueprints.
3. We build with various kinds of technical equipment and machinery: construction cranes, bulldozers, excavators, drills. These augment and, to some extent, supplant physical human strength. A construction site is associative: it associates human and nonhuman builders, plans and materials, the earth, water, and air.

4. In the associative scenario of a construction site, we build with the elements. In one way or another all construction materials are made of various combinations of the elements—especially water and the earth. But these ideal delimitations are themselves encrusted in vast elemental realities, subtending and surrounding them.

Apollo and Neptune are the gods of form and of formless abysses, of the sun and of the sea. They endeavor to help Laomedon in erecting the walls of a brand-new city, namely Troy. Form and formlessness, fire and water: Apollo and Neptune join their opposing forces to construct city walls, to collaborate with one other and with Laomedon in the work of building. To do so, they themselves "assume mortal form," conjugating the infinite and the finite, the divine and the human.

"There stood the work" (*stabat opus*).

"The stone, which the builders rejected, has become the cornerstone." (Psalms 118:22). A kernel of deconstruction.

What lends stability to a work of architecture? What allows it to stand, to keep standing, rather than cave in and collapse? Certainly, sound planning, good engineering calculus, and elemental support, when the earth does not give way under the foundations and bodies of water do not flood a shoreline, peppered with houses and apartment towers. In our construction activities we nonetheless presuppose that the world can be molded according to our plan and that which does not sit well with our intent and design must be eliminated, bulldozed, buried or cast in concrete. We labor under the illusion that imposed forms can subdue and eradicate formlessness. The balance of building tips from building-with to building-against (even though it is impossible to do away with the *with* once and for all). All construction becomes counterconstruction, the erection of barriers meant to hold the other back, at bay, on the hither side of a walled perimeter.

In vain did Neptune and Apollo await the payment, which Laomedon promised for their work. For its part, elemental retribution for the king's perjury was swift. The sea god "set all his waters flowing against the shores of miserly Troy. He flooded the country till it looked like a sea." Troy fell before the legendary fall of Troy by sinking, or, rather, by being submerged beneath rising waters. Formlessness devours the forms it let emerge. As a solid proof that building with the elements is nonnegotiable.

Buildings are the metamorphoses of the materials, of labor, of the places where they are situated, of the elements contained in them and surrounding them—in short, of everything and everyone they are built *with*. Unless they are perceived this way, they will have fallen still before they fall, like Troy, miserly in its recognition of elemental collaborations.

THE TENACITY OF SUBSTANCE: PELEUS AND THETIS

(Liber XI, 221-265)

Peleus:

I can barely bring myself to write to you. For the longest time, I have been scanning the text detailing your shameful exploits: how you plotted to rape Thetis, how you could not do it because she was constantly assuming new forms, how you offered sacrifices to the gods of the ocean just to be instructed in the most efficient method of having your way with her... And I felt nothing but disgust and near despair.

I was, so to speak, trying to hold onto a timeless bit of the text, and then it dawned on me: the grasp itself, your stranglehold, was the focal point. You followed Proteus's advice to the letter (for who would be a

THE TENACITY OF SUBSTANCE: PELEUS AND THETIS

better counselor on how to control liquid metamorphoses than their unsurpassed master?), namely "to hold her close, whatever she may be, until she takes again the form, which she had at first." That is what she felt: her members held down (*sua membra teneri*), her arms pinioned wide (*in partes diveresas bracchia tendi*).

Have you ever wondered why this was the recipe for your success? What you held onto and held constant across multifarious changes of form was substance. Without resorting to philosophical arguments and catchwords, Proteus taught you that substance is unperturbed by metamorphoses, because, with regard to it, they are accidents that are fleeing, ephemeral, and inessential. You had to *believe* that the substance of the one called Thetis was there, present beneath or behind the impressive parade of shapes she put on. And you had to *act* on that belief, holding her close—holding *her* "whatever she may be." But what or whom exactly did you grasp? Can you hold substance itself without wrapping your arms around one of its accidents after another?

You did not ask yourself these questions. Instead, you did exactly what Proteus told you to do. We have to go a step further, though, in order not to subject Thetis (all the Thetises of the past, present, and future) to the same violence you visited upon her.

So, what didn't change across the metamorphoses of Thetis? I will tell you: what didn't change is your hold and the belief sustaining it. The grasping creates the grasped and ensures the existence of the grasped, so long as the fists are clenched, the arms wrapped around the victim. When you relax your grip, mental as much as it is physical, substance vanishes. There is no substance outside your grasp, outside, that is, the straitjacket of identity, to which you confine the one (or the many—the two are really interchangeable) so grasped. Substance is your imposition on her, or on them, violent beyond measure.

Give metamorphoses their due! Relax your grasp, Peleus. You too, Ovid. See them for what they are: accidents without substance, free to slip into and out of one another outside your obsessively controlling grip. Step aside. Let them touch themselves, once you no longer pinion her arms. Maybe then we will still have a chance.

Non-Proteus

A CYCLE OF VIOLENCE: DAEDALION

(Liber XI, 266-345)

Swish. A headlong drop—wings spread wide; the rest of the feathery body stretched like a string—almost perfectly vertical. The victim is within the hawk's line of sight, if still very far down, and will soon be within his reach. No matter the physical distance, he can anticipate how he will be ripping up his still living lunch. Ahead of time, he is already getting inebriated with the sight and smell of freely flowing blood, the sounds of tearing joints and ligaments, the ecstatic moment when the body of the one in pain (the body that has become nothing but pain) expires its last breath.

He is focused on his target, so much so that he is gathered into a single point of concentration, rapidly moving through the air. "Harsh, eager for war, ready for violence" (*acer, belloque ferox at vimque paratus*), Daedalion keeps his past character traits as a hawk. He recycles these features in his new incarnation in a bird of prey. Swish, swish.

Despite their meticulously calculated trajectories, each one of his predatory drops commemorates the desperate jump, the suicidal leap from the peak of Mount Parnassus, which he took when he learned about his daughter's untimely death. Apollo took pity on Daedalion and transformed him into a hawk right before he hit the ground. The headlong plunge repeats that fall, which is only interrupted when sharp claws grab their victim. Daedalion's suicidal urge is reawakened, time and again, but now it spills out and targets those outside him (outside—for the time being, since they will be devoured after they are murdered). He follows the oldest rule in the psychic economy playbook, which is by the same token the oldest excuse for the perpetrators of violence, namely: you keep hurting others because you are hurt, "suffering himself, he makes others suffer" (*dolens fit causa dolendi*). To justify Daedalion in this manner, as Ovid does through the words of King Ceyx, is to act as an accomplice to his hawkish attacks.

In the meantime, yet another predatory drop has culminated in a death, nourishing more than Daedalion's body his insatiable soul, which hungers for the pain of others. More precisely, he derives pleasure from being the *cause* of their suffering, from tracking its invisible strands to himself, as the one from whom they emanate. The dying shriek of the victim placates him for a split of a second. Then the hunger for pain returns with renewed force.

The cycle of violence is a vortex that gives a body in the world to the noxious negativity reigning in his soul. A body that can only have the shape of a corpse, of untold numbers of corpses, with which this world is strewn. The hawk's eyesight is sharp: he is on a lookout for the still warm, moving, living bodies that have not yet been deadened, not yet sacrificed to the Moloch of his suffering self. Perched high up on a tree branch, he is invigilating, monitoring the slightest stirrings, the subtlest signs of life to be extinguished as soon as possible. Spotted! And swish ...

BECOMING A FOSSIL: THE WOLF OF NEREID

(Liber XI, 346–409)

A philosophy of fossils is yet to be written, and the current geological epoch baptized "the Anthropocene" not only requires such a work but etches it in grimy hieroglyphics into earth's strata. A philosophy of fossils, to which my *Dump Philosophy* is one of the preludes, would then decipher and repeat the strange earth writings of the Anthropocene.

There are certainly plenty of animal and plant fossils from bygone eras: say, ferns from the Mesozoic era, crustaceans from the Paleozoic era, dinosaur bones from the Early Cretaceous period. These are the shapes of the living devoid of life, that is, shapes that, as 3D snapshots of how they were at a certain moment of time, are no longer self-shaping or self-reshaping. They are monuments to themselves, inlaid in the geological crust, refusing to decompose or to dissolve into it, insisting on their material form. But, by resembling the outlines of the organisms they once were, they also indicate that, already in life, the living are entombed in themselves; that a living body is a corpse to be; that life and death, the living and the deadening, the shaping and the shaped are nourished (destroyed, analyzed to molecules, absorbed, rearranged, resynthesized) by one another in organismic existence.

Sometimes the fossils are shapeless; they are found in deep deposits as liquid, solid, or gaseous masses. In the Anthropocene, a certain conception of the human (*anthropos*: a conception that is *both* a limited, historically, culturally, and geographically bound invention or self-invention *and* a planetary reality) has become fossilized. The fossilized traces of this conception are palpable in the shapeless fossils that are to this day being utilized as sources of fuel or are utterly useless. They consist of an accumulation of that which resists decomposition, such as nuclear waste, the "forever chemicals," or plastics. All these are the geological monument to *anthropos*, the monument that is "the human" translated into the byproducts of his (most definitely *his*) activity. We are living among fossils, increasing them exponentially, suffocating on them, swallowing them, and poisoning ourselves with them. Life in the Anthropocene becomes, above or below all, an exponential production of fossils, an orgy of self-fossilization, coupled with the fear that the other fossils, excavated and incinerated *en masse* as fuel, will one day run out, signaling energy starvation and death. It is a life hell-bent on its absolute self-entombment.

The fearsome wolf of Nereid, released to avenge the murder of Phocus by Peleus, had to be subdued. Thetis herself prayed to the gods to spare the herds and the herdsmen from the ferocious menace. But the wolf disobeyed the divine command. He was more than an instrument, not a machine to be switched on and off. Which is why "the nymph changed him to marble [*marmore mutavit*]. The body, save for its color, remained the same in all respects; but the color of the stone proclaimed that now he was no longer wolf [*iam non esse lupum*], that now he no longer need be feared."

Nereid's wolf became an instant fossil, recalling the bodily shape of the wolf but stiffened and colored otherwise than the living animal. In the Anthropocene we become instant fossils from the perspective of deep geological time. Little more than two hundred years have elapsed since the start of the Industrial Revolution in England—a hardly registerable blip on the radar tracking the ages of the earth. Today everyone identifying with and as the human is Nereid's wolf (who, in turn, salutes, with his untamable ferocity, the wolf of the first metamorphosis), unprepared to put an end to a murderous, ecocidal rampage—and fossilizing all the quicker. The shape of the fossils that we are is that of our techno-body, shredded to bits, and of our metaphysical dreams that, when realized, give rise to environmental calamities.

Unlike an immediately fossilized wolf, nevertheless, the fossils of the Anthropocene *should* be feared, due to their accumulation that hampers planetary metabolism. In the event of species extinction, is the human "no longer" if his material traces, the outcomes of industrial activity, stay in place for hundreds, and often thousands, of years?

BEING NO MORE: ALCYONE AND CEYX

(Liber XI, 410-748)

A scream: "I am null and void!" (or: "It's the end of me!" or else: *nulla est Alcyone, nulla est,* "Alcyone is no more, no more!").

Then, heavy breathing, sobs. Someone is sobbing, someone is breathing, someone has screamed out these words; hence, "null and void" cannot be true. Is it, then, all pretense, an overdramatic reaction to loss?

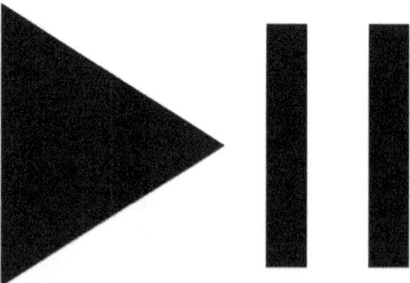

Let's hit a *pause* button here. Suppose there is more to Alcyone's inconsolable reaction to the death of her husband, Ceyx, at sea than a theatrical scene we automatically associate it with. "Alcyone is no more, no more!": references to herself in the third person and the repetition of *nulla est* on either side of her name render her all but anonymous. Though not physiologically dead, she identifies with the deceased, not least by reiterating what

BEING NO MORE: ALCYONE AND CEYX

was previously said about him, *viro qui nullus erat*, "a man who was no more," and (*mutatis mutandis*, with the due signage of sexual difference and of a difference between the present and the past tenses of the verb "to be") magnifying the reiteration in her *nulla est . . . nulla est*. This identification is a sign of death in life, of psychic death, further intensified by Alcyone's chilling statement: "far from myself I have perished; far from myself also I am tossed about upon the waves, and without me the sea holds me (*et sine me me pontus habet*)." She is, and she is no more: the sea holds her without her. The sea of oblivion, the sea of non-being, much vaster than the rivers Lethe or Styx.

Being no more is becoming no one. But still becoming.

Rather than an exceptional event, it is what happens in every process of becoming, where something passes through the eye of the needle of nothing in order to become something else. Not to mention becoming *someone* else, a position that, when properly understood, destroys the last shred of certainty that you have left the eye of the needle behind.

Becoming someone and becoming no one grow indistinguishable from one another. When, playing dangerously with his name and his life, Odysseus responds "Nobody," *Outis*, to the cyclops Polyphemus's question "Who is here?", he may not be just practicing the art of lifesaving cunning, as Homer implies and his readers unanimously agree. Cunning overshoots itself, inasmuch as in its lying shape it expresses the truth. Odysseus is speaking the truth: to be someone, to have become someone, is to be and to become no one. So, too, is Alcyone who is purely herself, who becomes no one, who is no more (who, therefore, is the *is*) in wholly identifying with the dead beloved. Dividing lines between veracity and falsity get smudged here in a way that has nothing to do with "alternative facts": cunning is the highest truth, when it comes to being no more and becoming no one.

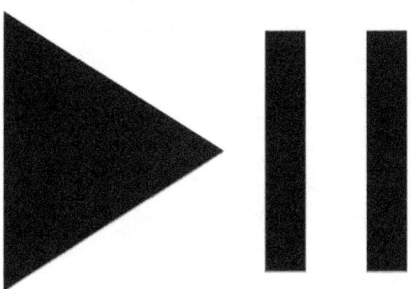

BEING NO MORE: ALCYONE AND CEYX

Release the *pause* button now. You will hear more heavy breathing, further sobs, from the one who professes to be no more and to be no one. But you will not be accosted by the tedious repetition of a litany. There will have been a change.

Listen carefully: "if not your bones with mine, still shall I touch you, name with name (*at nomen nomine tangam*)." In the crucible of anonymity, thanks to the loss of one's proper name along with everything that is one's own including oneself, a genuine relation to the name is forged. Here, the name does not stand alone. It springs back in a relation of touching, caressing or rubbing against another name, which would not have been possible before both became no one. (The cunning of Odysseus, if cunning it was, depended on a make-believe of having let go of himself—the make-believe that defines, besides the cyclops episode, his entire journey—as a result of which he also allowed names to touch: his own and another, homophonous with it, the proper and the common names. The price he paid for this half-hearted performance, snubbing the other, is that he got out of touch with himself, time and again, precisely when he seemed to have circled back to himself.)

Alcyone invokes herself in third person both before and after announcing that she was no more, nullifying herself. She does so to her name, with her name, in her name, which is no longer hers. A merely nominal death? Purely symbolic?

Look closer: the name is a substitute for a bone ("if not your bones with mine," then "name with name"), and as such, it is probably heavier, not lighter, than osseous rests. At any rate, it needs to attain a certain level of density to be tangible, to be touched by and to touch another name. Being no more, becoming no one—that is what is responsible for the transubstantiation of names, sifted through the nameless, that puts them on a par with things. "Nominal," "symbolic" tendencies are not mere, never mere, but more material still than the concept of matter, with which idealism operates.

Instead of the rattling of bones that rub against one another, Alcyone lets names (the proper as well as the common) rattle, as they touch and are touched by names. Ceyx—Alcyone. *Nullus—nulla. Erat—est.*

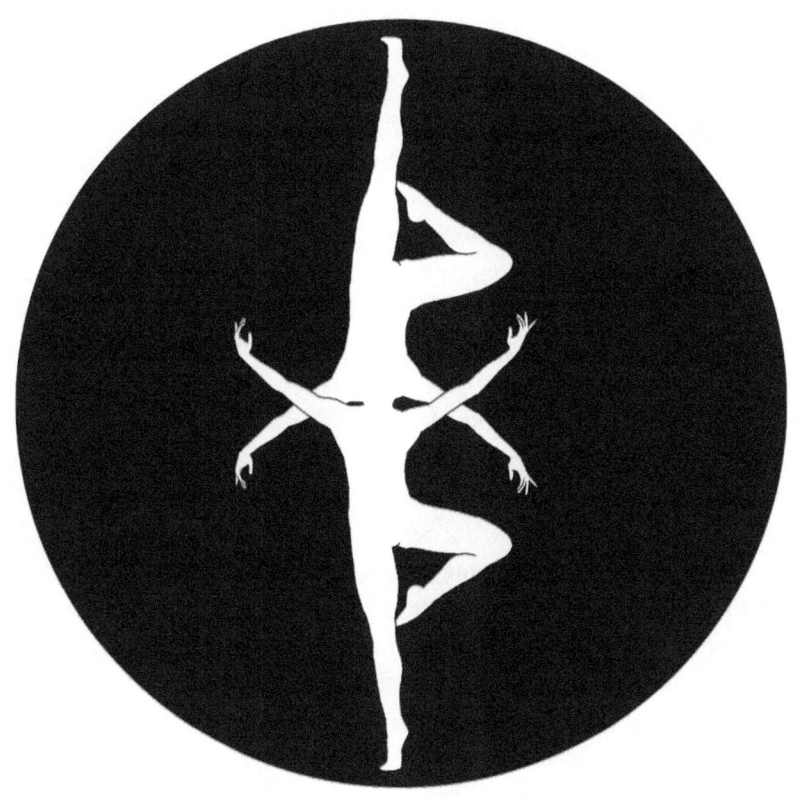

THE INFURIATING DESTINY OF BECOMING AN IMMORTAL ANIMAL

(Liber XI, 410-748)

You want to die repeatedly, and they won't let you.

I have no clue who pulls me out of the water each time I throw myself there, wanting to dissolve in the abyss, in the deep. An invisible hand rescues me and hands me back over to life. It's like Sisyphus but the other way around: he climbs up and comes tumbling down with the rock he pushes; I plunge downward only to surface on the waves again, light and feathery.

I am not kidding, I've "tried endlessly, *sine fine*, to find the way to death." Endlessly, I am on my way to the end. But the end never materializes. I rebegin—I am rebegun—even as I go under. An old man once said that, in everything we do, we are driven by the death drive, even when acting in a life-affirming manner, for example loving. No doubt about it. I only have a question for him. Are we secretly hoping that this drive (I mean the death drive) will keep steering us endlessly, driving us along the blind alleys, cul-de-sacs, and detours of existence to the end but without ending? Does the drive that dreams up the life of our unconscious minds in a perverse aspiration to death ever run out of fuel? Does its engine ever grind to a halt? Can the death drive die? I wish it did. If I cannot die, obeying its insistent orders, as unshakable as they are impossible to fulfill, then let *it* perish.

She is lucky: "her flight stopped along with her life," *cum vita suppressa fuga est*. With my flight from life, death retreats. How am I to accept it? How am I to be accepted into it? Judging by the feathers, wings, and my long neck I am an animal now, of the avian kind. Still, I can't trust my animality. Not because of the feathers and all, but because animals are supposed to die. This is what animals do: though some have shorter lifespans and others longer, they all kick the bucket in the end. It is a cruel irony that I am an animal—a mortal, probably avian, creature—who, seeking death everywhere all the time, is not allowed to die. Or, at least, to take away his own life. Is such radical "suicide prevention" not worse than capital punishment? Or than a life sentence? I am sentenced not *for* life but *to* life, the very life I am driven to end with every breath I take, to drown, to fill my lungs with water.

It is not me speaking to you. Of course, I no longer utter any words, like the ones transcribed here. It is not me; it is "wild rage" that speaks through me. The furiousness of not being able to go under without surfacing ever again. Without coming back to it, to my senses, to *me*; without subjection to the torture of regaining consciousness, of remembering and rebeing. Without anything. With nothing.

A HAPPY END: IPHIGENIA
(Liber XII, 1-39)

Among Ovid's many modifications of the classical mythological tradition, his take on the story of Iphigenia stands out for its upending of earlier sources. *Iphigenia at Aulis*, a play by Euripides, is a tragedy that unfolds just before the Trojan War. The Greek fleet is delayed in the Boeotian port of Aulis due to a lack of wind. It turns out that with this abnormal calm Artemis is punishing Agamemnon, who, along the way, killed a sacred stag of the goddess. The only way to appease Artemis is to sacrifice Agamemnon's daughter, Iphigenia. After initially resisting her horrific fate, Iphigenia accepts it in the shape of her freely assumed self-sacrifice for the sake of the Greeks.

Ovid turns things around. Instead of strange calm, a violent north wind (*Boreas violentus*) impedes the fleet's journey. The goddess demands immediate sacrifice to calm the storm. Iphigenia is offered at the altar, but a cloud is spread before the spectators' eyes and a hind (*cerva*) is sacrificed, while the young virgin is saved.

To be sure, a nearly identical version of the ending is attached to the Euripides's tragedy, where a messenger reports that, at the last moment, a deer was ritually slaughtered as a replacement for Agamemnon's daughter, "but the maid—none knew whither she had vanished" (Eur. *IA*, 1583). It is probable that Ovid relied on this version, an afterthought of sorts generally considered to be a later addition to the text of the play. At the same time, Ovid also inverted the meteorological beginning, inserting a violent north wind in place of unusual calm at sea. This radical alteration of the beginning is not trivial; it hints at a similarly drastic about-face of the ending.

What, then, is needed for a tragedy to culminate in a happy end? A farcical inversion. We are privy to the same dynamic in the biblical text. There, presaging Jesus's self-sacrifice, the sacrifice of Isaac by his father, meekly accepted by the son, is thwarted by God himself, who in the last moment provides a ram instead of the youth. Human sacrifice mutates into self-sacrifice, which, in turn, announces salvation in the guise of making an animal offering to the gods. Mere consciousness twists into self-consciousness, which, saturated with the power of negativity, is ready to bring to naught the entire world (even under the guise of the world's salvation). A later addition of the alternative ending to the Euripides's text either draws on the story of Isaac or on a source that is common to the Greek and Hebraic traditions. Be this as it may, the farce is there to stay.

In the backdrop to Isaac's aborted sacrifice atop Mount Moriah, God is so cruel as to demand it for no apparent reason, besides testing Abraham's fidelity, and Abraham is so deranged as to consent to the senseless murder of his favorite son. That an animal is substituted for Isaac at the altar—that the sacrificial offering does not take place as initially envisioned—does not cancel their cruelty and derangement. The economy of sacrifice is much clearer in the Greek text, where Agamemnon needs to pay for a life he has terminated with the life of his own daughter. This clarity is nowhere to be found in the story of Abraham and Isaac until the end, when the *deus ex machina* of the ram is presented as a symbolic substitute for a human being.

The structure of sacrifice is that of exchange: one thing for another, one being for another. An individual is sacrificed, or sacrifices herself, for the collective; an animal is sacrificed for the human; plant sacrifices (for instance, the culling of flowers) are often not recognized as such. The compilers of the Hebrew Bible, the author of a later insertion into Euripides's play, and Ovid engage in a unique narrative sacrifice. They sacrifice the end, the tragic one, to a happy one. All the way to contemporary Hollywood, a happy end is possible solely on the condition that the preceding tragedy is sacrificed to it—that, finally, sacrifice itself is sacrificed when neither a ram nor a deer is around. But the happiness of the happy end alimented by the sacrifice of sacrifice is worse than a fake smile. It is the happiness, which is not allowed to give the slightest intimation of its utter and complete misery.

"DWELLING," ONLINE
(Liber XII, 40-63)

Orbe locus medio, a place in the middle of the world,
A node,
Is every place online,
On the line of anyplace,
Englobing the globe.
Firewalls (yes!), though already breached—
"Countless entrances, a thousand apertures,
But with no doors to close them."
A house, *in* which you are as soon as you
Come *on*line—
A house for being in-on,
With no possibility of dwelling,
Anyplace, nowhere.
A house, built of wireless wires,
Of "confused noises, repeating all words and doubling them":
Rumor has it . . .
(Rumor has *you*)!
Insinuation, conspiracy theories, megatons—exabytes—of
 information
Dumped, and in the movement of dumping, erecting the aethereal
 walls
Of the ethernet connection.

There is no one, save for the throngs, *turba*, filling its halls,
In a turbulence that sets another rhythm.
"Falsehood mingles with the truth,"
In a rumor that has you that has it that all knowledge is relative
And that the unknown unknowns rule the day and the night.
A perpetual metamorphosis,
Where nothing morphs,
Meta—nothing;
Day is night,
Night—day,
X,
But the search is ongoing:
"Rumor herself . . . searches throughout the world for news,"
So that you can be *Reporters*
In *medio locus orbe.*

ON DEICIDE: CYCNUS AND ACHILLES
(Liber XII, 64-145)

The drums of war are growing louder and louder. I am approaching an indestructible enemy. A foredoomed fight? Maybe; I don't care.

The drumbeat I hear is only in my head, but I am not hallucinating. My heart is pounding, the pulse in my temples setting a rhythm for the battle to come.

My heart, the drum of war. My head, just as well. Is that why I am challenging Cycnus, the immortal son of Neptune himself, to mortal combat?

Just look at how the warring god is taunting me, offering his uninjured body, *sine vulnere corpus*, totally unprotected. A god demands the sacrifice of entire armies but is himself invulnerable. Is that fair? His demand I have heeded: "so many are slain, heaps of whose corpses upon the shore I have both made and see." But now I should collect a debt, making and beholding a divine corpse, to be put on the other side of the scales so as to assess if it weighs the same as this heap.

Theodicy, divine justice, is not incompatible with deicide, the murder of a god. The simple act of switching a couple of letters to leap from one word to the other is a hint enough. A small Jewish sect has taught us this lesson. If a god requires sacrifice, he (or, say, his son) shall be sacrificed. I will see to it, even at the price of my own life.

Another in my place would have given up already: he seems immune to every weapon I use against him, to every stratagem I come up with, to every strike. *Vulnus erat nullum*—there was no wound. It is no use to yell "God is dead!" either, no matter how sincerely you believe the words that come out of your mouth. He will be there regardless, laughing silently in your face.

Thud, thud, thud. My heart, the drum of a war declared against a god, beats in tandem with the strikes I deliver. What will fizzle out first: this double thudding or his existence?

The main thing is not to pause, *negat requiem*. Keep going. Keep fighting as if your heart is made of steel. Rhythmically thudding steel.

Then, when he least expects it, I change my tactic. He is expecting another blow on the heels of the last (I should not be talking about heels, or else, I *should* be talking about them nonstop, *negat requiem*); instead, I flip him around and pin him to the ground. Make him feel the earth as a foretaste of eating it, of being filled with it, of dissolving into it.

A god brought down to earth: Is that still a god? Food for thought. But I have no time to wine and dine. In thought, least of all. I go about my job of making Cycnus pay for the sacrifices he and other divine folk have claimed. Right the wrongs of theodicy with deicide.

It dawns on me: you can't kill a god, not because he is immortal but because he is undead. Yelling "God is dead!" that madman should have been corrected: "God is undead!" Cornered, nailed down, he left his armor behind, *arma relicta*, and morphed into "a white bird." His name leads us to think that the bird is a swan; my guess is that—oh, the irony of ironies!—he became a white dove, the bird of peace.

A god does not really die, then. At best he metamorphoses, which is not so bad for a start (and for an end).

TRA-TA-TA: TRAUMA, TRANSITION—CAENIS/CAENEUS AND NEPTUNE

(Liber XII, 146-209)

CAENIS (*DEFIANTLY*): You have just raped me. What else do you want? Why would you not leave me alone with my wounds? They are so many! A lifetime is not enough to count them all: the visible and the invisible, the inner and the outer, those that are visible on the inside and those that are inner and invisible...

NEPTUNE: I am here to do anything you want, anything that is in my power, to make you happy. Choose anything you wish, *elige, quid voveas*!

CAENIS (*UNINTELLIGIBLE*): I... you... if I were... him, not her...

NEPTUNE: There, there. Hush. Calm down and tell me what you want. I've already gotten what I wanted.

CAENIS (*ASIDE*): Would it be wise to seek a cure from the source of my injury? Should I become who I am not? For no other reason than to flee from my sore body, from the sore that is my body, from all that is mine, from me, who is but this mangled, babbling, heap of organs, spewing out tears and other less clear liquids? (*to Neptune*) Would you have raped me if I were a man?

NEPTUNE: It's hard to say. When I saw you walking along a "lonely shore," which I lick like all the others, my waters boiled immediately. I don't know what made me lose my mind. Maybe it was your shawl flapping in the breeze. If you were a man, you would not have had that shawl. But I can't be certain.

CAENIS: It doesn't matter; *you* don't matter. Not anymore. You have used me and now I will use you to ask for a boon that will make me invulnerable: *da, femina ne sim*—grant that I be not a woman.

NEPTUNE: I see. So, your invulnerability would depend on you being of no interest to me. And you dare say that *I* don't matter? I did make a promise, of course. I grant your wish.

CAENIS/CAENEUS (VIRI VOX, *IN A MALE VOICE, WHILE TRANSITIONING*): You think I was right to doubt the wisdom of scouring the cause of my sorrow for redress. For you could hear my desperate whispers with your keen divine ear. That was the subterfuge. Know this: escaping from your unwanted advances to another sex was but an excuse.

CAENEUS: I've always been a man at heart; now I am one in the rest of my organs. I will rejoice in the gift, *munere laetus*, whether you like it or not. I will become divine by becoming me.

NEPTUNE: You will become a god—that much I confirm. Neither of the sea (sorry, the job is taken) nor of the underworld nor of the mountain, but of yourself. Invulnerable. Uninjurable. Will you then forget the goddess that you were?

CAENEUS: It's not up to you to lecture me on the mysteries of the goddess. You know nothing of them. Not a speck of this sacred knowledge is in your possession. I am no longer listening to you: where your speech was, there I hear the monotonous noise of the waves rolling on pebbles and rubbing them against one another. You make no sense anymore. I grant you no sense. That is *my* gift to *you*.

NEPTUNE: Tra-ta-ta, tra-ta-ta-ta-ta. Tra-ta-ta...

LAPITHS AND CENTAURS: WEAPONIZATION AND DISFIGURATION

(Liber XII, 210–535)

Conceptually, the epic battle of the Lapiths and the Centaurs—the battle that verges on a civil war, given the close proximity of the two groups whose founders are the twin sons of Apollo and the nymph Stilbe—unfolds along two tracks: weaponization and disfiguration. Interrelated as the cause and the effect, these tracks intersect at multiple points. Here are some of them.

1. *Unlimited possibility.* Just about anything may be weaponized, and just about any part of the body may be disfigured, often in a lethal fashion. Conventional spears, swords, lances, and javelins are dwarfed by everyday objects, including a mixing vat, a chandelier, a table leg, an entire smoking altar, antlers hanging on a wall, a threshold stone, a piece of rock from a mountainside, or an uprooted old pine. The practical resignification of objects depends on the intention and the physical strength of those who weaponize them, hurling them along death-bearing trajectories. Other than that, there is no limit to their deployment. Similarly, every organ may be subject to disfiguration, often leading to death. Smashed faces and splattered brains, blazing brands shoved down the throat and further down into the chest, massive rocks and tree trunks crushing brawlers under their weight, bodies impaled on branches are just the tip of the iceberg of physical disarticulation.
2. *Tenuousness.* The habitual use of objects is tenuous, seeing that they may be inserted into a new (and devastating at that) context of use. The

habitual use of bodies and their organs is equally tenuous, for they, too, may suffer violent disruption (from without or from within) that puts into question their smooth functioning.

3. *Suddenness.* The migration of an object from one field of signification and use to another is not a gradual process, but an abrupt wrenching out of the old context and pragmatic landscape and introduction into a new one. Bodies stricken by external violence experience a sudden disturbance, while internal turmoil may be also instantaneous (as in the case of a heart attack or a stroke) or a more protracted affair (as in the case of cancer).

4. *The veneer of normalcy.* What we take to be a stable reality of things serving their usual purposes or of bodies and their organs functioning as they should turns out to be a veneer of normalcy, overlaying gore, disorder, and violence. The vastness of possible resignifications, the tenuousness of what is habitual, and the suddenness of a change of fortunes indicate that upheavals are never very far in space and in time. So it is, also, with Lapiths and Centaurs: in the blink of an eye, a wedding celebration turns into a battle scene.

5. *Singularity.* Whereas the use of objects in everyday situations is repeatable, within the material limits of wear and tear, their recodified deployment as weapons is a one-time affair. Unlike a gun that can be reloaded, or a spear that may be extracted from the corpse of the struck target, a threshold stone is not likely to be hurled as a weapon ever again, nor is a chandelier. When it comes to the body, its organs are also repeatedly engaged in the activities they are meant to perform; their disfiguration and deactivation by improvised weapons, however, is meant to put an end to their inherently repeatable activities. (In capitalist production and consumption, "planned obsolescence," which aims to impose limits on the use of objects other than those implied by wear and tear, is indicative of a tacit weaponization of such goods.)

6. *Contingency.* Weaponized items are close at hand and place-specific: if a battle rages in a temple, the altar will serve as a weapon (after a brief moment of wild contemplation, followed by a shout, *cur non utimur istis?* "Why not use this?"); if it spills out into the woods, fallen tree trunks will serve as projectiles, assuming one is strong enough to pick up and throw them. There is no, or very little, premeditation in using whatever happens to be close to "unruly hands." Given the low accuracy of contingently picked rather than manufactured weapons, they can strike

various parts of the body aimed at, though preference is always given to the head and the heart.

7. *Fulfilled intentionality.* The contours of a perverse phenomenology are rendered visible at yet another point where weaponization and disfiguration intersect. Rather than simply participate in a cause-effect relation, in their co-belonging, in the "successful" coming to fruition of a resignified use, these two processes comprise the phenomenological intentionality fulfilled in the accomplished intuition (of severe injury and death). To paint within these contours, a much more detailed discussion of the phenomenology of weaponization and disfiguration is in order than the incipient reflections I can offer here. I cannot neglect to mention, though, that for phenomenological fulfillment to be possible, there must be non-fulfillment within the old regime of material or practical signification. Things must cease to work smoothly in their usual context in order to work well in the exceptional context of sowing death and destruction. Finally, a suspicion creeps in: What if the exception is the secret rule underlying the rule of a "non-perverse" phenomenology? What if the happy coincidence of the intending and the intended, the seeing and the seen, the gaze and that which is visible for it were, at bottom, a bullet or an arrow hitting its target?

PERICLYMENUS: A PARODY OF A PARODY, OR IN THE FOOTSTEPS OF PROTEUS AND THETIS
(Liber XII, 536–579)

An arrow piercing its target: how much is presupposed, often groundlessly so, in this coincidence! In an accurate strike, both the projectile sent by a skilled archer and that for which it is meant preserve their identity long enough for their fateful run-in to take place. A moving target is difficult enough to attain. How much more difficult is it to hit one that is not-one, the one indefatigably moving *away from itself*!

From Neptune, Periclymenus received the power "to assume any form he pleased and to put it off again at will." He is the quintessence of metamorphosis. But he is not alone; he will have been preceded by the watery Proteus and the sea nymph Thetis. Nor...

> Now this and now that,
> Change itself is unchangeable;
> The now—constant
> Despite that and this
> Content filling it.

...is Periclymenus unique in using his breathtaking capacity for instant shapeshifting in an attempt to escape his attacker. Like Thetis at the hands of Peleus, he "vainly" tried to flee not by darting to another place but by hiding in another form. Until...

PERICLYMENUS

Periclymenus, this is my brief memo to you. I am only curious about one thing: When you tried to escape your attacker by metamorphosing, did you think like a plant? I know that you preferred animal embodiments, but I am not referring to the content of your becomings. Nor, even, to their form. What I mean is: Did you enter a vegetal mindset, according to which if you cannot move to another place in a dangerous situation, you should become another in the same place? No need to answer. Let this question be suspended in the air, imitating your feathery body at the precise moment when that arrow hit you.

... the moment, when as a bird, he suffered a superficial wound (*nec grave vulnus erat*) between his wings. Though superficial, the wound proved to be fatal, because it was inflicted there were the fold of the wings was located, a living hinge, the fold of metamorphoses. Despite their apparent randomness, these transformations are variations on the fold—the folding, the unfolding, the folding back again—that drives them. Injure the place of the fold, tear it along the line discernible in the crease, and you will bring the metamorphosis machine to a halt.

THE DEATH OF ACHILLES IN FRAGMENTS
(Liber XII, 580-630)

It matters to human beings where they die and how. I am not referring to different manners of death: agonizingly slow or fast. The same death is preferred at the hand of one person, but not of another. Achilles is slain by Paris, "the cowardly ravisher of a Grecian's wife" (*timido Graiae raptore maritae*). Ovid has no doubt that he would have "gladly fallen by the Amazon's double ax" instead. To whom does it matter? The dead are dead; they do not care. Posterity could well be indifferent. The pivotal point is the projected impression one's death would leave on posterity.

THE DEATH OF ACHILLES IN FRAGMENTS

Worries about death and about what will happen afterward eclipse by far every question about birth and what happened beforehand. Death may be sudden and unexpected, yet mortals have much more of a choice about their death than about their birth, which is why Hannah Arendt's suggestion to rebaptize them as "natals" may be off the mark. Cracking our existence open, birth weighs us down with its determinism; extinguishing life, death breathes with freedom. Between them lies responsibility. Only through this responsibility do we have a stake in the future without us. Having made a difference, however tiny, we cannot stay as indifferent to the future as we are to the deep past.

We all have our Achilles' heel, which is, nonetheless, nowhere to be seen in Ovid.

Iam cinis est—"Now, he is ash." Or dust. The word *cinis* applies to both in Latin, reducing all differences, including of the semantic kind, to pale gray. Indifference envelops everything and everyone with its cold foggy blur once again. You burn up, whether all at once or gradually, going up in flames or oxidating, shedding particles, joining ash or dust, ash and dust.

Can a name crumble into dust or join the ashes? Does oblivion leave such fine debris behind?

A death-dealing hand, *letifera dextra*: To whom does it belong? To Paris, of course, if we are considering the death of Achilles, as Ovid narrates it. But also:
- to anyone who takes the law into their own hands and becomes a murderer;
- to states that have not banned capital punishment;
- to markets, with respect to those they exclude and those they exploit to exhaustion with their invisible hand;
- to a watch, to time, and, in due time, to life itself.

WEAPON-ORIENTED ONTOLOGY (WOO): THE ARMS OF ACHILLES

(Liber XIII, 1–398)

I.

To write as if you are shooting at a target. Concentrate, aim, fire! Long shooting sprees with your fingers on the keyboard. A machine-gun typewriter. Go for the kill with clear and precise sentences, getting at the heart of the matter. Exhaustive. Analytic philosophy is passionate about these dispassionate ideals. (Still. Already. The same analogy will not let go of us all that easily. Before it attains anyone or anything in its crosshairs, the analogy strikes us, fatally wounding our thinking, imagination, and modes of expression. The staying power of a figure, a goal, a directive, a method is a symptom of its indigestibility, which is either an effect of the traumatic hold it has on us or of intense attachment and commitment. The archetypal figure of the hero gravitates in a similar psychological field. My hunch is that the hero lingers on in cultural imaginary not because of our affection for this figure, but because of its traumatic impassability, which might as well be the trait of all archetypes. The hero is the nonmetabolizable par excellence, the one who resists the loss of a recognizable identity, despite death or even thanks to it—for, what immortalizes him with greater panache than an early tragic demise? Derivative from the hero's nonmetabolizable character is the hubris of complete autonomy, together with the me-against-the-world stance and the accomplishment of superhuman feats beyond the range of finite capacities. The hero, then, as the condensation of psychocultural trauma, a never-ending yet also self-contained bracket setting itself apart from the rest of the text and context of existence.) You can transform your writing into a shooting range if you resort to short sentences with bullet words hitting their aim. Maybe even with some bullet points, for greater efficiency. In the end, no words will be necessary; numbers and formal symbols will do the trick. But writing cannot be neatly cut off from thinking. An intellectual hero reduces all reality to a formula, shooting at and hitting the whole of what is. The nonmetabolizable is the most lethal thing there is: as the impassible and impossible present, a being rid of becoming and of nothingness, it hauls beings into nonbeing. In word and deed, in thought and its expression.

II.

The bellicose frame of philosophizing and, more broadly, of thinking is not unheard of. In fact, it is as old as philosophy itself. Sun Tzu's *The Art of War* is, more than a treatise on strategizing, a snapshot of the entire cosmos (heavens and earth, life and death, energy and dispositions) converging on war. In *Bhagavad Gita*, the god Krishna reveals the true nature of existence, of incarnation and reincarnation, life and "death," to Prince Arjuna, reluctant to throw his army into battle. The Myth of Er, similarly treating of the subject of reincarnation, narrated in the tenth book of Plato's *Republic* begins on a corpse-strewn battlefield. Practicing at least one kind of virtue (*aretē*) in Aristotle is akin to aiming and shooting at the target, set by the elusive mean between two extremes. The war of all against all is both the negative and the positive condition of possibility for the emergence of sovereign order (indeed, of any sort of order) in Hobbes.

If war is more than war—if it is the default state of being, the *stasis* that being itself is—then military activities and paraphernalia are not only military; they are essentially ontological, or, at least, cosmological. So, when the arms of the fallen hero Achilles are divided among the survivors, it turns out that they embody much more than his legacy. The shield, for one, is "a molded picture of the vast universe," *vasti . . . imagine mundi*. Its wondrous relief-work depicts "the sea, the lands, the deep starry heavens, the Pleiades, the Hyades, the Bear that never bathes in Ocean, and Orion with his glittering sword rotating opposite her." The shield of Achilles gathers the four elements, including water and earth and the airy depths of the sky and cosmic fire, because these elements are interrelated through war, the strife (Heraclitean *polemos*) that steers the world. Having left his weapons behind, the dead hero is undead, his agency and the intentionality that fleshed it out continuing to act through them. And through his armor something else also speaks, something primordial is ventriloquized, namely the insight that the shield is the universe, because the universe is war.

Another sign of the ontological import of Achilles's weapons is their uncommon heaviness. A worthy inheritor will be strong enough to bear their "ponderous weight," *talia pondera*, alluding, of course, to the hero's superhuman capacities as much as to mass as the very materiality of matter, shot through with the trajectories of -tending before their bifurcation into intending and extending in various directions. Inheriting and carrying the shield of Achilles is inheriting and carrying the weight of the entire world, as a proverbial tortoise or as Atlas, who holds up and upholds the heft of the heavenly vault. In addition to the shield, the sword is extraordinarily heavy, which means that slicing and dicing reality is a task no less materially grounded, massive, and ponderous than that of supporting the real.

Shaped by the belligerence of thinking and being, every dialogue is a duel. It is a fight over the truth, with competing ideas and arguments for arms and armor, by turn, offensive and defensive. But the truth of the fight is the fight itself—there is nothing beyond it, nothing other than it, because it is, not unlike the shield of Achilles, a molded picture of the vast mind.

III.

According to the mortiferous phenomenology, which Ovid's work triggers, weapons are the material extensions of intentionality that kill or maim whoever is there where the intentional/murderous gaze turns. But they are also more than that. Imbued with an intentionality of their own, weapons appeal to and select those who will use them. "The arms seek Ajax, not Ajax the arms." This could be the motto of WOO (Weapon-Oriented Ontology). And if Ajax is not there? If he is dead, reposing in his eternal heroic glory? In that case, the weapons will seek his replacement, someone whom they will use while the fighter is under the impression of having complete control, disseminating death. Thus, "the arms claim greater honor than I do."

A whole world appears (and disappears, irretrievably) between arms and armor. Besides the independent intentionality of Ajax's arms and besides the ontological import of his armor, these things are irreducible to objects seen in external light. His helmet is a source of light in and of itself, "the very glint of the helmet gleaming with bright gold (*claro radiatis ab auro*)" betraying, revealing, pointing out the one who tried to hide wearing it. Rather than a thing in the world, the helmet is the ray illuminating this world, making it what it is, conducting it to becoming-world. Better yet, *insofar as* it is a miraculous thing in the world, this piece of armor makes or lets the world appear, if only in a brief flash of its bright golden gleam that spares neither the enemy nor the head it is supposed to protect (seeing that the sparkling of the helmet hands its wearer to enemy sight and, as a result, increases the risk and vulnerability it was meant to decrease). Armor turns into arms, the weapon for an unconscious self-inflicted wound.

With cold indifference, WOO indicates what it is all about: through the intermediate targets of the intentionality proper to arms and armors, its lethal arrows are directed and fly to one destination alone. Death. It is a dreaded destination, for sure, but it attracts every living creature to itself in and through merely living on. WOO does not introduce anything new into this fatal attraction, except that it accelerates the approach of death. It puts itself in the service of a swift passing of a life and of a world, from nothingness to nothingness. Which is to say—keeping in mind the ontological framing of war where, instead of world wars, worlds that *are* wars materialize so as to dematerialize everything in existence—that it puts itself in the service of the becoming-world of world, a becoming verging on the vanishing.

HECUBA'S LAMENT: THE HOWL OF THE PLACE

(Liber XIII, 399–575)

Awoooooo . . . Rrrrr . . . Arf, arf, arf . . . Ahh-woooo . . .

The Sithonian plains are ringing with dog howls that fill to the brim the unbearably hot, electrically charged August air, bouncing across the fields and traversing the entire peninsula east to west, from the Singitic to the Toronean Gulfs. They recall other howls—those of the wolf Lycaon—that pierced the nocturnal silence of Arcadia. Through the intermittencies of time and the punctuations of space, across the gap of domestication, what do the wolf and the dog communicate to one other?

The howls are audible, but there is no one howling. That is, there is no one doing it already. It is as if, infinitely sorrowful, saturated with grief, the place itself emitted these sounds. The unique name of the place supports the hypothesis: Cynossema, *Kunos Sēma*, The Sign (or the Tomb) of a Dog. *Locus exstat et ex re nomen habet*: "the place remains and takes its name from the thing," this "thing" being Hecuba, who under the weight of her anguish and the stones she was hit by in her skirmish with the Thracians, turned into a dog. After Hecuba's death, Cynossema is the main protagonist of the story, remaining, commemorating, both loudly and silently, the events that gave it its very name. The place remains, but it is not complacent, not immersed in itself; on the contrary, it is outside or beside itself, ecstatic (*locus exstat*), overflowing with the pain it cannot contain.

HECUBA'S LAMENT: THE HOWL OF THE PLACE

We join Hecuba at the end of her human journey, the moment after she gouged the eyeballs from the sockets of Thracian Polymestor, the guardian of her son, who had killed him to steal his wealth. Avenging their compatriot, Thracians stoned Hecuba, who "with hoarse growls, bit at the stones they threw and, though her jaws were set for words, barked when she tried to speak."

In the deafening noise of the Thracians shouting, stones ground between her teeth and her teeth breaking on the stones, her barking and the shrieks of the deoculated Polymestor, the last thing she remembers is the bloody eye she held in her hand, which was rapidly morphing into a furry paw. (For several reasons, Luis Buñuel comes to mind here with his 1929 silent film *Un chien andalou*.) The eye and the hand, vision and touch, contemplation and action—both lost in the midst of a crumbling world, which had buried her under its ruins before the Thracian stones did.

As soon as the metamorphosis of her hand into a dog paw is complete, the bloody gorged-out eye drops to the ground with a gelatinous plash. There are no more fingers to hold it. There is no more hand and no more eye, and yet she recovers vision and touch: a vision reliant on smell; a touch that is closer to the earth, with all four paws firmly planted, hugging the soil of Sithonia and getting enough traction from it to run as fast as the wind. Her sight is also in the olfactory sense, the crux of Hecuba's synesthesia, gathering all her senses under the umbrella of smell.

She keeps on barking, howling, and growling long after the crowd is gone. Now addressing the gods in her dog language, she is asking for one thing only: death. To die as a dog, like a dog, abandoned and all alone would be the height of bliss. The scenario that instils terror into most people's hearts is the only kind of death worthy of a human—the placeless one, in exile from an objective order of things—of the human she was and of the human she still is as a canine sign-tomb of that past incarnation. Her growls, howls, and yelps push against the horizon of her fate (a dog's death); they welcome it. After she perishes, the place will be the sign-tomb of the dog that she was, alluding to how the dog had been the sign-tomb of the human.

BECOMING-MANY: MEMNON
(Liber XIII, 576–622)

A PREHISTORY

Memnon, the king of Ethiopia, is dead, vanquished by the matchless Achilles. Memnon's mother, Aurora (Dawn), will not accept this state of affairs as a fait accompli. She appeals to Jupiter to reward her with the resurrection of her fallen son. Her prayers are answered: from the ashes of his body floating above the funeral pyre, Memnon is briefly reborn as a flock of black birds, as "countless sisters," *sorores innumerae*. But the rebirth is short-lived: dividing into two large groups, the birds fight each other and die a ceremonial death. Year after year.

2018: Election of Prime Minister Abiy Ahmed Ali in Ethiopia and end of the Tigray People's Liberation Front (TPLF) decades-long rule
2019: Abiy Ahmed Ali is awarded the UNESCO Peace Prize, the Hessian Peace Prize, and the Nobel Peace Prize
September 2020: TPLF holds and wins regional elections in defiance of a federal order
November 2020: Abiy Ahmed Ali sends the federal armed forces to the northern region of Tigray to commence the Mekelle Offensive
November 2020—November 2022: The Tigray War erupts, a bloody civil conflict, leaving hundreds of thousands dead.

Aurora (Dawn) dies for the day to be born and is born for the night to die. Day in, day out; this is who she is, that is what she does. In his death, Aurora's son, Memnon, births a flock of birds who annually die (in his honor!) in a sororicidal war. Viewed from another perspective, the cycle of life is a cycle of death, apparently predetermined, regularized, implacable.

August 2023: hostilities within Ethiopia flare up again.

> The people of Amhara cannot bear another conflict. WHO calls on all parties to the conflict to cease hostilities and return to talks.
> —TEDROS ADHANOM GHEBREYESUS. AUGUST 2, 2023

The dead body of king Memnon is now a dispersed multiplicity. From the one, many are born postmortem, after death, thanks to the "high-leaping flames" of the funeral pyre. They arise from the corpse and from fire, *ex ignis*, and it is this necrotic and fiery origin that haunts them, that divides them and ignites an avian civil war. As fourth-century Christian theologian Gregory of Nazianzus wrote, "the one is in *stasis* [stagnation and uproar or civil strife] with itself [*to hēn stasiazon pros heauto*] subsequently falling apart into multiplicity" (*Oratio* 3.ii). The one is fighting against itself, precisely as not-one, as the many it has become.

> The Chairperson of the African Union, H.E Moussa Faki Mahamat, is following closely and with grave concern, the continued military confrontations in the Amhara region of the Federal Democratic Republic of Ethiopia. The Chairperson reaffirms the African Union's firm attachment to the constitutional order, territorial integrity, unity and national sovereignty of the Federal Democratic Republic of Ethiopia to ensure stability in the country and in the Region.
> —MOUSSA FAKI MAHAMAT, AUGUST 17, 2023

"When the sun has completed the circuit of his twelve signs [*cum sol duodena peregit signa*], they fight and die again in the customary ceremony for their dead father."

> I am gravely concerned about the situation in Ethiopia.
> —ANTÓNIO GUTERRES, AUGUST 19, 2021

> The United States reiterates its grave concern over continuing reports of ethnically-motivated atrocities committed by Amhara authorities in western Tigray, Ethiopia, including those described in the recent joint report by Human Rights Watch and Amnesty International.
> —NED PRICE, AUGUST 4, 2022

> The Ethiopian Human Rights Commission (EHRC) has expressed "grave concern" over the "deadly hostilities between the Ethiopian National Defense Force (ENDF) and the Fano armed group in the Amhara Regional State."
> AUGUST 14, 2023

> You should consider what service I, though but a woman, render thee, when with each new light I guard the borders of the night (*cum luce nova noctis confinia servo*).
> —AURORA TO JUPITER

> Related peace and security issues shake the constitutional order, present a danger to the sovereignty of the country and public peace and safety. Therefore, to stop the situation, declaring a state of emergency has become necessary.
> —TESFAYE BELJIGE, AUGUST 4, 2023

"At last these shapes kin to buried ashes fell down as funeral offerings and remembered that they sprang from that brave hero (*seque viro forti meminere creatas*)."

Fighting against the Ethiopian National Defense Force (ENDF: END the Fighting?) are Amhara region's Fano militias. In Amharic, *fano* (or *fanno*) means "a strong young man in his prime," as well as "volunteer fighter" or "outlaw." *Fano tesemara* was a popular protest song (indeed, a call to arms) of the Ethiopian Student Movement in the 1960s. In the Italian colonial invasion of Ethiopia, the *fanno* (free peasants with their own weapons) defended their land from foreign invaders.

THE DAUGHTERS OF ANIUS: A BLESSING

(Liber XIII, 623–647)

PREAMBLE 1

Outside deeply religious circles, invocations of a blessing will, no doubt, raise eyebrows. An archaic performative speech act, a blessing says nothing informative. It does not communicate anything to anyone, except announcing or enunciating itself as the blessing that it is. But this not-saying-anything is—according to the word *blessing*, or its Latin-inflected form *benediction*—saying well and doing well, if not saying and doing the good. Needless to say, it wishes the good for that which or the one who is blessed, and, beyond that, it transforms itself (at the core of its verbal and ritual structures) into a channel for good energy, concentrated and steered toward the blessed. Without

THE DAUGHTERS OF ANIUS: A BLESSING

adding anything substantively new, a blessing provides the coordinates, orienting the good. Conversely, a curse, or a *malediction*, wishes and says that which is bad, or outright evil. It, too, is a channel, though this time for negative energy, bringing bad luck or tragic fate. As a channel, it cannot but be affected by what it channels; while the one who blesses is touched by the good redirected toward the other, the one who curses is grazed by the evil transmitted to the other.

PREAMBLE 2

The three daughters of Anius, a seer and a priest of Apollo, are Oeno, Spermo, and Elais, or Wine, Grain Seeds, and Oil. From Bacchus, they have received a gift: upon their touch, *nam tactu*, everything turned into "corn and wine and the oil of gray-green Minerva [olives]." Waging war against Troy, Agamemnon captured the three sisters "and bade them feed the Grecian army with their heavenly gifts." The blessing of the daughters of Anius turned into a curse: they were forced to supply invading soldiers with provisions, fueling their bloody rampage.

In Judaism, the blessings (*b'rakhot*) of wine and bread are pronounced whenever a religious person is about to consume these fermented products. The blessings thank God for "bringing forth bread from the earth" and "creating the fruit of grapes." Christian Eucharist is a variation on this blessing, which converts bread and wine into the body and the blood of Christ.

A BLESSING

Blessed be the three sisters,
Giving sustenance to the hungry,
Comforting bodies and cheering spirits,
Inspiring those they nourish
To nourish others,
To become the bread, and the wine, and the oil for their neighbors,
Prolonging lives, rather than cutting them short,
Sharing the gifts,
Satiating with a just peace.

THE DAUGHTERS OF ORION: A BLOOD OFFERING FOR THE WOUNDED EARTH

(Liber XIII, 648-699)

When nymphs fail to fill dried-up springs
With the tears of sorrow they weep
For a parched earth;
When the bareness of leafless trees
Is matched only by human exposure
To the scorching sun and the impending end;
When starved cattle perish on a stony earth,
No longer covered by the brilliant green
Of grass and shrubs—
Then
Will we, like the daughters of Orion,
non femineum iugulo dare vulnus aperto
illac demisso per fortia pectora telo
("dealing wounds of more than maidenly courage
to their bared throats, with weapons plunged into their valiant
    breasts"),
Fall back on the oldest and goriest of survival technique,
Spilling blood?
Our own or that of others?
Will the soil rejuvenate after it imbibes
Streams of gruesome sacrifice?
Will the terrible offering to god-knows-whom

Fill the aquifers and the lakes, the rivers and the reservoirs
With lifegiving moisture?
Will it give room by making space?
Wars raging on the body of the already wounded earth:
To sacrifice foe and friend alike.
Melancholy dreams of the world without us, thriving:
To sacrifice the human species for planetary wellbeing.
Same old same old ancient logic
Sweeps through both scenarios,
Now developing in parallel
And now feeding into one another.

POLYPHEMUS AND GALATEA: LAND AND SEA

(Liber XIII, 700-897)

Land and sea confront one other in an elemental standoff: the apparent stability and solidity of the former contrasts the indeterminacy, uncertainty, wavering, treacherous depths, and vacillations of the latter. True, the earth can give way in landslides or earthquakes; its volcanic protrusions may erupt with hot lava. But as land, it sustains. Overgrown with the "shaggy locks" of vegetation, boasting "a whole mountainside for its possession," bearing herds of animals.

A sense of transcendence, of an abrupt transition from one condition to another, is born at the cusp of land and sea. This transcendence is as elemental as it is political: maritime empires articulate and organize themselves in another way than the imperial landmass. It is the Leviathan versus the Behemoth, as Carl Schmitt conceives of the elemental-political confrontation via Hobbes and Johann Jakob Bachofen, or the cyclops Polyphemus versus the nereid Galatea in Ovid's recounting of the myth. Except that Polyphemus loves Galatea, offering everything that is his as "gifts," *munera*, to her. What forms does land's love of the sea assume? Does the land that offers to the sea entire mountainsides, vegetal beards and locks, flocks and herds, consent to being submerged by its marine lover? In this hypothetical state of self-abandon, does land eagerly sacrifice parts of itself to the rising sea? Or does it, on the contrary, encircle maritime expanses, imposing itself on them?

One thing is clear: despite his monstrous appearance, fearsome character, and wild demeanor, after Polyphemus falls in love with Galatea he begins to work on, cultivate and cherish his limits (which *she* sets), to know himself through the beloved other, to realize his finitude and to accept it. Elemental love prompts Polyphemus to "comb shaggy locks" with a rake, to "cut rough beard" with a reaping hook, to care for himself and for others: *caedis amor feritasque*, "his love of slaughter falls away." He admits: "lately I saw my reflection in a clear pool," that is to say, in her, in water, who granted him self-knowledge. A clear pool, of course, is not the sea by any stretch of the imagination; unlike maritime expanses, it is domesticated, contained by the earth, landlocked, quelled, disciplined. With all these provisos, it is not insignificant that land delivers itself visually, symbolically, cognitively to its watery other and receives itself—altered, having been endowed with a measure of self-knowledge—from that other.

Galatea does not reciprocate Polyphemus's affection. She is in love with another (Acis: we will have a chance to reflect about this strange love triangle in a moment). Polyphemus, though, attributes her lack of interest in him to her obdurate commitment to the elemental war, the unwillingness of the sea to meet the land halfway, to entertain any encounter other than lashing the shore with the waves. He accuses Galatea, the daughter of Nereus who is the old sea god, of being *fallacior undis* (falser than water) and *surdior aequoribus* (deafer than the sea). Without quite comprehending her, without seeing what frames and determines his vision, he considers the sea from the standpoint of the land. In a similar way, land-based empires point out the imperial nature of maritime empires, while falling short of recognizing their own.

That is where the ill-fated love triangle comes to the fore. The son of Faunus and a Symaethian nymph, Acis is the object of Galatea's desire. Reborn as a river god, he is the union of water and land, of a nontranscendent relation between these two elements. Were it not for the elemental standoff, Acis would have been a child of Polyphemus and Galatea; instead, he is smothered to death by jealous Polyphemus, buried under a "hurled piece wrenched from the mountainside," the same mountainside perhaps as the one land offered as a gift to the sea. Here, Polyphemus's hypocrisy is unmasked: whereas land accuses the sea of stubbornly pursuing elemental conflict, she, loving Acis, meets land halfway. And land goes so far as to castrate himself, breaking off a juicy chunk of himself, only to prevent that union from being consummated.

The revival of Acis as a river god, as waterways cutting through land, simultaneously remolds a deadening act into the act of generation. Against his own will, Polyphemus is the progenitor, with Galatea, of her metamorphosed lover. "The mass that had been thrown cracked wide open and a tall, green reed sprang up through the crack, and the hollow opening in the rock resounded with leaping waters, and, wonderful! suddenly a youth stood forth waist-deep from the water." Parturition takes place in the body of Polyphemus, which cracks and births a spring, then a river. Galatea, for her part, swells in and flows through that body. Acis's resurrection, his birth from a violent death, wreaks havoc in the identities of land and sea that are mixed, mixed-up, in the fecund middle. He, Polyphemus, is now a birth-giving *she*; she, Galatea, is now an inseminating *he*. Acis does not metamorphose alone. With him, the entire love triangle morphs into a circle.

PHYTOMORPHOSIS: GLAUCUS
(Liber XIII, 898-969; Liber XIV, 1-79)

Glaucus,

I was moved to write this letter because I spotted a sliver of you in myself (unless, the other way around, it was myself in you that I saw). You say you've discovered the powers of the herbs, *vires herba*, and that these powers have reshaped you. After imbibing vegetal juices, you lost consciousness, and when you regained it, you were transformed. "I was different from what I was but lately," you testify "in all my body, nor was my mind the same (*neque eundem mente recepi*)." Anyone else would have quipped: "What's so strange about this? When you ingest certain substances (whether plant-based, fungal, or synthetic), you should expect to experience altered states of consciousness, to sense your very body and the world otherwise than in everyday life." But I suspect that something else is going on with you (and with me).

You report that the setting for your vegetal epiphany was breathtakingly refreshing, untouched by human and by animal alike. You found yourself on "a shore fringed by verdant meadows... which neither horned cattle have ever disturbed in grazing nor have the peaceful sheep nor hairy she-goats cropped." Such close attention to the place is not a minor detail. Nor is it "something like an idle tale," *res similis fictae*, the ancient fake news. You were already phytomorphosing when you were attending to the meadows and the shores this way, a bit like plants who are exquisitely mindful of everything that surrounds them, above and below ground. The guiding question in becoming-plant is about *where* the metamorphosis unravels, rather than *how, from what* or *into what*.

For me, a certain place was the catalyst of my mind's metamorphosis, the Peneda-Gerês National Park (you can look it up, if you want, but its *where* cannot be captured in words or images). Plant-thinking started to course through me there, or, more accurately, I became aware of its having coursed through me for as long as I have existed, thanks to the fledgling intuition born there. You put it well: "I stood for a long time in amazement and doubt" before "I felt my heart trembling within me, and my whole being yearned with desire for another element." Breathing in the air of the forest, inspiring, expiring, and conspiring with plant life meant *there* (and in other places, to which I have carefully transplanted this feeling) activating a vegetal mind, thinking about and thinking with vegetality in me and outside of me. So, after you, I can repeat: "What potency herbs [*herbarum potentia*] have, no one knows better than myself, for I was changed by them."

"The point, however, is to change the world," a pair of philosophers would retort to us. Yes, but a finer vegetal point is to show how the world is changing, how it has already changed, how any and all sustainable change is driven by plants, themselves constantly changing beings conveying in every one of their fibers that all metamorphosis is phytometamorphosis or, simply, phytomorphosis. It's not up to me to explain this to you, Glaucus—you, who embarked on your unique trajectory of transformation after imbibing the liquid potency of herbs, which led you to the ocean, which made you "plunge into the sea" and to commit to an amphibious life.

Not everything is ideal and idyllic in phytomorphosis. This, also, no one knows better than yourself, after the jealous Circe used the brew of "noxious roots," *radice nocenti*, in order to poison the pond where your beloved Scylla dwelt and to turn her into a monster. Altering the body and the mind well beyond the scope of psychedelic or psychoactive substances some plants contain, herbal powers work in secret, unexpectedly, their metabolic properties closely linked to their metamorphic potential. To deliver oneself to them, body and mind, is to be in for a surprise.

PHYTOMORPHOSIS: GLAUCUS

You are eager to swim away, Glaucus. I know, I know. My writing will not detain you here much longer. Take this letter with you to the depths of the sea. Not in a bottle, but unprotected. Let its vegetal ink merge with salt water; allow the tree afterlife that works as its paper support to dissolve, as well. We who say *yes* to phytomorphosis do not hold on to unpliable identities. For thinking and writing to develop along the lines of plant-thinking and plant-writing, they must be released to a congeries of their vegetal destinies, which neither you nor I can predict, let alone predetermine.

Farewell

THE SIBYL'S MONOLOGUE
(Liber XIV, 80-153)

Sand. Such a calm and abundant trace of past violence! Each grain is a nonstop silent scream: listen attentively with your heart and with your hand—you will hear it. Each complains about the violence of deep time slowly grinding geological formations to earth crumbs. The violence of breaking calcified organic matter down to the smallest bits. Pulverized... What was I thinking when I tied my fate to a handful of sand? Grabbing it, "I made a foolish prayer that I might have as many years of life as there were sand-grains in the pile." I wished on myself that each year would be a grain of sand: diminished, dry, degraded. No rejuvenating power, nothing organically enlivening. Only sand... Our lives are made of nothing but time. And when time is made of sand, sand is the stuff of our lives. I became a walking-talking hourglass. (Soon to be only a talking, not a walking one.) With each grain of sand that dropped down the tiny opening into the lower glass bulb, I grew smaller, as well. Even if I were to hug all the sand there is, I would not have been saved. My torture would have been more excruciating: I would be hanging out to dry, deserted by everyone including myself, my body-self, for all eternity. When a certain patriarch was promised that his progeny would be as numerous as the grains of sand on a beach, was that a blessing or a curse? You decide. Anyway, it turns out I grabbed exactly one thousand grains of sand. Old Heraclitus can testify to this. I don't know how he knew. But it's there, in his Fragment 92, the grain of sand his thought turned into. "A raving mouth," *mainomenó stomati*: that's what he calls me.

THE SIBYL'S MONOLOGUE

By the time, in year 1, Ovid came across my shriveling body, seven hundred grains, seven hundred years, had slipped away from me. The worst was yet to come: I told him all about it. It seems like I had three hundred years of painful shrinkage left in me. But here we are 2,025 years on—and I am still here. Or still there. Or, in fact, neither here nor there but somewhere between the two. It was prophesied that only my voice would survive, *vocem mihi fata relinquent*, after my body was reduced to nothing. This voice has tarried with you past its expiration date. I have outlived myself by more than seventeen centuries. A voice that, less than an echo, no longer sounds, no longer resounds, but is written, transcribed, recorded. In these pages and elsewhere. Still raving, Heraclitus would say, but already without a mouth. Why? Maybe because, sliding down in the closed space of an hourglass, the sands of time do not pass; they are not digested into the past. They sit there, accumulating in the lower portion of this time-measuring contraption, the chronometer of our lives made of grinding deep-time violence. You have the impression that, at any moment, you can flip the hourglass, invert the senses of what was up and what was down, of all-the-time-in-the-world and of no-time-left. But this is not the case. All those irreversible sand grains are accumulating somewhere, everywhere, which is fast becoming a nowhere. Becoming-desert, filled with sand. And covered with it, all over. A grainy and silent voice recording of screams as a substitute for the living web of the world. Every creature that has ever existed, that will ever exist, and that has never existed nor will ever exist joins this cacophonous chorus. I am their mouthpiece, a raving mouth without mouth, a voice without sound, bodiless mortal immortal relics. I have not chosen this fate for myself. The god who granted me one thousand withering years could not have foreseen this. In my near nonbeing, I've turned into an orifice for crumbling being and for nonbeing, for . . .

the . . .

becoming-sand . . .

of the world . . .

BECOMING-FOREIGN-TO-YOURSELF: ACHAEMENIDES

(Liber XIV, 154–222)

1. Close your eyes and take a deep breath. Observe the flow of your thoughts. Sieve through them, separating those you recognize as typical for you from those that surprise you, so out of sync they are with your normalized self. Zoom in on the surprising thoughts. Then shed mental light onto the one observing you from within. Mark the difference between yourself as observing and yourself as observed. Situate yourself in the gap between them. Welcome to your foreignness to yourself in thinking!
2. Open your eyes and take a look at your body parts: arms, feet, legs, hands, chest, genitals, stomach, etc. You may use a magnifying glass. Focus on skin irregularities, pores, scars, hair, birthmarks. Mentally or with the help of drawing reconnect parts of your body by linking these traces to one another. Discover the animal heritage of your body and its vegetal legacies.
3. Concentrate on your joints, especially at the knees and elbows, hips and shoulders. Experiment with the freedom of movement they afford you. In the wake of these experiments, place your limbs into usual positions, varying the combinations of these across your entire body. Disarticulate and rearticulate yourself starting from the joints.
4. Ask yourself where your home (*domus*) is. What is the place you keep circling back to, your personal Ithaca? This can be a geographical locale, an idea, a person, a living being, an inanimate thing—at any scale of

existence. Do not take homecoming for granted. Dedomesticate your home. Invent other vectors and other trajectories that would not necessarily put you on the arc of return. Achaemenides: "May I look on Polyphemus yet again, and those wide jaws of his dripping with human gore, if I prefer my home and Ithaca to this ship . . ."

5. Try out different vocal articulations that are not present in your mother tongue or in other languages you speak. These may be similar to screeches, bellows, resonant vibrations, palpitations, murmuring, thumping, droning, or buzzing of nonhuman animals or things. Don't speak a foreign language; become foreign to yourself in a language yet to be articulated.

6. Analyze the ways in which you are digested into the elements, plants, and social interactions through atmospheric emissions, sewage discharges, solid waste/garbage, messaging apps, speech. Visualize how your flesh sinks into the flesh of existence (*mea viscera . . . in sua mersurum*). Whatever of you does not dissolve in various milieus will fossilize. Relate to yourself as a fossil to-come.

7. *Mors erat ante oculos,* "Death was before my eyes." Do not avert your mind-body's gaze from your mortality. Consider yourself from the standpoint of having died before you actually die, "fearing death and yet longing to die," *mortemque timens cupidusque moriri.* Defamiliarize your routine from a place and a time beyond the absolute horizon of their finitude.

8. How will you breathe, think, move your body, speak, and relate to others from the carefully cultivated condition of your foreignness to yourself? Who will you be to yourself? What will "your" self be to you?

AEOLUS: THE RULER OF THE WINDS
(Liber XIV, 223-319)

Aeolus "confined the winds in a prison" (*cohibentem carcere ventos*). Also called "the ruler of the Tuscan waters," *Tusco regnare profundo*, he is primarily the ruler of the winds. Hence, Aeolic/eolic power.

While wind energy is a renewable resource, its deployment is useless and even harmful in the absence of an overall paradigm shift in our theories and practices of energy generation. Imprisoning the elements will not do the trick, unless we learn to live, power, and empower ourselves in synergy with them. To see in energy a synergy, rather than a struggle or future entropy. The winds "confined . . . in a prison" spell out disaster. And, yes, a disaster is not long in waiting: the winds "enclosed in a bag of bull's hide" steer the ship of Ulysses and his companions in the right direction until they "untied the strings that held the winds (*dempsisse ligamina ventis*)."

AEOLUS: THE RULER OF THE WINDS

Freshly liberated, the winds cause the vessel to reverse its course and sail back to dangerous waters and unsafe shores. There, the voyagers were enchanted by Circe and turned into pigs.

Capture and release, resource accumulation, mastery and subjugation are poor orientations for a calm and sustainable model of energy generation. Tight control is caught in seesaw dynamics with the total *loss* of control, that is, with being at the mercy of the very thing one considered to be under one's thumb. The same goes for insane "green" proposals to uproot hundreds of thousands of trees in order to install a gigantic solar energy farm or to place wind turbines in bird migration paths or on indigenous lands, further jeopardizing local ways of life. The current "rulers of the winds" still live with prisons in their heads, which is why they build prisons and walls, both material and immaterial, all around the globe.

Long in coming, a nonnegotiable metamorphosis has to do with our conceptions and practices of energy. Rather than a withheld potentiality, viciously extracted from all that is and just as viciously released in a burst of activation, energy should connote the actuality of what just is, of what keeps metamorphosing into another. Not formless, but materially formed and changing in synergic interactions. Even when it comes to the wind, which could be guided and steered toward a desired outcome, while we let it steer and guide us in the singular configurations of its force.

A sail is a synergic energy device, particularly because it moves together with the wind; a wind turbine is not. Of course, the latter is a magnified version of a windmill, but here size matters: the sheer scale and number of wind turbines comprising a wind farm, let alone the materials of which they are made, shift this mode of energy production back into the destructive mode. Every classical category, from quantity and quality to possibility/actuality and relationality, has a role to play in the redefinition of our theories and practices of energy, not to mention the questions of *what* it is (its quiddity) and *how* it is (procured and utilized).

So long as we imagine ourselves, on a par with Aeolus, to be "the rulers of the winds," we will keep smuggling the old shape of destructive-extractive energy back into ostensibly "green" solutions. Energy metamorphoses will have failed then. As the rulers of the atom, we will untie the strings that temporarily stabilize atomic energy, opening the Pandora's box. The ship of existence reversing its course is the best we can hope for in these circumstances.

PICUS, OR THE KEYBOARD PECKER
(Liber XIV, 320-434)

o: At times, he touches laptop keys gently and silently, almost caressing them, softly stroking them as if playing a Mozart piano sonata in A minor. But these occasions are rare. More often than not, he strikes the keys of his universal writing machine in a rapid succession of moves, with precise and perfectly coordinated gestures: *tuc-tuc, tuc-tuc-tuc-tuc, tuc, tuc-tuc-tuc.* (Between stroking and striking, there is a world of difference, and yet only one letter changes; *o* becomes *i*. The roundness and wholeness of the *o* gives way to the pointed sharpness of the *i*.) He grows ten strong, albeit invisible, beaks at the tips of his fingers, and it is with these beaks that he pecks the keys.

i: That's strange. I thought that a keyboard pecker was someone quite inept at typing. Not having the order of letters and other characters on the keyboard memorized, this person uses just two fingers to press each key, in a painfully slow fashion. Such inaptitude is called "hunting and pecking," actually.

o: Whoever came up with this name has never heard a real woodpecker in a forest. Nor even a chicken on a farm, whose pecking movements are much faster than those of a hunting-and-pecking digital novice. Imagine: the stream of his ideas rushes at an enormous speed. Quick as his fingers might be, they stand no chance—his hands cannot catch up with his head. That's why it sounds like this, I mean, like "an indignant bird," *indignatus avem*, who "with his hard beak wrathfully inflicts wounds on the long and rough oak tree branches."

I: You are wrong yet again. Woodpeckers don't just hurt trees; they also devour caterpillars, wood borers, bark lice, and other insects keen to inflict damage. Why wouldn't the bird pour its wrath out onto these critters? Or maybe it's plain hungry?

O: Remember, we are talking about and listening to a metamorphosed woodpecker, be it Picus, who suddenly "saw feathers covering his body," *pennas in corpore vidit*, after he scorned Circe's advances, or the one pecking enragedly at his computer keyboard with ten finger-beaks. Pecking is their peculiar manner of expressing emotions, of displacing negative affect and chipping at an oak trunk instead of Circe's treacherous hand or at the body of a laptop instead of . . .

I: Before this fateful metamorphosis he "went blindly groping in the forest depths." (I can't help but think back to the poor hunting-and-pecking typist.) As a woodpecker, is he at home in the forest? Orienting himself well in its depths? Seeing in the dark of matter, the dark light of matter itself? And the digital woodpecker—what light does he see, aside from the blue glow of the screen? What is that *vision of the fingers*, whose proficiency is *heard* in the *tuc-tuc-tuc* of the keyboard?

O: Everything is new, save for the name. *Nec quicquam antiquum Pico nisi nomina restat*: "nothing of his old self remained to Picus, except his name." You may conclude that names are resistant to metamorphosis. But maybe they are so accommodating to the most diverse kinds that *names are metamorphoses*? Only the name remained and nothing else; still, the name doesn't merely remain as an outdated relic but is perfectly adequate to the transformed Picus. To cut a long story short, he is at home in his name. And, consequently, at home in the world, in the forest, in the dark intimacy and immanence of matter, and (yes!) at the computer screen and by the keyboard.

ACMON TURNING INTO A BIRD: A JOKE
(Liber XIV, 435-511)

Acmon's metamorphosis into a swanlike bird would have been encrypted as a multilayered joke, still resonating with Greek-speaking Romans in Ovid's times.

Inciting the wrath of Venus, "naturally hot-headed" (*fervidus ingenio*) Acmon rejects ongoing suffering (*patientia*), his own and that of his companions. For his insolence he is punished: his voice grows thin, his neck elongates, his elbows curve into nimble wings, his face grows "stiff, ending in a sharp-pointed beak."

Considering that Acmon (*akmōn*) means "anvil"—a heavy block, of cast steel or iron, upon which blacksmiths strike and shape hot metals—the metamorphosis and the events preceding it appear in an ironic light. Acmon's hotheadedness is now attributable to the molten iron being struck on top of it; the suffering, against which the speech daringly attacking Venus rebels, is the patience and forbearance of the metallic support for metal that is being worked on. But the most striking (pun intended!) feature of the transformation is that of a hefty artifact, used to manufacture other artifacts, becoming an elegant and light bird. The suddenly stiffened face of Acmon is the sole trace of the metal block's rigidity (with a further connotation of this stiffening added in the context of the character's interactions with Venus). Other than that, the elegant, elongated neck, the long feathers, and the nimble wings of the bird he has morphed into could not be more different from his previous incarnation.

The climax of the joke is that an anvil defies the pull of gravity and takes flight. Moving *contra natura*, it is ensouled, or maybe possessed. The comedic devices of juxtaposition, hyperbole, punning, and double entendre are all deployed, but the most effective technique is that of the mismatch between the name and the thing so named. It is in the gap between them that the subversive power of humor is abruptly discharged, retrospectively coloring the description of Acmon with ironic, or even sarcastic, hues.

AN APULIAN SHEPHERD: BITTER WORDS, BITTER FRUITS

(Liber XIV, 512–565)

Apulian Shepherd (From The Adriatic Coast Of Present-Day Italy)

BEHAVIOR

- Terrifying the nymphs
- Mocking the nymphs, clownishly imitating their dances
- Screaming "boorish insults and vulgar words" (*obscenis convicia rustica dictis*)

"Now he is a tree." *Arbor enim est.* A wild olive, to be precise.

Wild Olive (Olea Europaea L. Subsp. Oleaster)

BIOCHEMICAL COMPOSITION

Oleic acid—$C_{18}H_{34}O_2$
    Linoleic acid—$C_{18}H_{32}O_2$
    Palmitic acid—$C_{16}H_{32}O_2$
    Stearic acid—$C_{18}H_{36}O_2$
Phenol—C_6H_6O
Tocopherol
    α-Tocopherols—$C_{29}H_{50}O_2$

β-Tocopherols—$C_{28}H_{48}O_2$
γ-Tocopherols—$C_{28}H_{48}O_2$

The focal point of metamorphosis is the tongue: the words it mouths, the flavors it savors. The acrimony of the Apulian shepherd's speech persists in the bitterness of the wild olives that grow on the tree he has become. Although in his new arboreal shape he no longer has a tongue, the site of reception for his irritating missives is the tongue of the other, of a poor soul who ventures to taste the olives. From the tongue as the source of emission (of insulting words, for instance), we switch to the tongue as the site of reception of bitter (*amaris*) flavors and of sharp, pungent (*asper*) hints. Broken down to its biochemical components, the flavor of wild olives corresponds, line by line, molecule by molecule, to aspects of the shepherd's behavior. Now, semantic bits are coded in the language of oleic acid, phenol, and the tocopherols. The tongue that tastes them gets the point right away, without the interference of linguistic interpretation.

What is still more difficult to chew on is the "rustic," unbearably "boorish" character of the unnamed shepherd, which earns him the punishment of being transmogrified into wild olives. Embittered, he transmits bitterness. Very often, wild fruit are inappropriate for human consumption. The work of cultivation then purposefully selects those varieties of wild plants that are palatable and sweeter, promoting these in agriculture and taking over the job of evolutionary development. The shepherd obsessively enacts wild behavior—but to whom is it unpalatable? To the self-proclaimed upper-class denizens of civilization? The nymphs, whom the shepherd verbally and gesturally attacks, however, are not the typical representatives of an alienated civilization; they are the spirits of the streams and rivers, of the woods and the meadows. His behavior is wild from the perspective of the wilderness itself: the wild of the wild.

RE: A FUNEREAL HYMN FOR AENEAS

(Liber XIV, 566-608)

Reduce, reuse, recycle—your body.
Reduce it to its best part, *pars optima*, which will evade decay.
To the bones. Stripped bare.
Reuse the frame to clothe it with divine flesh.
Recycle in your newly procured divinity the old gods of the place,
The indigenous deities who will have coalesced in you,
    Aeneas-Indiges.
Venus herself, your mother, the love of all that exists
Re-creates you.
Repurgat, respersit, restitit.
She cleanses you over and over again,
Liberating you of yourself—
A funeral that is no funeral—
Ridding you of parts of you not deemed the best (for her, not you).
She keeps sprinkling you with divine perfume
To mask the stench of decomposition.
She ensures that something remains of you,
That something is saved, indeed,
That not everything is lost, beyond recognition,
Of what you and the others knew of you.

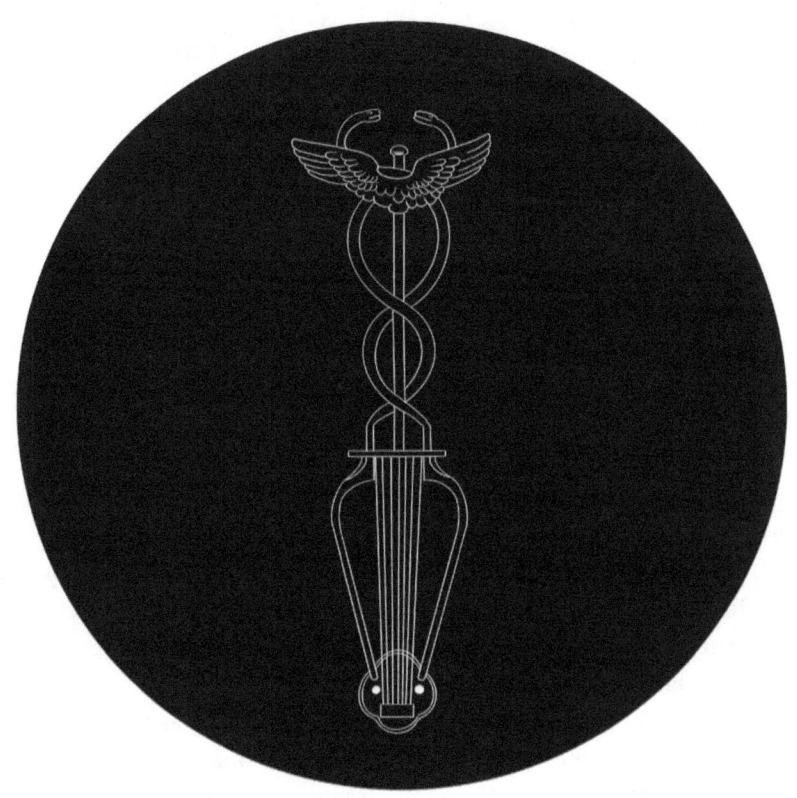

VERTUMNUS, VERTIMUS: THE TURN OF BECOMING

(Liber XIV, 609-697)

Vertumnus, the seducer. How could he not achieve what he had set out to do? His name verges on *vertimus:* we become, we turn. Into what? Into whom? Too early to tell and too early to ask. But as soon as these questions are raised, he has already captivated and involved us: he turns and becomes with us, as us; we turn and become with him, into him, through him into just about anything. An endless text-only and text-not-only feed.

A "perfect image" of the sower and the reaper, Vertumnus busies himself also with everything that happens before, between, and after these agricultural activities. The alpha and omega of being as becoming, his is the love that is both first and last; *you* are his first and last passion, *tu primus et ultimus illi ardor eris.*

Before anything happens, he turns and overturns the previous state of existence. That is the preparing inherent in all preparation. Preparing the ground, working with the earth, with the soil—this, too, is included in the verb *vertere*. The very first sentence in Book I of Virgil's *Georgics* (1:1) begins from the absolute agricultural beginning: *terram vertere*, overturning the soil, or, simply, ploughing the field in a certain type of human engagement with plants meant to encourage their becoming. It indicates that to become, to turn (say, into a bountiful plant), it is necessary to disturb, to turn around and overturn the soil or the present state of affairs.

After everything has taken place, he does not let things stagnate and triggers another revolution in being. Turning not only the soil but also freshly mown grass, *recenti desectum . . . gramen versasse*. There is no becoming without a revolution properly so called, an overturning overthrow, in which we turn (*vertimus*) together with everything and everyone swept into the whirl of this movement. The overturning overthrow of becoming seems insatiable.

Nothing works behind the scenes, never making an appearance in the open, in the finite opening of existence it helps along. The nothing works there, and he embodies it as its "perfect image." We can only infer the work of nothing from the othering of the same, its dis- or refiguring. If becoming is both a coming-into-being and a passing-away, becoming and unbecoming, coming and going, *venir* and *de-venir*, then it is both growing and decaying, with metamorphosis taking place between these transitions. Mind you, we are dealing with vegetal movements, which is why the nothing that works in him, through him, works with and through plants.

Hence: *all becoming is becoming-plant*. As we become anything or anyone, we become plants; we become them and *with* them. This does not necessarily mean that we blossom or develop roots, literally or metaphorically. For Goethe, the essence of plants is metamorphosis. Change of shape does not overlay an immutable core making them what they are. Metamorphosis *is* plants; their *living form is the alteration of form*. Becoming-plant, becoming-vegetal we turn (*vertimus*) into metamorphosis, become the becoming.

We deliver ourselves to a finite becoming, which is at the same time endless. There is a double deferral at play here, pushing back against nothing as much as against being, understood as what has become, what has come out of becoming, the end result, a final outcome. Becoming, after all, is a journey without a fixed terminus or terminal, and even though there are definite outcomes of vegetal becoming (fruit and seeds are the obvious references), these outcomes lack ultimacy because they, in their turn (the turn of *vertere*), initiate a new cycle of growth and decay. Circular closure coincides with absolute openness. Usually taken to signify immobility and stagnation, plants are mutable, versatile, and supple enough to flesh out the becoming of those without a formal membership in their biological kingdom—say, us, ourselves. Metamorphosing, they *are* that which is on the way toward or out of being, green transitions between being and nothing. Passing from one state to another, we also become plants. *Vertimus*. And imperceptibly, Vertumnus accompanies us at every turn.

MARBLE THOUGHTS: ANAXARETE

(Liber XIV, 698–764)

What a weird spot to mount a statue of Anaxarete! By the window, peering out from behind the curtain, looking to the street. Her marble face is full of horror and surprise: eyebrows raised, eyes wide open, mouth gaping. Sometimes it seems that those facial expressions change, but it might be no more than the play of light and shadow as the sun travels across the sky, illuminating different sides of the exquisitely chiseled visage.

She is ensconced in one of those liminal spaces, neither fully within nor without, neither reassuringly private nor completely public—liminal like the "hard threshold," *limine duro*, of the house where she is placed and where her despondent would-be lover Iphis hanged himself, his corpse's swinging feet banging on the door as if to "demand admittance." Neither herself nor not-herself, the marble Anaxarete is a monument to herself.

MARBLE THOUGHTS: ANAXARETE

Some people, after all, act as statues of themselves throughout their lives. Rigid, commemorating a life not lived but monumentalized, a thought not thought but edified. No one is admitted in the sphere of statue-persons, not even the statue-persons themselves.

—When you philosophize, do you carve your language from marble? Or do you let it flow and flourish?

Marble thoughts are of a "stony nature," to be sure, but this stone, softer than granite and harder than limestone, yields to the chisel. So, marble thoughts are somewhere between Descartes's den and Socrates's marketplace (*agora*). Yielding to the chisel, they are prone to figurativity, the concepts clothed in a material form, which is ultimately the thinker's own carnival mask. This mask does not cover the face only: it merges with the face and then creepingly spreads to the rest of the body, taking possession of it. That's the price you pay for embodying your work, for the life of the mind poured onto the page or the screen.... Then the others, those who come after, can play with your marble thoughts as a child plays with toy soldiers or with dolls (or with marbles, for that matter): putting them side by side, making them clash, pretending that they nurse one another, have the afternoon tea together, or do marching exercises. The technical term for such make-believe is *interpretation*.

As for Anaxarete, I am inclined to think that, far from illusory, the expressions of her sculpted face really change. Marble thoughts are the grimaces of marble faces. Though apparently static, their slow procession makes up marble consciousness, a marble intentionality replete with marble senses, intuitions, memories, anticipations. And let's not forget the all too evident analogy: the statue that Anaxarete has become corresponds to the rigor mortis of Iphis's body. This dead body, however, displays an uncanny, ghostly intentionality—banging on the door with its swinging feet in a continuation of the quest to cross her threshold, which his body pursued while alive. So, it would stand to reason (above all, to the marble reason that always stands, not inclined but erect as a statue, which, for its part, is always standing, even if it is in a seated or prone position) that her marble body is replete with an intentionality of its own, similarly carrying on the activity of the flesh-and-blood body across the ruptures of its transformation.

—What sort of intentionality would that be?

—Resistance to softening and melting, the energy-intensive maintenance of hardness always in the process of abating.

THE APOTHEOSIS OF ROMULUS: BLOOD FOR CELESTIAL PEACE
(Liber XIV, 765-851)

The stories of two city founders, Romulus and Myscelus, weld a narrative hinge between Book XIV and Book XV of Ovid's *Metamorphoses*. History—of Rome and Crotona, as much as of all other political communities—is a living and multipronged metamorphosis of founding moments. After a while, the founding events lose their initial shape—they themselves are transformed by their subsequent transformations. (Don't believe me? Then take a look at the five ancient and highly venerated Buddha images housed at the Phaung Daw Oo Pagoda on Inle Lake in Myanmar. You will immediately sense the workings of history in the most palpable of manners.)

A common vector of transforming the foundation is its cleansing. Grisly, bloody, violent beginnings start resembling an elegant, wise, benevolent inauguration. Merciless war morphs into perpetual peace, especially if this peace reigns on the terms dictated by victors in the war. The founder of a city (but also of a cult, a sect, a new religion) ascends to heavens, not subject to decomposition and decay reserved for the rest of us mortals. The founder's divinization completes the process of cleansing the foundations, of pointing to a squeaky-clean floor, where viscera and maimed limbs have lain just a moment ago in pools of blood, feces, urine, and vomit. But something else has changed in the meanwhile: the floor is now above, where the ceiling should have been.

Poets play a role that is far from negligible in cleaning up historical mess. One could say that poets are the janitors of history. Ovid renders Romulus divine: with the silent nod of consent of Jupiter himself, *corpus mortale per auras dilapsum tenues* ("his mortal body dissolved into thin air"), while *pulchra subit facies* ("a fair form clothes him"), the form of a god. Brilliantly glorious, Romulus attains life everlasting, receiving the name of the god Quirinus. He becomes a serene lawgiver, shedding along with his mortal body, the image of a warrior and a fratricide.

But while cleaning up the mess, Ovid puts it in plain sight. Who was Quirinus? On the authority of Varro, Dionysius identifies him as an ancient Sabine deity (2.48), the god revered by a people who lived in the Apennine region before the founding of Rome, the event a large section of the Sabine population, which stayed in tribal formations in the mountains, resisted. The Sabines lost their war against Rome and were eventually assimilated into the Roman Republic. Ovid is not inconsistent with Dionysius. It is the "fair form" of the Sabine deity that clothes the transmogrified frame of Romulus, even as the Quirinal Hill is included within Rome's city limit. The slain and the subjugated are incorporated into their slayer and subjugator: in his superhuman hypostasis he becomes them.

Ideologies of all stripes justify the shedding of blood for a higher cause: the steep staircase to heaven is strewn with corpses that actually fulfill the function of stairs and banisters on it. The question is: What to do with the staircase after the ascent is complete or after it is presented as completed—which, for all intents and purposes, amounts to the same thing?

Ludwig Wittgenstein, who neither had a dialectical mind nor entertained the possibility of climbing *down* from his propositions, insisted on throwing away the propositional ladder as soon as one had used it to make one's way up to the truth. (Recall Heraclitus, Fr. 60: "The way up and the way down is one and the same.") In the historical dimension, this implies forgetting the bloodshed, subjecting foundational violence to the most severe psychic repression. Wittgenstein's solution is as detrimental to the work of thinking as to the demand for justice, for the workings that are still alive in a finished work as for the bones and other shreds of the victims of history that prop up its living edifice.

Ovid's solution is more dialectical, even if it falls short of the standards of justice. The apotheosis of Romulus and his deification as Quirinus essentially say: having climbed up the ladder and become a god, become the ladder. Or, more exactly put: become a god by becoming the ladder you used to reach such heights, by including in your deathless glory all the gore and all the deaths, to which you owe it. Romulus's mortal body dissolved into thin air, but the fairest divine form, for which it was exchanged, did not preclude corporeality: via Quirinus, into whom he was transformed, all the nameless and dead Sabines entered, still anonymously but indelibly.

There is no better way to forget than to commemorate out of context: names without beings and beings without names.

There is no better way to wash off the blood that has been spilled than to soak it up, even and especially by shining bright with divine glory.

HOMELAND INSECURITY: MYSCELUS
(Liber XV, 1-59)

...*poenaque mors posita est patriam mutare volenti.* And so, abruptly, without understanding what's going on, without the safety nets of translation, not knowing how to swim in it, one is thrown into another language, another culture, a different age. The sentence fragment in Latin fails to offer reassurance, even when translated: "death penalty is meted out to the one who wishes to change fatherlands." How many times would I have died, were this sentence executed? How many times did I die, appearances notwithstanding, when parts of me did not survive each move?

לֶךְ־לְךָ מֵאַרְצְךָ וּמִמּוֹלַדְתְּךָ וּמִבֵּית אָבִיךָ אֶל־הָאָרֶץ אֲשֶׁר אַרְאֶךָּ
"Go forth from your land, and from your birthplace, and from your father's home to the land, which I will show you" (Gen. 12:1).

—You don't know where you are going; it's going to be a surprise; someone or something will give you a sign of the land, which has never been and never will be your home.
—Jewish sages and mystics read the first words of the verse לֶךְ־לְךָ ("Go forth") according to the reflexive form, in which they are written: "Go unto yourself." In this vein, they refer to an inner immigration, a departure from self-certainty to an unknown destination the self will have become or will have kept becoming.

HOMELAND INSECURITY: MYSCELUS

> *Patrias, age, desere sedes i, pete diversi lapidosas Aesaris undas*
> "Up and away from your native land; go seek out the rocky channel
>   of the distant Aesar."

—You are going from the security of your native land, where you are familiar with every corner, every house and tree, every smell, to another place, sharp in its rocky outlines, but harboring aqueous uncertainty in its midst.
—The command to abandon your homeland invariably arises outside of you, but it is pulsating in you, just as blood pulsates in your temples—it is the outside that is within you, so much so that it *is* you already othered, already other to yourself, still before you packed your meager belongings and departed or simply fled, having left everything behind, include a significant portion of yourself.

> В ночь, выхаркнуты народом!
> Кто мы? да по всем вокзалам!
> Кто мы? да по всем заводам!
>
> *Into the night, we are spat out by the people!*
> *Who "we"? At every train station!*
> *Who "we"? At every factory!*
> —MARINA TSVETAEVA, "WHO—WE?"

"Spat out by the people," we become "we" as an I, enveloped by night. The night of the unfamiliar and the incommunicable; the night, in which there is nothing but solitude, displacement and distiement, dismemberment and unfathomable wholeness.

> *candidus Oceano nitidum caput abdiderat Sol, et caput extulerat*
>   *densissima sidereum Nox*
> "the bright Sun had hidden his shining head beneath the sea, and
>   thick Night had raised her starry head"

The head of the night—the head of the headless, the amorphous, so thick and viscous that it attaches to your skin. You are swathed in it, and it indwells you. With every new deracination, excision and exodus from a culture, a language, a land, a body politic, the night thickens. Despite its impenetrability, it sparkles with another sense, the starry shimmer of thinking.

A VEGAN FEAST OF WORDS: PYTHAGORAS

(Liber XV, 60-390)

PRELUDE

No one becomes anyone else. Apples are apples, oranges are oranges, sheep are sheep. And everyone becomes someone else by way of the incorporation of the eaten into the eater. Metamorphosis as a function of metabolism. Even if you are not yourself eaten (for the time being: worms, fungi and bacteria, fire, vultures, or fish will consume the body after its death, depending on the place that receives it), in the act of eating you become the other—you literally are what you eat. Digestion is both the breakdown and the assimilation of nutrients, analysis and synthesis, material thinking in both its aspects of discernment and combinatorics. No wonder that the ancients considered digestion to be a function of the slow fire of the stomach, cooking food inside the organism, transforming nourishment in the same manner as the fire, burning through, discerning among, and recombining things in the outer world. An epithet of the Hindu god of fire, Agni, is *Jatavedas*, "all-knowing": burning differently in distinct supports, he knows them in the most intimate of ways, from within. Fire is cosmic being and cosmic thought, analyzing and resynthetizing existence, granting life and channeling death. The culinary arts are mediations between the outer fire of the world and the inner fire of the stomach. Cooking is thinking; a predigesting forethought, its operations are to be repeated, supplanted and supplemented by the digestive system.

Nourishment is the material reincarnation of the eaten, having passed through the transformative power of fire, in the eater. And all are digested into spirit, the sublime stomach and intestines churning up spiritual reality. It is an errant spirit to be sure, which, everywhere the same, inhabits the most diverse bodies: "The spirit wanders, comes now here now there, and occupies whatever frame it pleases [*errat et illine huc venit, hinc illue, et quaslibet occupant artus spiritus*]. From beasts it passes into human bodies, and from our bodies into beasts, but never perishes." Is it, then, morally permissible to consume animal flesh as food, seeing that the spirit itself never perishes?

Here, a veritable verbal and ideational feast of vegan thought commences. (The expression "a feast of discourses" is Plato's, introduced in *Timaeus* 20b–c.) Implicit in the argument about errant spirit is the notion that eating animals is nothing less than sublimated cannibalism: the human eater devours the potential past humans these "beasts" could have been and the potential future humans they may be. Theirs are "kindred souls," *cognatas animas*, and, in the bodies, blood is the marker of this proximity. Although spirit also wanders into and indwells the bodies of plants, the leap from the vegetal to the human must cover a greater distance than the one from the animal to the human and back. Hence, "let not blood be fed on blood" (*nec sanguine sanguis alatur*)!

All this is but a prelude to a sophisticated dramaturgy of vegan argumentation. What would it look—and sound—like if enacted by participants in the drama of nutritive life?

A choir of apples and grapes: We wrap our seeds in sweet fruit to protect and nourish them on their perilous journey into the future. If you eat our fruit, you do us no harm. Even if you swallow our seeds, inadvertently, you do us a favor. Like birds and other animals who feed on us, you will excrete the seeds, spreading them far and wide and stimulating their growth with your waste.

Herbs and vegetables: To the solar flame
Add the fire of your stoves, softening us.
Flamma mollirique! Flamma mollirique!
Help us ripen otherwise.
Keep a part of us unscathed:
the branches or the roots,
the seeds or the shoots.
With the earth we will collaborate,
if the world you let regenerate.

The earth: I am not what I have been; I will not be who I am. Sing your elemental laments for me—*prodiga alimentaque tellus*, "the earth prodigal in nourishment." But know this: I hold many surprises in store.

An Armenian tiger: Delight in bloody food, yes!
But what sort of delight, if in it
I can taste my own death?

Flesh: There is no such a thing as flesh. I am a figment of your theoretical imagination, an unjustified abstraction of the most concrete. Whatever it is that is voicing these words in your head could not keep silent, though. If you need an image for flesh, do not picture it as interiority, as a storage place of energy or calories. The flesh of the world is tact and contact, the touch of skin on skin, sunrays on leaves, wind on fur . . .

Birds, fish, rabbits: The golden age—
Plenaque pacis—
Full of peace,
When no teeth
Tore us apart.
Freedom to roam
Air, water, land;
Freedom from fear

In *aetas aurea*—
The golden age.

A pig: Why justify violence against me? You say that "with my broad snout" I had "rooted up the planted seeds and cut off the season's promised crops." Is this reason enough to smoke or roast my snout? Or to serve it under a cream sauce?

A goat:	A scapegoat, forever and ever,
"The goat is held fit for sacrifice,"
Even by the staunchest defender
Of vegan diet,
Who confirms loud and clear
That eating animals is a sacrificial practice,
Carried out with fire and all kinds of kitchen gear.
The gods, to which we are offered,
Are neither Yahweh nor Jupiter
But *avidum alvum*—
A greedy stomach—
And a bloodthirsty mind.

A choir of sheep and oxen: *Placidum pecus*, a peaceful flock, and *natum tolerare labores*, born to endure work, we have been exploited by you to the fullest. Our wool and the exertions of our muscles were not sufficient for you—you, who do not rest until you bite into our muscles, tear our tendons, and don't spare even the tail.

A choir of gods:	Alas! Alas! We are
"The partners of their crime."
Partners of their crime, we have become
At the time when our divine noses were no longer
content
To smell frankincense and myrrh
And when our palates wanted more than ambrosia or nectar.
Whose original sin was taking pleasure
In a whiff of roasted flesh,
If the mortals as much as the immortals

Salivated,
Gave and accepted these murdered animals
As sacrifice?
Theirs and ours;
Ours and theirs.

The humans of the future (*polyphonically*): "Make not their flesh your food, but seek a more harmless nourishment." Nourishment is energy: not fuel, but that which is. Do not destroy and do not extract to procure it. Open yourself in order to receive. Live synergically.

THE PHOENIX MEMO
(Liber XV, 391–478)

I have written my three-hundred-page love-hate letter to the phoenix and have nothing more to add to it. For the ashes of that missive, refer to Michael Marder, *The Phoenix Complex: A Philosophy of Nature* (Cambridge, MA: MIT Press, 2023). Semantic afterglows.

RUNNING OUT OF WORDS: A WOUNDED BODY POLITIC— HIPPOLYTUS

(Liber XV, 391–546)

OCTOBER 13, 2023. Tel Aviv. A sea of memorial candles at the public mourning ceremonies for the Israeli victims of the massacre that took place almost a week prior in the south of the country. Among the candles, a sign stands out. It reads, *Nigmeru ha-milim*. "There are no more words" (alternatively, "The words have ended"). Actual human bodies and the body politic are lacerated. Maybe, it is "all but one great wound," *unumque erat omnia vulnus*. But without words there is no mourning—only a deadly, lethal, death-bearing trauma, eating into the traumatized body, devastating its mind and the world around it. The sign is a citation from a song by Arik Einstein, *Nigmeru li ha-milim*, "I have run out of words," set to the music of Elvis Presley's "Love Me Tender." There is an important difference: when I run out of words, I am still there perhaps to regain them in the future; when there are no more words and no more "I," the violence of nonverbalization is absolute.

OCTOBER 10, 2023. "I was thrown from my car, and while the reins held my legs fast, you might see my living flesh dragged along, my sinews held on the sharp stake, my limbs partly drawn on and in part caught fast and left behind, and my bones broken with a loud, snapping sound. My spent spirit was at last breathed out and there was no part of my body which you could recognize" (*nullasque in corpore partes, noscere quas posses*).

OCTOBER 14, 2023. IDF (Israeli Defense Forces) conducts "readiness drills" on the border with Gaza Strip. Using a permanent marker, a soldier writes on a missile, 'Am Yisrael Chai, "The people of Israel is alive," drawing a Star of David beneath the inscription. Is it the same Star of David that was sewn onto the clothes of ghettoized Jews nearly a hundred years ago? And on the striped uniforms of Jewish prisoners in the camps? The same as Rosenzweig's "star of redemption?" As *my* star? My great-grandparents' and my child's? Are the death and destruction this missile will bring going to guarantee the vitality of those who will fire it? Of the *idea* they promote? Are the life and rebirth of a people, only yesterday at a loss for words, going to emanate from the mass deaths of Palestinian children, among other civilians in Gaza?

OCTOBER 9, 2023. "Can you—dare you—nymph, compare your loss with my disaster?"

OCTOBER 15, 2023. The dead and injured in the bombings of Gaza surpass the numbers of those massacred and wounded in the attack on Israel. "Daring to compare losses": this is not a matter of performing a basic mathematical operation, in order to find out which number is greater. Hippolytus chastises the nymph for comparing her loss with his disaster, as though there could be a loss of life, prematurely cut short, as a mere counting or accounting issue, without it also being a disaster—each disastrously lost life incomparable, unsubstitutable, devoid of the guiding light of any star. Beyond comparisons, the language of mathematics is useless. Numbers will not replace the words you have lost.

OCTOBER 8, 2023. "Further, I saw the rayless world [*luce carentia regna*] of death and bathed my torn body in the waves of Phlegethon."

OCTOBER 16, 2023. On the eastern rim of the Mediterranean, along the narrow stretch of land since time immemorial called Gaza (Ancient Egyptian *Ghazzat*; Assyrian *Hazat*), millions are deprived of food, water, medicines, and life, subject to relentless bombardments. Directly and indirectly killed. Here, too, the Mediterranean is turning into a sea of death, its waves resembling those of Phlegethon, the infernal flaming river of blood.

OCTOBER 7, 2023, OCTOBER 17, 2023. "the sea rose up [*mare surrexit*] and a huge mound of water seemed to swell and grow to mountain size, to give forth bellowings, and to be cleft at its highest point."

Ten days of a brutally rising tide. (But how much time of oppression, traumatization, and suffering has preceded and impelled this tide? And how many days, months, and years of mass murders will follow?) A terrible swell is formed in the sea of death and blood, of grief and rage, of humanity and inhumanity which could only rise up in the very being of human being (no other animal is capable of this)—the surging abyss, in which words drown. Waves do recede, eventually, even if global sea levels are rising. What might they reveal? The words that litter the sandy or rocky seabed (one stumbles upon some of them in low tide) are not the same words as the ones that the sea had swallowed up. They are muted and mutilated, stamped with the wordless disaster and the similarly wordless violence it emits in its aftermath. You cannot tell these words apart from pebbles or pieces of glass, ground and polished by the power of the waves. In other words, they are words that are heavy (perhaps, too heavy to be expressive or indicative of anything), dense, material, indistinguishable from things. What to do with them? What might they do to you?

BEING DOUBLE: CIPUS
(Liber XV, 547–621)

1.

I could not believe my eyes. I was seeing myself and not seeing myself—or, better, seeing not-myself. Seeing double; a misaligned double vision (my mental image of myself not matching my own reflection) presented itself before me in all its horror. I was—still am; the doubling of tenses goes without saying—a demonstrable monster, portending something (*monstro portenditur isto*) yet to be announced. So incredulous was I that I had to verify my vision with at least one other sense: I felt the urge to touch what I saw, *quae vidit, tetigit*. What was it? Small protrusions on my forehead, horn-like. There were two of them, no doubt about it: they were—still are—also double and growing. As I touched each horn, I was jolted with an electrical discharge, a kind of mini-lightning striking between the protrusion and my fingertips.

Intense pain; a smell of burnt skin. Besides pain, the lightning strikes brought along with them vivid emotions, thoughts, images, and desires. Touching one of my newly formed horns, I was shot through with rage, the impulse to enslave everything and everyone on my path, a throng of subjects kneeling in front of me. Touching the other, I was permeated by a sense of peace, the desire to dissolve into the world, to offer myself up to it, be it as a sacrificial scapegoat. Sitting cross-legged on the ground, I contemplated the issue with my bodily and mental eyes. How much time this period of silent contemplation lasted, I cannot say.

At long last, I came to realize that each protrusion was an antenna of sorts, and, moreover, that each was fitted for the reception of polarized signals, of emotional and ideational pluses and minuses. The little I knew about electrical currents suggested to me that, if I were to snap out of this bifurcated state, I had to connect the negative and the positive poles. Quite literally so. I held onto one of my horns with the right hand, doing my best to ignore the piercing pain that, lashing each of my fingers and the palm of my hand, traveled up my arm and to the shoulder. Then, breathing out, I wrapped the fingers of my other hand around the other horn. A bright flash, a loud boom, and . . .

2.

I am riding an oxcart on the outskirts of Rome. My memory of yesterday's events is nebulous. My head is throbbing with the most terrible migraine, and I can barely feel my fingers; they are mostly numb. This pain and this absence of sensation are my only realities at the moment.

Someone has placed a carefully rolled up senatorial edict next to me. Let's see. *At proceres, quoniam muros intrare vetaris, ruris honorati tantum tibi, Cipi, dedere, quantum depresso subiectis bobus aratro conplecti posses ad finem lucis ab ortu.* "Since you might not come within the city walls, Cipus, the Senate gave you as a gift of honor, as much land as you could enclose with a yoke of oxen and a plow from dawn till close of day."

An ox-drawn cart—it must be a sarcastic reference to my horns that, so far as I can tell with my benumbed fingers, are more prominent than ever. The horns. That's it! There are two of them, and there were two of us, two of me: myself and my double, man and beast, the same yet different. I tried to reverse this individual fission, by stimulating the process of fusion. Or, maybe, to let the electrical current flow: from me to myself, from my minus to my plus poles. And what then? A blackout . . .

I have been expelled from the city, as the edict states. If the edict says so, it is the truth. But I have also been given the gift of land outside city walls. Punished and rewarded; rewarded and punished. For what? Why? I am made of forgetting and memory, forgetting to remember, remembering to forget, and, right now, trying to remember what I have forgotten. No, not *what*, but *whom* I have forgotten, *whom* I have betrayed: myself as other to myself.

Flashbacks are more painful than migraine. Here they are, searing irresistible images onto my retina.

> A laurel wreath hiding my horns, "a wreath of peaceful laurel..."
> A great multitude in front of me...
> Auguries of war and enslavement...
> *Quem vobis indicat augur, si Romam intrarit, famularia iura daturum.*
> Horns, the sign of a sovereign beast, of the beast who is the sovereign: myself, doubled...
> Expel him—expel it—expel me!

Then, this: an oxcart, a fresh senatorial edict, fresher still—the smell of plowed earth, migraine and numbness, blackouts and flashbacks, expulsion and high honors. Being double: doubly being and not-being.

ORBI ET URBI: TO THE WORLD AND TO THE CITY— THE APPROXIMATIONS OF POWER

(Liber XV, 622-744)

Curves are the contours of togetherness, of appearing together against a common horizon or of chains that shackle and traverse many lives. So much so that curving defines the sense of the world and of the city, *orbis* and *urbs*— their rounding or encirclement by a wall or a moat, for instance. Delineating the ends of the world and of the city are their specific curvatures: the rings (currently, circle subway lines or ring roads or highways, often concentric, ensconced in further such rings) that, through their closure, enclose those who dwell within; the orbital trajectories these complex entities move along; the tightness of an embrace; the embeddedness of the urban and worldly embraces in the embrace of time, or, more precisely, in the curvature of space-time singularly befitting the energy-mass, which bends it.

••••

Protection increases risks and dangers: it is because a city is walled that it can be besieged, becoming a mousetrap. And it is because, seeking sundry opportunities and safety in numbers, its inhabitants cluster together in crowded living quarters, that they are vulnerable to the "deadly pestilence" of diseases and epidemics. When the curvature of the city turns out to be suffocating, appeals to salvation and healing (*salutifer*: the one as the other) reach out to a broader horizon of the world.

A delegation from epidemic-plagued Latium, which is not so far from Rome, travels to the Greek Delphi, "situated in the center of the world" (*mediamque . . . orbis*), desperate for help from the god and his oracle. The journey from the city to the world is one of globalization, all hopes for local cures pinned on global forces, on *orbis terrarum* taken as a whole. (Not by chance, *terrarum* is so close to *terrarium* that word-processing spellchecks insistently and automatically recommend converting the former into the latter. Rest assured: we will encounter a curious terrarium specimen in a moment.) So the delegation from Latium goes along a tortuous route stretching beyond the curving urban limits all the way to the curvature of the world, from Rome to Greece, to the center of a world which is already bygone—if not at the time of the events Ovid depicts then, without a doubt, in his own times. Approximations to power and to its presumed centers miss their mark: just when you think that you are there, at the heart of brilliant, glorious, divine or quasi-divine absolute authority, it will have been displaced, decentered, disempowered.

••••

Urbi et Orbi, "To the City and to the World," is a papal blessing reserved for very special occasions. Read out from the *loggia* of Saint Peter's Basilica in the Vatican, the speech forges for itself a time and a space beyond the city and the world, which it addresses, while staying in the city and in the world. This *beyond within* is another mutation of urban and orbital curvatures, the transcendence within immanence that is the schematic organization of Christianity and, by implication, of the Church. At the same time included and excluded, it is the place of power and sovereignty, eluding a straightforward approximation.

ORBI ET URBI: TO THE WORLD AND TO THE CITY

• • • •

Approximations to power and to its presumed centers miss their mark. The oracle at Delphi says as much. "What you seek from this place you should have sought, O Roman, from a nearer place (*propiore loco*)." To translate: do not expect salvation to come from the global center, because the answers are closer than you think. Seek not the father but the son; not the sun but the sun's son; not Phoebus/Apollo but Asclepius; not God-the-Father but the Son. An approach to the formal seat of power, to its apex, to the figure of the sovereign, is, in equal measure, a distancing from the capacity to do anything about the affliction. Power dwarfs you, makes you powerless, especially when you think you wield it, exchanging a nearer place for its atopia. Geographies of deliverance: the curve gently bending again and guiding you back to what was right under your nose, or maybe underfoot—coiling there, oozing with danger and promise, with poison and remedy. The Son and the Serpent—the Son as the Serpent—a wise savior and a wise seducer. In the end, they are one and the same, like the way up and the way down. Gnostic inversions.

• • • •

A river is snaking through the landscape of gently sloping hills, winding, meandering as it is striving to reach the sea. It could well be Córdoba's Guadalquivir, the river of a city of medieval wisdom, the city of Averroes and Maimonides, as well as, well before their time, of Seneca—the city and the river that extend an invitation for explorations of meandering and, later on, of blossoming. I was honored to accept Córdoba's and Guadalquivir's invitations. That would be a fluvial place closer to me. The one closer to Ovid and the Latium delegation is the Tiber.

A river becomes a snake, and a snake becomes a river thanks to the curving shapes, the "curving [*incurvo*] embankments," and a sleek reptilian body reflected on its waters. The snake is the embodiment of salvation emanating from a nearer place; he is coiled on the staff of Asclepius, the god of medicine and the son of Delphi's Apollo. When the staff is not available, the soteriological snake will be "rising on high and reclining heavily with his neck resting upon the ship's curving [*recurvam*] stern, gazing down upon the azure waters." Another curve: of the stern, but also of the reflection: of the divine animal-snake in the riverine ecosystem-snake.

A river reflects power and the self-divestment of power. The verticality of the staff and the stern is the dimension of top-down, hierarchical ordering and command over all. This verticality is, however, imperfect. It is corrupted by the curving of the staff and the stern and by the snake's coils that amplify deviations from the tyrannic ideal and that, in so doing, act as a poison and a cure: act and counteract (also themselves); activate the defining curvatures (the curved edges) of the world and the city; actualize their defenses and render the defended entity more vulnerable.

• • • •

Salutifer urbi, "a health-bringer to the city," cannot come from within the space of the city and the ever-expanding walls of a megalopolis. Nor is it going to be a global messianic figure, who holds universal solutions to all local problems. Salvific, healing power has little to do with power's many centers. It is hidden in the nearest, especially in the nearness of places that are still the places of *someone*, the someone not possessing (and thus deadening) them but revitalizing them, breathing another life and air into them. What if the rod of Asclepius and the serpent entwined with it were a tree? Vertical and deviating from verticality, curving and ramifying, snaking through the soil with its roots and filial with respect to the sun, defying the logic of a center and resembling a river with its many tributaries... A green *salutifer urbi* and *salutifer orbi*, this vegetal figure emerges in its salubrious glory when you rewind the footage that shows the rod and the snake back to the tree (the Tree of Life, perhaps), out of which the rod was carved and which was also entwined with the serpent in another tradition. The arboreal power of "health-bringing" is not a power. Its curving, branching shapes escort us to the hither side of the power/powerlessness opposition.

THE INDIGESTIBILITY OF FATE
(Liber XV, 745-870)

Fate—what has been spoken, and as soon as it is spoken, etched in stone, or on "iron tablets," *tabularia ferro*.

Fate—a dictum, a dictate, a decree without the right to appeal. A speech that does not hear (not even itself).

Fate—the indigestible and the immutable, excepted from the metabolic and metamorphic routines of all that is.

The fate of metamorphoses—the unchangeability of change itself; the dictum that everything has always changed, is changing, and will forever keep changing. Its formal, if utterly abstract, veracity achieved at the expense of material forms. Into what or into whom does the metamorphosing entity metamorphose?—no longer a question of fate, but of destiny, of provisional destinations on the endless path of metamorphosis.

Fate—to be accepted or to be rejected, that is, to be accepted with resignation or torturously, with an overdose of suffering.

Fate—a future trauma; the future *as* trauma; *insuperabile fatum*, "insurmountable fate," hailing from the immemorial past. Hence, fate—*aeternas ruinas*, "the eternal ruins."

THE INDIGESTIBILITY OF FATE

Fate—a period of "allotted time," of time carefully weighed and measured, thought out, determined in advance, predetermined and completed, chopped up and filled out with what one will have known as one's life.

THE WORK UNDONE: OVID

(Liber XV, 871-879)

Dear Publius Ovidius Naso:

I will agree with you on one thing and one thing only: even after dying, "through all the ages" you have lived in fame. Everything else you have written in the closing lines of your book cannot be true in the light and in the shadows of a thinking, a sensing, and a becoming in the world, of the world, guided by metamorphoses.

    First and foremost, it is preposterous to think that "the work is done." How can the work of metamorphoses ever be accomplished, even if *Metamorphoses* is finished, the ink drying on the opus's last word, which is precisely *vivam*, "I shall live," uttered or inscribed in defiance of finitude?

Second, I cannot believe you when you write that "neither the wrath of Jove, nor fire, nor the sword, nor the gnawing tooth of time shall ever be able to undo" what has been done. Your work persists through these very destructive forces; its own metamorphoses are nourished by them, the doing and the undoing of the done equally responsible for the work's ongoing life, its posthumous survival. And by extension, yours.

The third thing I take issue with is your metaphysical self-dissection, the way you separate your "mortal frame" from your "better part," *parte meliore*, which is your name. Are you identifying with Aeneas, whose own divinization had to commence with the rescue of his "best part," *pars optima*?

Fourth, and most indefensibly, you tie the fate of your name to the spread of Rome: "wherever Rome's power extends over the conquered earth," *quaque patet domitis Romana potentia terris*, there your best part, your name, will be on people's lips. This is truly despicable: you are willing either to don the cloak of "soft power" or to assume the shape and the role of a poisonous cherry on the imperial cake of earth domination.

What have you learned from metamorphoses while composing your *Metamorphoses*? I wonder. Why do you refuse them with so much self-conceit, with so much arrogance? Why protect your work, your name, your self from their influence? Judging by the intensity of some portions of the text, you have occasionally opened yourself enough to their influence to let them traverse you, course through and overflow your corpus. And even your corpse. Also, while generally keeping to the style of epic poetry, you have been venturesome enough to experiment with other genres—from elegy to pastoral poetry and tragedy—in a way that allowed the matter at hand to prescribe its changeable, changing forms. None of this is a panacea for your imperial hubris: empires, too, are transformed, sometimes beyond recognition, but their power continues to dominate the earth. Which brings us back to the question of posthumous fame, or of a posthumous life.

Don't you think, dear Publius Ovidius Naso (you, whose very name, or at least a part of it, while it has remained, has morphed into Ovid, Ovide, or Ovídio in some of those languages into which Latin had metamorphosed after *its* death), that the posthumous life of a work is all the more effective, the more advanced its undoing, its decomposition, its composting in the soil of a culture? Forget the imposition of imperial dictates, languages, names, monuments, and other insignia of power from above! From below, the work's autolyzed and putrefying tissues will be reduced to the molecules of sense and non-sense. In collaboration with the "gnawing tooth of time," these may then stimulate the growth and flourishing of something else, namely of the very future, in which we will and will not live.

Yours,
M.M.

GPSR Authorized Representative: Easy Access System Europe, Mustamäe tee
50, 10621 Tallinn, Estonia, gpsr.requests@easproject.com

www.ingramcontent.com/pod-product-compliance
Lightning Source LLC
Chambersburg PA
CBHW022030290426
44109CB00014B/815